A UNIVERSAL FAITH?

PEOPLES, CULTURES, RELIGIONS, AND THE CHRIST

Louvain Theological and Pastoral Monographs is a publishing venture whose purpose is to provide those involved in pastoral ministry throughout the world with studies inspired by Louvain's long tradition of theological excellence within the Roman Catholic Tradition. The volumes selected for publication in the series are expected to express some of today's finest reflection on current theology and pastoral practice.

LOUVAIN THEOLOGICAL & PASTORAL MONOGRAPHS

9

A UNIVERSAL FAITH?

PEOPLES, CULTURES, RELIGIONS, AND THE CHRIST

Catherine Cornille & Valeer Neckebrouck

Essays in honor of
Prof. Dr. Frank De Graeve

PEETERS PRESS
LOUVAIN

W.B. EERDMANS

ISBN 90-6831-429-7
D. 1992/0602/65

TABLE OF CONTENTS

INTRODUCTION

In the face of the event of secularization and the need for a true encounter with other religions and cultures, the question of the Universality of Christianity has become one of the most challenging theological issues of the day. It has come to threaten our conception of mission and to shake the very roots of fundamental theology. While most have only recently become aware of its implications, decades ago a visionary few discerned this phenomenon and have since sought to ride the crest of its development. In this spirit, we present these essays on the occasion of the emeritus of Prof. Dr. Frank De Graeve, s.j., who has long been one such visionary.

In addition to the classical disciplines of theology and philosophy, Frank De Graeve was trained in the then gradually emerging study of the various non-Christian religions. He studied with some of the most eminent specialists of his day: anthropology with Evans-Pritchard, archaic religions with Goets, Hinduism with Johanns and Ashby, Buddhism with Lamotte, Tucci and Kitagawa, Zoroastrianism with Duchesse-Guillemain, Judaism with Kaplan, and Islam with Hodgson. To conclude his academic training, De Graeve worked for two years as a postgraduate fellow with Mircea Eliade. He thus became an exemplar of that early generation possessing synthetic knowledge of the field of Comparative Study of Religions. Without much concern for publishing, De Graeve can with as much authority expound on an obscure African tribe, intricate points of debate at the early Buddhist councils, or subtle aspects of the Moorish influence in Spain. It is thus not without reason that he has come to be known as "the walking encyclopedia."

All of this, combined with a profound knowledge of, and commitment to Christian theology made Frank De Graeve uniquely disposed to become a driving force in the development of the discipline of what has since come to be known as the "theology of religions." Convinced that "the Christian theological discussion of the non-Christian religions should be actively cognizant of the religiously pluralistic nature of its horizon" and that that "encounter being the only Christian hope, we had better be theologically prepared for it," he instituted the courses of "Theology of the Interreligious Encounter" at the University of Notre Dame, and "Theology of non-Christian religions" at the University of Leuven. The notion of inculturation and the related questions of the Universality of Christianity and the Uniqueness of Christ were thus at the very heart of Frank De Graeve's thinking and teaching throughout his career.

It is thus only fitting that the colloquium held on February 21 and 22, 1991 to honor the work and mark the emeritus of Frank De Graeve would focus on these subjects which are both lifelong interests of his and current imperatives for us all. Those who spoke at the colloquium have been involved in missionary activities in various continents and/or stand as prominant thinkers in the area of the theology of religions. Its first part dealt mainly with distinct issues of inculturation connected to particular cultures and religions into which the Christian mission has penetrated, while the second part focussed on the theological and dogmatic issues pertaining to the encounter with different cultures and religions. To the papers presented at the colloquium, a few essays have been added by former students of Prof. De Graeve from the Filipines: Jose De Mesa and Jimmy Belita.

Though particular problems of inculturation should not be separated from general questions concerning the theology of religions, the first seven essays of this volume deal with inculturation: in general, in India, in Japan, in the Muslim world, in Africa, and in the Filipines, respectively. The final three concern purely theological aspects of our topic.

The opening essay of the volume is a general introduction to the concept of inculturation by one of its main theorists and advocates, Aylward Shorter. He offers a discussion of alternative concepts which have been proposed, explains his own preference for the term "inculturation" and argues, as his title suggests, for the inculturation of the Gospel and the decentralization of authority as premises for the Universality of Christianity. However, as subsequent essays show, the process of inculturation has preceeded its conceptualization. While pointing to the complexity of the Indian context with its many cultures, religions and dehumanizing poverty, the essay by Jacques Dupuis shows that certain early attempts at inculturation in India may be paradigmatic for the Church as a whole. Some Indian theologians have made creative attempts toward inculturation which hold far-reaching implications for theology at large. Conversely, Jan Van Bragt discusses the need and possibilities for the inculturation of Christianity in Japan by reflecting upon the past failure of the Christian mission in Asia. He compares this with Buddhist successes and, on this basis, advances some provocative proposals for Christian inculturation.

Interreligious dialogue is one of the main components of inculturation. While real dialogue is often regarded as a rather recent development in the encounter between religions, Arnulf Camps reconstructs a dialogue which took place in the first half of the nineteenth century between the Abbé F. Bourgade and the Muslims at Carthage.

If inculturation is, as W. Reiser puts it, "the process of a deep, sympathetic adaptation to, and appropriation of, a local culture in which the Church finds itself, in a way that does not compromise its faith," its first step consists of listening to the people. This is exemplified in the essay of Lambert Bartels, in which the Oromo people of Ethiopia are themselves invited to express their views on God, Creation, Heaven, the Scriptures, morality, and Jesus Christ. Not all cultures, however, have been receptive to Christian attempts at evangelization, whether or not through inculturation. This represents a serious challenge to the idea of the Universality of Christianity.

The focus on inculturation represents a reassessment of the past as well as a program for the future. Some peoples, such as the Filipinos, have been very receptive to the Gospel message, even if brought to them in Spanish form. The challenge for Filipino theologians is then that of providing a solid cultural analysis which would make way for true inculturation. This is argued and offered in the essay of José de Mesa. But it is also that of explicitating and evaluating spontaneous forms of inculturation. This can be found in Jimmy Belita's account and interpretation of the *Santo Nino* cult in the Filipines. As every particular form of inculturation in its turn informs theology at large, Belita shows how the notion of the *Santo Nino* throws a particular light on the question of the Uniqueness of Christ.

The essays dealing explicitly with the theology of religions are opened by that of Gavin D'Costa who has become a recognized authority in the field. After providing a survey of the different theological approaches developed toward religious pluralism, D'Costa defends a trinitarian theology of religions based on his own two theses. This trinitarian approach is one way of addressing the central question of the theology of religions, and of the universality of Christianity: that of the Uniqueness of Jesus Christ. Wiel Logister focusses specifically on this problem by discussing old and new Christological models, and by advancing Biblical, historical and dogmatic foundations for a true openness to other traditions. There are (almost) as many approaches to the questions of the Uniqueness of Christ and the Universality of Christianity as there are theologians. To a certain degree, however, they all build upon the original insights and intuitions of pioneers of the current theology of religions such as Frank De Graeve. Already during the Second Vatican Council, he developed Eleven Theses toward a Christian Theology of Interreligious Encounter. In the concluding essay, Catherine Cornille discusses these theses and shows the current relevance many still retain.

Catherine Cornille

INCULTURATION
THE PREMISE OF UNIVERSALITY

Aylward Shorter

Introduction

This paper attempts to explore the relationship between inculturation and universality, on the understanding that the Catholicity of the Church is jeopardized so long as inculturation is not wholeheartedly adopted in practice. "The Latin Church," wrote Jean-Yves Calvez, "must renounce its superiority complex and monopoly of forms of expression."[1] Ten years ago the Zairean theologian, Oscar Bimwenyi, described the Christian life of Africans in uncompromising terms.

> They pray to God with a liturgy that is not theirs. They live according to a pre-existing morality which is not the conversion of their own previous morality under the action of God's grace and the breath of the Holy Spirit. They are ruled by a Canon Law which is not a law born from the conversion to Christ of social and juridical realities inherent in the universe to which they belong... They reflect — when indeed they reflect — using philosophical and theological systems secreted by the meditation and reflection of the other Christian communities which evangelized them.[2]

Various authors speak of "earthing," "rooting," "grounding" or "inserting" the Gospel.[3] Such metaphors echo Paul VI's concern that the Gospel should be transposed into cultural or anthropological language, and not merely into a semantic or literary one.[4] It is useless to proclaim the Gospel, if it is not

---

1. Jean-Yves Calvez, "The Real Problem of Inculturation," *Lumen Vitae*, vol. 40, 1985, no. 1, pp. 70-80.

2. Kweshi Oscar Bimwenyi, "Inculturation en Afrique et attitude des agents de l'evangelization," *Bulletin of African Theology*, vol. 5, 1981, pp. 5-17 (author's tr.).

3. One of these is Gerald A. Arbuckle, *Earthing the Gospel* (London, Geoffrey Chapman, 1990); another is Nicolas Standaert, "L'histoire d'un neologisme," *Nouvelle Revue Theologique*, no. 110 (1988) 555-570.

4. *Evangelii Nuntiandi*, 63.

allowed to take root. Christianity's growth depends on this, and
this condition, in turn, implies the abandonment of monocultural
uniformity. A theologian from India bluntly declares:

> Christianity, with its universal message, cannot grow as a religion
> today, unless it abandons its preference for western culture, with its
> rational, technically minded, masculine bias, and opens up to the
> feminine, intuitive understanding of reality in the east. [5]

The "Enlightenment" strengthened the conviction of European
Catholics that they were in possession of absolute cultural norms,
but although lipservice is now paid to cultural pluralism, Euro-
American Catholicism has not wholly shed its culture blindness. [6]
This is shown by a conscious or unconscious process of theological obfuscation. Before exploring this phenomenon, it is necessary to achieve some degree of terminological clarity and even to
take sides in the debate concerning terminology.

Context and Culture

A number of writers prefer the terms "context"/"contextualization" to "culture"/"inculturation." This is partly because "inculturation" had prior sociological associations before it was reinterpreted theologically, and because "contextualization" was felt to
be a more neutral term. [7] A more common reason, perhaps, is
because "context" is felt to be a more comprehensive concept
that includes secular modernity, technology, social justice and
politics, as well as traditional "culture." [8] Tang criticizes the term

5. S.M. Michael, "The Role of the Church in the Transformation of Culture,"
Indian Missiological Review, vol. 11, no. 11 (1989) 79-95.

6. Jean-Yves Calvez, "The Real Problem of Inculturation", p. 72. Aylward
Shorter, *Toward a Theology of Inculturation* (London, 1988) 17-30, Edmund Hill,
"Christianity and Cultures," *New Blackfriars*, vol. 67, nos. 793/794 (1986) 324-
329.

7. Robert J. Schreiter, *Constructing Local Theologies* (London, S.C.M. Press,
1985) 5-6.

8. Ruy O. Costa, *One Faith - Many Cultures* (New York, Orbis Books, 1988)
XII; Edmund Tang, "Context and Contextualization," *Pro Mundi Vita Studies*,
no. 4 (1988) 10-12; Krikor Habblian, "The Problem of Contextualization,"
Missiology, vol. 11, no. 1 (1983) 95-111. This definition explains the term's

for being too socio-political and inattentive to multi-faith situations.[9] While Costa, although he prefers "context," wonders whether the term is not itself the child of western, self-critical, rationalized religion.[10] "Contextualization" arose in Protestant circles connected with the reform of theological education and one sympathizes with Arbuckle's rejection of the word as suggesting a communications tactic of evangelizers.[11] There is also the problem of defining contexts. Schineller emphasizes their extreme complexity and diversity — "contexts within contexts," like nests of Chinese boxes — and Stackhouse asks about their spatio-temporal characteristics, concluding that they do not define themselves.[12] This author also makes the verbally ingenious distinction between the "textuality" of the Church — its fidelity to the Gospel — and its "contextuality" or fidelity to the contemporary scene.[13]

In fact, the preference for "context"/"contextualization" is often based on a misunderstanding of the anthropological notion of culture.[14] Kroeber and Kluckhohn listed 164 definitions of culture, but they are all reducible to a few basic ideas.[15] Culture is not to be equated merely with "folklore" or even "the arts." It is a comprehensive concept that embraces society and the social system and all that individuals acquire as members of society. Indeed, many definitions concentrate on the social origins or social functions of culture, in learning process or in group

popularity in South Africa, cf. Albert Nolan, *God in South Africa* (London, Catholic Institute of International Relations, 1988.)

9. Edmund Tang, "Context and Contextualization," p. 10.

10. Ruy Costa, *One Faith - Many Cultures*, p. XIII. Costa dismisses "inculturation" as being an apologetic term on a par with "indigenization," p. XII.

11. Gerald A. Arbuckle, *Earthing the Gospel*, p. 18; David J. Hesselgrave and Edward Rommen, *Contextualization: Meaning, Methods, Models* (Leicester, Apollos, 1989) 33 also explain contextualization as translating the Gospel into verbal forms meaningful to people in particular existentive situations.

12. Peter Schineller, "Inculturation as the Pilgrimage to Catholicity"; *Concilium*, 204, pp. 98-106; Max L. Stackhouse, "Contextualization, Contextuality & Contextuation," in Costa, *One Faith - Many Cultures*, pp. 3-13.

13. Max L. Stackhouse, "Contextualization, Contextuality & Contextuation," p. 6.

14. Tang, "Context and Contextualization," p. 11.

15. Alfred L. Kroeber and Clyde Kluckhohn, *Culture: A Critical Review of Concepts and Definitions* (Cambridge, Mass., Harvard Univ. Press, 1952) 38-40.

identity. For others, following Geertz and those who offer a semiotic analysis, culture is ultimately a pattern of meanings embodied in symbols.[16] Culture is unique to the human being who is the "primary constituent of culture" and who is, as it were, suspended in his or her own web of meanings.[17] These control one's perception of reality and enable a person to relate cognitively, affectively and behaviourally to experience.[18] Cultures offer different conceptions of reality and different adaptive strategies for living and surviving.[19]

The concept of "culture" is no less complex than that of "context," there being clusters of sub-cultures and a spectrum of different cultural levels, among which religion, or the absolute which replaces it, is the most profound and most dynamic.[20] There is also a complementarity and a dynamic among the diverse cultures which belies the impression of relativism and incapsulation conveyed by popular contemporary sociology. Cultures are not discrete, isolated systems, but relate to one another in a historical process of intercultural communication. Acculturation, or the mutual influencing of cultures in their respective development, is only to be lamented when there is unwelcome cultural domination. "Culture is not a sacred monolith that it is wrong to confront."[21] Nor are cultures necessarily harmonious and well integrated; they may be dysfunctional and unstable. Taking these factors together, "culture" seems to be a more workable concept than "context."

"Inculturation" and "contextualization" are terms that denote the presentation and re-expression of the Gospel in forms and

16. Clifford Geertz, *The Interpretation of Cultures* (London, Hutchinson, 1973) 89; cf. also Robert J. Schreiter, *Constructing Local Theologies*, p. 53.

17. International Theological Commission, "Faith and Culture," *Omnis Terra*, no. 198 (1989) p. 264; Robert J. Schreiter, *Idem*, quoting Geertz and Weber.

18. Cf. Shorter, *Toward a Theology of Inculturation*, p. 5.

19. John M. Huels, "Interpreting Canon Law in Diverse Cultures," *The Jurist*, no. 47 (1987) 249-293; Michael, "The Role of the Church in the Transformation of Culture, p. 86.

20. D.S. Amalorpavadass, "Réflexions théologiques sur l'inculturation," *La Maison Dieu*, no. 179 (1989) 60; International Theological Commission, "Faith and Culture," p. 264.

21. John Ball, "Adaptation, Translation, Contextualization: Christian Tradition and the Cultural Process," *The Outlook*, vol. 20, no. 3 (1986) 68.

terms proper to a culture, processes which result in the reinterpretation of both, without being unfaithful to either.[22] It is a
creative development which, as the International Theological
Commission rightly says, participates in the dynamism of cultures
and their inter-communication.[23] Definitions of inculturation
tend to put the emphasis on one or other term of the equation —
Gospel or culture. Here are examples of both:

> The process of a deep, sympathetic adaptation to, and appropria-
> tion of, a local culture in which the Church finds itself, in a way
> that does not compromise its basic faith.[24]
> The process by which a particular people respond to the saving
> Word of God and express their response in their own cultural forms
> of worship, reflection, organization and life. This is how a local
> church is born and continues to live.[25]

Inculturation is a process which involves the destigmatization
of alien cultures, and the self-emptying (*exinanitio sui ipsius*) of
both communicator and receptor cultures.[26] Several writers make
much of the fact that inculturation/contextualization helps cultures to transcend their own limits. Thus, for Stackhouse, the
ultimate criterion of contextuality is intercontextuality, and for

22. Joseph Masson, "L'église ouverte sur le monde," *Nouvelle Revue Theologique*, vol. 84 (1962) 1038, uses "inculturation" in adjectival form. This would
appear to be the first use of the term, but Charles Chossonnery, "Toute église est
en inculturation permanente," *Bulletin of African Theology*, vol. 6a, no. 11 (1984)
134, quotes Meinrad Hebga's assertion that the term was invented by the
anthropologist Melville Herskovits in the 1970s.

23. International Theological Commission, "Faith and Culture," 2:29; Pedro
Arrupe, "Letter to the Whole Society on Inculturation," in Jaime Aixala, (ed.),
Other Apostolates Today (St. Louis, Society of Jesus, 1981) 172. Aidan Kavanagh,
"L'inculturation de la liturgie: un regard prospectif," *La Maison Dieu*, no. 179
(1989) 69, has questioned my use of Arrupe's phrase "new creation." It should be
obvious, however, that "creativity" does not preclude the original use of pre-
existing sources. If it did, it would, *per impossible*, lift inculturation out of the
intercultural process altogether.

24. William Reiser, "Inculturation and Doctrinal Development," *Heythrop
Journal*, vol. 22 (1981) 135-148.

25. Michael Amaladoss, "Dialogue and Inculturation," *Inculturation*, no. 314
(1988) 22.

26. Lamin Sanneh, *Translating the Message: The Missionary Impact on Culture*
(New York, Orbis Books, 1990) 1; Karl Muller, "Accommodation and Inculturation in the Papal Documents," *Verbum SVD*, vol. 24 (1983) 358.

Kraft, transculturation.[27] However, cultures are already by definition categories of interaction, and evangelization merely intensifies and channels their intercommunication.

Syncretism and Desyncretization

Closely associated with inculturation/contextualization is the problem variously described as "culturalism," "contextualism," "over-inculturation" or simply "syncretism."[28] Acculturation is necessarily accompanied by a greater or lesser degree of syncretism, or anomalous conflict of meaning. For Christian writers, syncretism occurs when culture appropriates the Gospel and distorts its meaning, or when unabsorbed cultural elements with conflicting meanings are juxtaposed with Gospel values.[29] Inso far as inculturation is concerned, syncretism must not be allowed to invalidate the Gospel. Inculturation, therefore, implies a measure of desyncretization, and this was the experience of the earliest Christians in their efforts to detach themselves from Judaic religious culture. Today we observe many Christian syncretisms: South African *apartheid*, new religious movements or sects, western politicians claiming the "moral high ground," or Christianity allied to political nationalisms. Eugene Uzukwu has discovered an "operative theology of identity" between the priestly and hierarchical model of the Church" and the worship of spirits and taking of titles among the Igbo of Nigeria.[30] Nearly twenty years ago Philip Turner discovered a similar Christian

27. Max L. Stackhouse, "Contextualization, Contextuality & Contextuation," p. 6, Charles H. Kraft, *Christianity in Culture* (New York, Orbis Books, 1919.)

28. Shorter, *Toward a Theology of Inculturation*, p. 224; Max L. Stackhouse, "Contextualization, Contextuality & Contextuation," p. 8; John M. Waliggo, "Making a Church that is truly African," in John M. Waliggo, *et al.* (eds.), *Inculturation, Its Meaning and Urgency* (Nairobi, St. Paul Publications Africa, 1986) 11-30.

29. It can also occur in reverse, when — in the absence of true dialogue — the meaning of another faith is subverted by Christianity. Cf. Wole Soyinka, *Myth, Literature and the African World* (Cambridge, Cambridge Univ. Press, 1976) 121-122.

30. Eugene E. Uzukwu, "Church and Inculturation: A Century of Roman Catholicism in Eastern Nigeria," *Sedos Bulletin*, 85, no. 10 (1985) 217-222.

syncretism in the kingdoms of Uganda.[31] William Biernatski points out that syncretism occurs when enthusiastic missionaries conduct a superficial adaptation in ignorance of the true meaning of cultural symbols, and Lamin Sanneh shows that cultural domination has also been a cause of syncretism, particularly in Latin America.[32] Robert J. Schreiter takes a sympathetic view of syncretism and has been criticized for this.[33] It is, however, clear that syncretism is present to a greater or lesser degree in every form of Christianity from New Testament times.[34] Inculturation is a task always yet to be achieved, because it involves a never ending appeal to cultural conversion.[35] There is no ready-made model for Christian cultures, least of all the Euro-American model, so often presented as a model of successful inculturation.[36] As Lesslie Newbigin remarked, "The Gospel escapes domestication."[37]

Writers on inculturation point to an evolution of the Church's thinking about cultures, and this is often expressed in terms of successive missionary strategies. Schreiter's three models: translation, adaptation and contextualization have been widely echoed.[38] Kraft's opposition between translation and transculturation has also been found useful.[39] While Hiebert's elaborate historical sequence from "non-contextualization," through post-colonial contextualization to "critical contextualization" is mat-

31. Philip Turner, "The Wisdom of the Ancestors and the Gospel of Christ: Some Notes on Christian Adaptation in Africa," *Journal of Religion in Africa*, vol. 4, no. 1, pp. 450-468.

32. William E. Biernatski, "Home Hard Sayings about Symbolism and Inculturation," *Inculturation*, vol. 3, no. 3 (1988) 20-25; L. Sanneh, *Translating the Message*, p. 91.

33. Robert J. Schreiter, *Constructing Local Theologies*; Adrian Edwards, "God Above and God Below," *New Blackfriars*, vol. 69, no. 812 (1988) 20.

34. Sanneh, *Translating the Message*, pp. 37-91.

35. Gerald A. Arbuckle, *Earthing the Gospel*, p. 110.

36. Casimir Guanadickam, "Inculturation and the Local Church," *Lumen Vitae*, vol. 40, no. 1 (1985) 67; Amalorpavadass, "Réflections théologiques sur l'inculturation," p. 58.

37. Lesslie Newbigin, "The Enduring Validity of Cross-Cultural Mission," *International Bulletin of Missionary Research*, vol. 12, no. 2 (1988) 50.

38. Robert J. Schreiter, *Constructing Local Theologies*, pp. 5-6 ff.

39. Kraft, *Christianity and Culture*; Hesselgrave and Rommen, *Contextualization: Meaning, Methods, Models*, p. 65.

ched by Kaplan's scheme: "toleration," "translation," "assimilation," "Christianization," "acculturation" and "incorporation."[40] Such schemes point to a growing acceptance — at least at a theoretical level — of the need for inculturation in a Church, faced by the modern, empirical and pluralist understanding of culture.

Inculturation and the Culture-Differential

Historically, Christian evangelization has enjoyed its greatest successes wherever there was a technological culture-differential between communicator and receptor. This explains, for example, why the Church today is stronger in Latin America and Africa than in Asia. This differential also underlies the contemporary consciousness of a "global village" or "one world." Euro-American technocratic culture is a totalitarian world process that has created a global monetary system, provoked a worldwide industrial revolution, internationalized productive capital and — for good or ill — influence global ecology.[41] At the global, or macro-level cultural diversity is disappearing under the influence of this process of modernization, the chief instrument of which is urbanization.[42] By the end of the twentieth century half the world's population will be urban dwelling. Besides creating ecological problems, modernization/urbanization is a force for secularization, for cultural disorientation at the micro-level and for increasing the disparities between rich and poor.[43] It is not surprising that inculturation assumes considerable importance in once-colonial countries where the recovery or redefinition of

40. Paul G. Hiebert, "Critical Contextualization," *International Bulletin of Missionary Research*, vol. 11, no. 3 (1917) 104-111; S. Kaplan, "The Africanization of Missionary Christianity: A History and Typology," *Journal of Religion in Africa*, vol. 16 (1986) 166-186. See also, among many others, Shorter, *Toward a Theology of Inculturation*, pp. 10-11, 17-30.
41. Peter Rottlander, "One World: Opportunity or Threat for the Global Church?" in *Concilium*, no. 204 (1989) 108.
42. Johan Baptist Metz, "Unity and Diversity: Problems and Prospects for Inculturation," *Concilium*, no. 204 (1989) 80; Aylward Shorter, *The Church in the African City* (London, Geoffrey Chapman, 1991.)
43. Shorter, *Ibid.*

traditional culture is jeopardized by the world process.[44] At the macro-level there is no "exotic" alternative to Euro-American modernization, as the demise of the various indigenous socialisms has proved. While it threatens to wipe out local, cultural traditions, the world system itself fails to meet the basic needs of humanity, and, indeed, has no real substance as a cultural system.[45] On the contrary, it appears to undermine human sensibilities and render human beings less compassionate.[46] It is, as it were, a worldwide movement of "anti-culture."[47]

If this viewpoint is accepted, it is difficult not to agree with Johan Baptist Metz that "the secular Europeanization of the world is not an innocent vehicle" for the universal propagation of the Church's message.[48] The alternatives are spelt out by Rottlander. Either the Church concludes that inculturation is a piece of hopeless romanticism and jumps on the Euro-American capitalist bandwagon, or it accepts inculturation and makes a credible bid for a polycultural Christianity.[49] The first alternative implies the subversion of the Gospel itself; the second, in the words of Michael Amaladoss, "is a call to uphold human and religious values as the basis and inspiration of culture in a secular and technological world" — a world which separates religion and culture as a matter of course.[50] This is not a question of expediency, but one which belongs to the Church's own vocation to meet "others in their otherness."[51] It is, in fact, another aspect

44. Amalorpavadass, "Réflections théologiques sur l'inculturation," p. 58.

45. Peter Rottlander, "One World: Opportunity or Threat for the Global Church," p. 108; Johan Baptist Metz, "Unity and Diversity: Problems and Prospects for Inculturation," p. 80.

46. Michael Drohan, "Christianity, Culture and the Meaning of Mission" *International Review of Mission*, vol. 15, no. 299 (1986) 298-299; cf. also Edmund Hill, "Christianity and Cultures," *New Blackfriars*, vol. 61, nos. 193/194 (1986) 324-329, where Hill speaks of "Christianity's all too successful inculturation in a violent, arrogant and aggressive culture," p. 326.

47. Aylward Shorter, *Toward a Theology of Inculturation* (London, Geoffrey Chapman, 1988) 231; cf. also Marcello de Cavallho Azevedo, *Inculturation and the Challenges of Modernity* (Rome, P.U.C., 1982.)

48. Johan Baptist Metz, "Unity and Diversity," p. 80.

49. Peter Rottlander, "One World: Opportunity or Threat for the Global Church," pp. 110-112.

50. Michael Amaladoss, "Dialogue and Inculturation," p. 24; Peter Rottlander, "One World: Opportunity or Threat for the Global Church," p. 113.

51. Johan Baptist Metz, "Unity and Diversity," p. 83.

of the preferential option for the poor. Non-western cultures are resisting the logic of Euro-American secular domination, and it belongs to the Church to side with those who feel threatened, not to assist in the process itself by drawing others into the secularizing vortex. It may even be that Euro-America needs to draw on the spiritual resources of the Two-Thirds World to fight its own battle with the secularizing and dehumanizing process.

There is a further, unanswerable argument against the fantasy of a Christian world culture, which is best expressed in the words of John Paul II.

> ... the synthesis between culture and faith is not just a demand of culture, but also of faith. A faith which does not become culture is a faith which has not been fully received, not thoroughly thought through, not fully lived out.[52]

If the language of faith is that of the receptor culture, then attempts to speak a universal language result in a superficial standardization that, at best appears culture-bound and irrelevant, and at worst encourages syncretism.[53] This is the dilemma of every "universal" document, issuing from a centralized *magisterium* to the lived pluralism of the Church: from typical editions of liturgical books, apostolic exhortations and encyclical letters to a universal code of Canon Law and the text of a universal catechism. Even in the realm of theology, while we have conceded the existence of a plurality of theologies, we still gratuitously assume a universal concept of theology itself.[54] All that can be realistically achieved at the macro-level is to develop theological "bridging categories" (Metz), a canonical *loi cadre* (Legrain), a "cross-cultural hermeneutic." (Huels).[55]

52. *L'Osservatore Romano*, 28th June 1982, pp. 1-8.

53. This was the point of view of Pedro Arrupe at the 1977 Synod of Bishops. Cf. *African Ecclesial Review*, vol. 20, no. 1 (1978) 32-33.

54. Johan Baptist Metz, "Unity and Diversity," p. 85.

55. Johan Baptist Metz, "Unity and Diversity," p. 85; Michel Legrain, "Young Churches and the New Code of Canon Law," *Theology Digest*, vol. 31 (1984) 217-218; John M. Huels, "Interpreting Canon Law in Diverse Cultures," *The Jurist*, vol. 47 (1987) 249-293.

Eurocentrism in Official Inculturation Theology

Inculturation is now so much a part of theological discourse in the Church that there are few neo-conservatives sufficiently courageous to contest it explicitly. One of the few is Aidan Kavanagh of Yale University who acquiesces in the label "reactionary."[56] Kavanagh fears that inculturation will lead to the local politicization of the liturgy and the "dispersal of the Church itself as a worshipping community."[57] He writes:

> Our First World will necessarily influence the other Worlds of the planet, even decreasingly, because our World is the one farthest ahead in power in all its aspects — intellectual, economic, military, educational, and so on. Our World's inevitable cultural power, even in decline, is necessarily far greater now than anything the British brought to bear on their colonies in the nineteenth and early twentieth century.[58]

It is rare to find such complacency in the face of Euro-American secularising world culture. Kavanagh sees the answer as loyalty to the Gospel in the cultural forms of the communicator, and, although he tries to disarm in advance the critics who would accuse him of advocating a *laissez-faire* policy, he appears to believe that inculturation is a mystery that will develop organically by itself.

Another well-known exponent of western monoculturalism is Cardinal Josef Ratzinger who puts his faith in the worldwide spread of European thought and in "the universal significance of Christian thought as it has evolved in the West."[59] That so eminent and influential a personality in the Church should identify universality with western cultural forms is disturbing, to say the least.

---

56. Aidan Kavanagh, "Liturgical Inculturation: Looking to the future," *Studia Liturgica*, vol. 20 (1990) 98 (cf. also *La Maison Dieu*, no. 179 (1989) 67-82, which gives a French version of the same paper, delivered to the 12th *Societas Liturgica* conference in York, 1989); "You may still find me reactionary, but at least you will know more about what sort of reactionary I am... ."

57. Aidan Kavanagh, *Ibid.*, p. 98.

58. Aidan Kavanagh, *Ibid.*, pp. 98-99.

59. Josef Ratzinger, (with Messori, Vittorio), *The Ratzinger Report* (San Francisco,??? Press, 1985) 103.

Generally, however, those who oppose cultural polycentrism in the Church take refuge in abstract and minimalist versions of inculturation theory, while upholding Eurocentrism in practice. Gregory Baum notes the curious contradiction between official affirmations concerning inculturation and the participatory society, on the one hand, and the *magisterium's* return to centralization and authoritarianism, on the other. As in other areas of doctrinal and moral teaching, the Church's failure to follow its own pronouncements fatally weakens the power of its message.[60]

A major form of abstractionism consists in assuming that the "Church," "Gospel" or "Faith" pre-exists, and accompanies, the act of evangelization in a culturally disembodied form. The idea seems to be that there is an "essence of the Gospel,"[61] that there are "core values" or an "invariant core"[62] that culture is an extrinsic, separable phenomenon, a "husk" enclosing a "kernel," "soil" receiving a "seed," a "form" requiring "content," or accidents in relation to substance in Thomistic philosophy.[63] In fact, religion is by definition a "cultural system" and is, as we have seen, integrally linked to culture.[64] This is equally true of the Christian Gospel, the supra-cultural validity of which consists in its capacity for cultural re-expression in a series of historical inculturations stretching back in a trajectory of meaning to the events and outlooks of the New Testament, and appealing to authentic values in every human cultural tradition.[65] Because of this, writers, such as Metz, Geffre, Reiser, Calvez and Shorter have pointed out that the parallel drawn between inculturation

60. Gregory Baum, Introduction to *Concilium* 204 (1989) XIV-XV.

61. *Evangelii Nuntiandi*, 63.

62. John M. Huels, "Interpreting Canon Law in Diverse Cultures," p. 288; Max L. Stackhouse, "Contextualization, Contextuality & Contextuation," pp. 3-13.

63. Robert J. Schreiter, *Constructing Local Theologies*, pp. 5-6; Amalorpavadass, "Réflections théologiques sur l'inculturation," pp. 63-65; Max L. Stackhouse, "Contextualization, Contextuality & Contextuation, p. 6.

64. Clifford Geertz, "Religion as a Cultural System," Michael Banton, (ed.), *Anthropological Approaches to the Study of Religion* (London, Tavistock Publications, 1966) 1-46.

65. Max L. Stackhouse, "Contextualization, Contextuality & Contextuation," p. 8.

and the Incarnation is only partially correct.[66] We do not live in a world of essences, nor do magisterial faith statements arise in some privileged supracultural sphere; rather the Gospel travels throughout history from one inculturated form to another.[67]

Minimalization consists in playing down inculturation as a two-way process. In Roman documents considerable emphasis is placed on the Church or Gospel which "penetrates," "transforms," "heals," "elevates," "enriches," or "recenters" cultures.[68] Cultures are said to be "introduced into the life of the Church."[69] *L'Osservatore Romano* even want so far as to entitle an address of Pope John Paul II in 1983: "The Church Creator of Culture in her Relation with the Whole World."[70] The Church is thus envisaged as a cultural entity, standing over against all other cultures. Little or nothing is said of inculturation leading to a new creation, or bearing new fruit for the Church; of cultures discovering, interpreting, realizing or re-expressing the Gospel; of new insights that can enrich the universal communion of particular Churches.[71] Nicolas Standaert has even noticed that a papal quotation from *Evangelii Nuntiandi* edited out the reference to the cultural re-expression of the Gospel and stopped short at the evangelist's work of transposition.[72]

Another minimalist tactic is to exaggerate the need for slowness in carrying out inculturation, in order to lessen its assumed risks and dangers. Writers, such as Adrian Hastings and Gerald A. Arbuckle, point out that sound inculturation does not suddenly happen, but is encouraged to grow, depending, as it does, on a

66. The parallel was drawn in *Ad Gentes Divinitus*, 22; cf. Johan Baptist Metz, "Unity and Diversity," p. 147; Aylward Shorter, *Toward a Theology of Inculturation* (London, Geoffrey Chapman, 1988) 79-83.

67. Francesco R. De Gasperis, "Community and the Newness of Faith in the Mother Church of Jerusalem," in Paul Beauchamp, *et. al.* (eds.), *Bible and Inculturation* (Rome, 1983) 60; Jean-Yves Calvez, "The Real Problem of Inculturation,", p. 77; Robert J. Schreiter, *Constructing Local Theologies*, pp. 5-6.

68. Nicolas Standaert, "L'histoire d'un neologisme," p. 564.

69. International Theological Commission, "Faith and Culture," p. 265.

70. Casimir Guanadickam, "Inculturation and the Local Church," p. 67, quoting *L'Osservatore Romano* of January 19th 1983.

71. Nicolas Standaert, "L'histoire d'un neologisme," p. 564.

72. Nicolas Standaert, *Idem*, p. 564; *Evangelii Nuntiandi*, 63.

14   AYLWARD SHORTER

personal and cultural conversion.[73] Others, however, call for patience because they do not believe in the need for any effective intervention to bring it about.[74] Against this, other writers — especially from Africa — speak of inculturation as requiring vital and urgent action.[75] This is because they feel that the *status quo* is deteriorating; Christians lead a divided life; religious education is superficial; syncretism and secularism are fast gaining the upper hand. Worse still, expectations are being created by official teaching which are not being fulfilled in practice. Inculturation requires urgent practical implementation if there is to be effective evangelization.

Without a doubt, minimalism reflects and upholds the actual *status quo* in the Church, according to which centralized authority usurps the culturally pluriform vernacular of faith. This leads us into a discussion of the question: Who are the agents of inculturation? And ultimately into the realms of ecclesiology. Before following this path, it is necessary to consider the prior question: Who or what is inculturated?

The Subject and Agents of Inculturation

Certain possibilities have already been ruled out. The subject of inculturation is not the Gospel, in the sense of a core or essence rationally paraphrased into propositional form. As Metz points out, the dogmas and faith-statements of the past require decoding, if we are to understand them today, because they belong to alien inculturation.[76] The Gospel is not a theological

73. Adrian Hastings, "Western Christianity Confronts Other Cultures," *Studia Liturgica*, vol. 20, no. 1 (1990) 24-25; Gerald A. Arbuckle, *Earthing the Gospel*, pp. 190-191.

74. Aidan Kavanagh, "Liturgical Inculturation: Looking to the Future," p. 105; cf. John Paul II's Address to the Zairean Bishops in 1980, *African Ecclesial Review*, vol. 22, no. 4 (1980) 4-5, in which he implied that inculturation in Africa could take as many centuries as in Poland.

75. Cf. John M. Waliggo, "Making a Church that is truly African," in John M. Waliggo, *et. al.* (eds.), *Inculturation: Its Meaning and Urgency* (Nairobi, St. Paul Publications Africa, 1986) 11-30; and J. Mutiso-Mbinda, "Inculturation: Challenge to the Local Church," in John M. Waliggo *et. al.* (eds.) *Ibid.*, p. 76.

76. Johan Baptist Metz, "Unity and Diversity," p. 86.

treatise, but a history, at the centre of which is the God-Man, born in Bethlehem and raised up in Jerusalem.[77] What is inculturated is a trajectory of meaning which goes back through the events of Church history to those of the New Testament. The person of Jesus Christ is made *imaginatively credible* to people of the receptor culture, through evangelization/inculturation. Through grace, the receptors are enabled to respond to Christ's self-gift, and to inform and construct their lives in accordance with the "Christic model."[78] For Christians, engaging in cross-cultural mission, there is, in the final analysis, no other absolute. Lesslie Newbigin has expressed it very eloquently.

> It is an illusion to suppose that we can find something larger, greater, more inclusive than Jesus Christ. Jesus when lifted up draws all people to himself. We must not relativize the name of Jesus in favor of some other absolute. It is an illusion to suppose that we can find something more absolute than what God has done in Jesus Christ.[79]

The fact that the Gospel is basically a history of events which carry a coherent meaning, going back to Christ in the New Testament, entails two further consequences. One is that the cultures of the Bible are necessarily privileged and respected as the *ne plus ultra* in cultural decoding.[80] The second is that a historic Church accumulates a currency or patrimory of cultural elements, either contingent or necessary, which is communicated through acculturation and which survives in great part as a syncretic component in Christianity's inculturated forms.[81] There is still a dangerous tendency in official Church documents to imply that this patrimony is a "culture," and even to equate it with a universally significant Euro-American culture. This patrimony includes the residue of previous inculturations, as well as

77. Titus Pressler, "Christianity Rediscovered: A Reflection on Vincent Donovan's Contribution to Missiology," in *Missiology*, vol. 18, no. 3 (1990) 272.

78. Edmund Hill, "Christianity and Cultures," p. 328; Shorter, *Toward a Theology of Inculturation*, pp. 59-63; Nolan, *God in South Africa*.

79. Lesslie Newbigin, "The Enduring Validity of Cross-Cultural Mission," p. 52; cf. also Jozef Tomko's critique of Paul Knitter, *No Other Name* (London, S.C.M. Press, 1985) in Jozef Tomko, "Missionary Challenges to the Theology of Salvation," *Inculturation*, vol. 4, no. 4 (1989) 7-12.

80. Aylward Shorter, *Toward a Theology of Inculturation*, pp. 64-65.

81. Aylward Shorter, *Toward a Theology of Inculturation*, pp. 65-67.

the outcome of mutual invigoration and enrichment in the contemporary communion of Churches.[82] It is a multicultural phenomenon which assists the Church in passing "from one kind of clarity to another" in its developing understanding of the faith.[83] It is a naive oversimplification to identify this patrimony with the culture of Europe, even if that culture is seen to be what it is in reality, a complex phenomenon of astonishing diversity.

Jean-Yves Calvez has written: "Inculturation is diversification," and other theologians have spoken of a "polycentric Christianity" with a diversity of cultural roots.[84] Who are then the agents of a polycentric inculturation? The obvious response is that they are the regional particular Churches. Even Aidan Kavanagh wants inculturation left to practising, baptized Christians, rather than to hierarchs, commissions, theologians or even pastors.[85] This liberality, however, is somewhat negated by his insistence on rigid control by episcopal conferences and Roman curial congregations. We come, in the final analysis, to the question of ecclesiology. In the documents of the Second Vatican Council an ecclesiology of communion emerges from the background of an older, pyramidic universalism. Angel Anton has argued convincingly for the collegiality represented by episcopal conferences, provinces and patriarchates, in spite of recent attempts to deny their theological significance.[86] *De facto*, episcopal conferences are being given more and more responsibilities and they constitute in reality a form of communion among the particular Churches or dioceses. Anton shows that the episcopal function is by its very nature collegial and that episcopal ordination is a collegial act, carried out by a neighbouring bishop or bishops.[87] Collegial responsibility and action belong, therefore,

82. *Evangelii Nuntiandi*, 63, 64.

83. William Reiser, "Inculturation and Doctrinal Development," p. 137.

84. Jean-Yves Calvez, "The Real Problem of Inculturation," p. 73; Peter Rottlander, "One World: Opportunity or Threat for the Global Church," p. 112; Johan Baptist Metz, "Unity and Diversity, p. 79.

85. Aidan Kavanagh, "Liturgical Inculturation: Looking to the future," p. 104.

86. Angel Anton, "The Theological Status of Episcopal Conferences," in Hervé Legrand, *et al.* (eds.), *The Nature and Future of Episcopal Conferences* (Washington, Catholic University of America Press, 1988) 185-219.

87. Angel Anton, *Ibid.*, p. 202.

to the episcopal function. For Reiser, the praxis of inculturation is a genuine development of the theology of the local Church.[88]

By definition, the *analogum princeps* of the local or particular Church is the diocese, but it is clear that a diocese can seldom be identified with the culture, cluster of cultures, or context that is the object of inculturation.[89] Although the diocese is, in reality, a flexible unit, being large or small in extent, densely or sparsely populated, as the case may be, ethnic cultures frequently overlap diocesan boundaries and even those of national episcopal conferences. There are also unstructured, culturally similar or identical, groups of nomads and migrants, present in dioceses which are not even geographically contiguous.[90] For these reasons, bilateral, regional, and even continental, relationships among episcopal conferences may be of greater cultural or contextual significance than relations among individual dioceses.[91]

Inculturation, Diversification and Universality

The joint initiatives of dioceses and episcopates are at present firmly controlled by the Holy See, under the provisions of the 1983 Code of Canon Law. According to Legrain, the code's catholicity is open to question and its compromise between centralization and decentralization is poorly formulated.[92] More disturbing still, is the fact that its understanding of mission is outdated. The code envisages missionary activity going from the centre to the periphery, from Euro-America to the South, when — from a missionary point of view — the Church is more than ever before a *koinonia* of local churches, reaching out to one

88. William Reiser, "Inculturation and Doctrinal Development," p. 136; cf. *Lumen Gentium*, 23; *Ad Gentes Divinitus*, 22.

89. Angel Anton, *Ibid.*, p. 193 ff.

90. Cf. "The Apostolate to the Nomads" in Eastern Africa which unites, the Diocese of Moroto in Uganda, the Dioceses of Ngong, Lodwar, Marsabit and Garissa in Kenya, and the Diocese of Arusha in Tanzania.

91. Jesus Hortal, "Relations among Episcopates," in Hervé Legrand, *et. al.* (eds.) *The Nature and Future of Episcopal Conferences*, pp. 174-180.

92. Michel Legrain, "Young Churches and the New Code of Canon Law," p. 217.

another in their needs.[93] Ecclesial maturity is today measured by
a capacity for interdependence, by the ability both to give from
poverty and to receive in humility. Although, pastoral sensitivity,
diversity of application, conflict with established custom and
grants of dispensation ensure a varied exercise, the 1983 code of
Canon Law remains bound to its culture of origin. This can be
seen, for example, in the cultural parallelism which results from
the implementation of the Church's marriage law, or from the
extraordinary attempt — in Canon 1083 — to fix an age of
maturity for marriage for the entire world.[94] If there is one
conclusion to be drawn, it is that of the canonist, Piskaty, that
the Roman Curia cannot make binding decisions for the local
Church.[95] Many, if not most, local episcopates have yet to be
persuaded of this.[96]

If inculturation cannot be conferred upon the local Church by
a centralized administration, this authority is nevertheless all too
capable of obstructing the process, chiefly by witholding permission for experimentation and approval for local initiatives. Yet,
even here, it has been pointed out that the spontaneous initiatives
of oral cultures frequently escape the surveillance of the literate
bureaucracy which needs texts and documents submitted for
approval or disapproval. The early history of the Zaire Mass is a
case in point. This is "inculturation from below," the only valid
inculturation, and it explains the importance of initiatives taken
at the grass-roots, particularly in the basic communities.[97] When
inculturation becomes a lived and popular reality, it is unstop-
pable, and official disapproval runs the risk of provoking schisms
and secessions.

93. *Ibid.*, p. 218.

94. Steven Bwana, "The Impact of the New Code in Africa," *Concilium*
no. 185 (1986) 103-109; Kurt Piskaty, "The Process of Contextualization and Its
Limits," *Verbum SVD*, vol. 24 (1983) 163-171; Michel Legrain, "Young Churches," p. 218.

95. Kurt Piskaty, "Process," p. 170-171.

96. Julien-Efoe Penoukou, *Églises d'Afrique: Propositions pour l'Avenir* (Paris,
Karthala, 1984), discusses the role of the local Bishop as guarantor of inculturation; see also Shorter, *Toward a Theology of Inculturation*, p. 194.

97. Shorter, *Toward a Theology of Inculturation*, pp. 251-254; 261-271.

Conclusion

True universality takes account of the Church's lived pluralism and seeks to develop a culturally polycentric Church. Inculturation is the necessary premise of Catholicity. As Edmund Hill has pointed out, the universalism of Christianity, or of the Gospel, is not a given. As a mark of the Church, it is not automatically present. On the contrary, it is a vocation, a call, "a task imposed" by Christ; and we have far to go towards its realization.[98] Let us give the last word to Lesslie Newbigin. In the final analysis, the Gospel only retains "its proper strangeness, its power to question us," when we are faithful to its universal, supranational and supracultural nature.[99]

98. Edmund Hill, "Christianity and Cultures," p. 328.
99. Newbigin, "The Enduring Validity of Cross-Cultural Mission," p. 50.

INCULTURATION AND INTER-RELIGIOUS DIALOGUE IN INDIA TODAY

Jacques Dupuis

Introduction

If one single term were to be used to characterise the mission-ary thrust and theological approach which has developed in the Church in India during the post-Vatican II period, "contextualisa-tion" would probably be the least inadequate. "Contextualisa-tion" says more than "inculturation" while it includes it. It means a constant reference to the context in devising a missionary policy and a search for relevance which takes the context as starting point of theological reflection. The context is understood as a true *locus theologicus*. Contextualisation implies, therefore, an induc-tive method. Unlike the deductive method which, taking its point of departure in universal truths and principles, seeks to apply these to concrete reality, an inductive method starts from contex-tual reality itself and asks what the Christian message and revelation in Jesus Christ have to say to it. A reversal of perspec-tive is involved here as a result of which theology is viewed as interpretation in context, that is, as hermeneutics.[1]

Contextualisation supposes in all situations a keen attention to reality; in the case of India, however, the demands it makes on theology are especially serious. The reason is the complexity of the Indian context. In general terms, the contextual reality of India may be described as made up of three principal elements: a great variety of cultures, a plurality of religious traditions, and the dehumanising poverty of the masses crying for integral libera-tion. None of these elements characterises the Indian context in an exclusive manner, but probably no other country combines the three to the same degree of intensity. It has been noted that, while

1. See Claude Geffré, *Le christianisme au risque de l'interprétation* (Paris: Cerf, 1983.)

the dehumanising poverty of large masses of people is a distinc-
tive feature of all "Thirdworldness," the coexistence not only of
various cultures but of many religious traditions is a specific
characteristic of "Asianness;"[2] and, one might want to add,
among Asian countries, the same defines "Indianness" even more
strikingly.

A few concrete data suffice to indicate the complexity of the
Indian context. 40% of the Indian population of over 800 million
people live even today on the poverty line or below. In each State
of the Indian union several major languages, with their specific
cultures, and innumerable dialects coexist. India, which is the
cradle of several of the great Oriental religions, is also the land
where virtually all the religious traditions of the world coexist and
meet in the daily life of people. In addition, Christianity itself is
represented in India by a large variety of groups. Among these
are: Roman Catholics; the Churches of North and South India
into which the Anglican Church, some Orthodox and several
Protestant Churches have united; and a host of Christian denominations. The Catholic Church in its turn includes three "individual" Churches: the Latin Church, and two Oriental Churches,
the Syro-Malabar and the Syro-Malankara. This diversity notwithstanding, Christianity accounts in India for 2.5% only of the
overall population, numbering some 20 million people among
whom 12 million Catholics, while the Hindu majority represents
over 80% of the total population. Islam, with over 70 millions, is
the first religious minority in the country, a number which keeps
India among the four countries in the world with the highest
Muslim population. The other religious minorities are all inferior
in number to Christianity, with Sikhism coming in third place
and Buddhism in the fourth.

The complexity of the Indian context — the various elements
of which intermingle in various ways — raises for the contextualisation of mission and theology methodological problems which
cannot be eluded. To start with the cultural element: In the
diversity of Indian cultures can some widespread elements be

2. Cf. for instance, Aloysius Pieris, *An Asian Theology of Liberation*, Maryknoll (New York: Orbis Books, 1988) who writes: "The Church must... step in the
baptismal waters of Asian religion and... pass through passion and death on the
cross of Asian poverty" (p. 63).

singled out which would serve as common foundation for a process of inculturation? Is there such a thing as one Indian culture, with the consequence that one model of inculturation can be devised which would be valid for the whole country? Or, on the contrary, are the differences between the various cultures so great that the inculturation process must follow distinct models in different places? Perhaps there is no a priori answer to these questions, neither in one or the other direction, with the result that both common elements and differences need to be taken into account in each concrete situation. Inculturation is by itself a complex process.

Coming to the religious element: The differences between the various religious traditions, Hinduism and Islam for example, are so great that a universal model for inter-religious dialogue between them and Christianity remains necessarily problematic. Each religious tradition constitutes a partner *sui generis*, to be met by Christianity on a bilateral basis. This is not to say that multilateral dialogue between Christians and others is a priori excluded; nor that a Christian theology of religions in general is impossible which would view them all as related, though differently, to the mystery of Jesus Christ and Christianity. But, once again, the scope left open for general statements and overall evaluations is limited, and attention to particular reality is required in each case.

Where Hinduism is concerned, to which the majority community of India belongs, there is the further question whether it can be viewed, as some have suggested, as only a cultural reality without a specific religious faith; or is it, on the contrary, a religious faith in its own right, with a specific culture attached to it? The question has important implications as becomes manifest when it is asked whether it is possible for one person to be a "Hindu-Christian." Is hyphenated Christianity understood in this way an acceptable concept? Once more, there seems to be no absolute answer to this question. Some have answered it positively but in the process have reduced Hinduism to a philosophy or a cultural reality, endowed with a strong social organisation, yet without a specific religious faith, its multifaceted beliefs and practices notwithstanding, or — perhaps — due to this variety

itself.[3] The problem of being a "Hindu-Christian" would amount
then to that of the inculturation of the Christian faith and
practice in the majority culture of India. Others, refusing what
appears an undue simplification, have sought to combine the two
religious faiths, the Hindu and the Christian, in their personal
experience, in an attempt to hold them together, admittedly in a
precarious state of tension as the intellectual synthesis of both
seemed to escape their grasp.[4] Others still have thought such an
intellectual synthesis of both faiths possible and have advocated
a "Hindu-Christian" theology.[5]

However this may be, one thing is certain which needs to be
stressed: Inter-religious dialogue in general, and "Hindu-Christian" dialogue in particular, in order to be sincere and authentic,
requires that both partners, while holding to the integrity of their
own religious faith, endeavor to enter personally, as far as is
possible, into the religious experience and world-view of the
other. Such an "intra-religious" dialogue is, on both sides, a
prerequired condition for the inter-religious dialogue between
persons belonging to the two different faiths.[6] What is said here
directly about Hindu-Christian dialogue holds good — *mutatis
mutandis* — in the context of Buddhist-Christian dialogue as
well.[7] It may further be noted that, where the Oriental religions

3. See Hans Staffner, *The Open Door* (Bangalore: Asian Trading Corporation,
1978); *Jesus Christ and the Hindu Community: Is a Synthesis of Hinduism and
Christianity Possible?* (Anand: Gujarat Sahitya Prakash, 1988.)

4. Henri Le Saux (Swami Abhishiktananda) is a striking example of such a
symbiosis between Hinduism and Christianity in which, however, a complete
intellectual integration seems never to be reached. See especially *Intériorité et
révélation* (Sisteron: Editions Présence, 1982); *La montée au fond du cœur: Le
journal intime du moine chrétien - sannyasi hindou (1948-1973)* (Paris: OEIL,
1986.) See also James Stuart, *Swami Abhishiktananda: His Life Told through his
Letters* (Delhi: ISPCK, 1989.)

5. See on Raymond Panikkar, Robert Smet, *Le problème d'une théologie
hindoue-chrétienne selon Raymond Panikkar* (Louvain-la-Neuve: Centre d'histoire
des religions, 1983.)

6. See Raymond Panikkar, *The Intra-Religious Dialogue* (New York: Paulist
Press, 1978.)

7. See John B. Cobb, "Christianity and Eastern Wisdom," *Japanese Journal of
Religious Studies* (1978) 285-298; "Can a Buddhist Be a Christian Too?," *Japanese
Journal of Religious Studies*, 1980, pp.35-55; *Beyond Dialogue: Towards a Mutual
Transformation of Christianity and Buddhism* (Philadelphia: Fortress Press, 1982.)
See also David Lochhead, *The Dialogue Imperative: A Christian Reflection on
Interfaith Encounter* (London: SCM Press, 1988.)

are concerned, the distinction between culture and religion, its theoretical validity not-withstanding, is largely unpracticable: both spheres are inseparable in reality, mutually integrated as they are in a single holistic approach to reality. The result is that no dialogue with culture is devoid of religious connotations, and vice versa.

The third element of the Indian context also raises problems of method. Can the uplift of the masses from their dehumanising poverty and involvement in the liberation of the oppressed people be viewed as an isolated concern, kept apart and separated from a project of inculturation? To say that it can would betray a distorted view of culture. Surely, induced poverty and injustice are no part of human culture; they are anti-culture with deep adverse effects on the life of a people. No inculturation project can then be devised which would not take into account the socio-economic reality and the disability suffered by the weak classes of society. In situations of oppression there can be no inculturation without human liberation and social uplift. The same must be said where social concern and inter-faith relations are concerned: no inter-religious dialogue program can make abstraction from, or remain indifferent to the dehumanising condition of the poor. Indeed, part of dialogue must consist in a mutual critique by religious traditions and institutions as to the impact, positive or negative, they have had on society and its structures and the liberative potential enshrined in them for human liberation. Have they not often been accomplices to the powerful in maintaining the status quo and perpetuating injustice? In a context of human poverty and oppression inter-religious dialogue cannot dispense with a common involvement of members of the various religious traditions in a liberative praxis; nor can a theology of religions be kept separate from a theology of liberation.

The three fundamental elements that together make up the Indian context thus appear so intimately connected that no mission or theology program can dissociate them. The same is true where the Asian scene in general is concerned and has been clearly perceived by the Federation of Asian Bishops Conferences (FABC) ever since its creation in 1971. In a document published by their first General Assembly held at Taipei, Taiwan (April 1974), in anticipation of the Synod of Bishops on evangelisation due to take place in Rome in the same year, the Asian bishops took as the "primary focus of (their) task of evangelisation... the building up of a truly local Church" (9). Such a local Church, they said, would be one "incarnated in a people, a Church indigenous and inculturated. And this means concretely a Church in continuous, humble and loving dialogue with the living traditions, the cultures, the religions — in brief, with all the life-realities of the people in whose midst it has sunk its roots deeply and whose history and life it gladly makes its own" (12). They further explained: "In Asia especially this involves a dialogue with the great religious traditions of our peoples" (13). They added in like manner: "A local Church in dialogue with its people... means (in) dialogue with the poor" (19); "this dialogue... involves genuine experience and understanding of (the) poverty, deprivation and oppression of so many of our peoples. It demands working, not *for* them merely (in a paternalistic sense), but *with* them, to learn from them... their real needs and aspirations... and to strive for their fulfilment, by transforming those structures and situations which keep them in that deprivation and powerlessness" (20).[8] In brief: Dialogue with cultures, religions, and the poor; or, equivalently: inculturation, inter-religious dialogue, and human liberation. The three components of "Asianness" are seen in their inter-relatedness and unity, as making up together the context against which the evangelising thrust of the Asian Churches is defined.

This consistent thrust of the Asian Churches has been well observed by an Asian theologian who wrote recently:

> From 1971 onward it has been affirmed — most clearly by the FABC General Assembly of 1974 at Taipei — that the "basic mode of mission in Asia" must be dialogue. *Missionary* dialogue, of course. We must explore the interface of the Gospel's meanings and values with the realities of Asia and its many peoples — its histories and cultures, religions and religious traditions, and especially its "poor masses" in every country. These realities — cultures, reli-

8. "Evangelisation in Modern Day Asia," Statement and Recommendations of the First Plenary Assembly of the Federation of Asian Bishops' Conferences, Taipei, Taiwan, 27 April 1974, in *For all the Peoples of Asia. The Church in Asia: Asian Bishops' Statements on Mission, Community and Ministry, 1970-1983*, Volume I: Texts and Documents (Manila: IMC Publications, 1984), pp. 25-41.

gions, life-situations of poverty — make up the ambience and context wherein the Gospel is to be proclaimed; these realities define the "place" for the localisation of the Church and the inchoate "*real*-ization" of God's kingdom.

This overarching program of dialogue with the cultures (i.e., inculturation), with the religions and religious traditions (i.e., inter-religious dialogue), and with "our peoples, especially the poor multitudes in Asia" (i.e., development/liberation), has been the thematic background of both the pastoral and missionary activity of the local Churches of Asia in the past twenty years. In the 1979 international Mission Congress (Manila) it was used as the overall framework for reflection on mission and the tasks of mission in the 1980s.[9] For the 1990s these dialogues remain the headings under which the concerns and activities of Christian mission are collocated. It is in the endeavor to bring these dialogues into life and practice, and in the ongoing reflection on the process they have initiated, that the way of theologising on mission must surely be constructed in the decade to come.[10]

Where India is concerned, the same threefold focus is explicitly given to the Church's mission as it seeks to respond to the three dimensions which together define "Indianness" even more clearly than they determine "Asianness." To show this, it is enough to recall Pope John Paul II's address to the bishops of India in New Delhi (1 February 1986) during his visit to the country. Having reaffirmed the Church's duty to proclaim the good news, the pope immediately went on to lay emphasis on a threefold task: "to ensure the true development and liberation" of the deprived sections of society (5.3); inter-relgious dialogue which constitutes, he said, "a serious part of your apostolic ministry" (5.4); and "the great challenge of inculturation" (5.5).[11] Two months later, during the Plenary Assembly of the episcopal conference held at

9. The proceedings of this congress are found in Gaudencio B. Rosales *et al.* (eds), *Toward a New Age in Mission: International Congress on Mission, 2-7 December, 1979*, Books I-III, 2 vols (Manila: International Mission Congress, 1981.)

10. Catalino G. Arevalo, "Mission in the 1990s: Agenda for Mission," *International Bulletin of Missionary Research* 14 (1990/2) 50.

11. See *The Pope Speaks to India* (Bombay: St Paul Publications, 1986), pp. 25-34.

Goa (April 1986), Cardinal Simon Pimenta, Archbishop of Bombay and President of the Conference, reminded the bishops of the threefold focus of the pope's speech to them. He quoted the pope to the effect that "in the name of bearing witness to the Gospel the Church endeavors to ensure the true development and liberation of millions of human beings"; and added: "One cannot... miss (the pope's) insistence on inter-religious dialogue and inculturation as two important imperatives for the Church in India with its multi-religious background and its (diverse) traditions of spirituality."...[12] Once again, human liberation, inter-religious dialogue and inculturation are viewed as inseparable components of the Church's evangelising mission.

Yet, holding together the various elements of the Indian context in an effort to "contextualise" the Church's evangelising mission as well as theological reflection raises further fundamental questions which it is necessary to touch upon, even if only rapidly. One concerns the local Church as the agent of the local mission and her relationship to the Church universal. Contextualisation of mission requires that the primary focus in ecclesiology be placed on the ecclesial reality of the local Church with the legitimate autonomy it needs to be able to devise concrete ways of living, celebrating and witnessing to the Christian message and mystery. The local Church, however, must maintain communion with all other local Churches engaged in the same mission in their own circumstances, and indeed foster that communion. The universal Church appears in this perspective as the communion of all the local Churches — a communion to which the Church of Rome and its bishop presides in charity. The mystery of the Church is, therefore, at once one of diversity and unity.

A second question — which is derived from the first — regards the plurality of theologies in the unity of the Church's faith. Theology cannot be contextualised without becoming plural. But again there is a complemetary truth: all the local theologies must maintain communion in the unity of the Church's faith. As truly as the universal Church is the communion of local Churches, so too universal theology must be conceived as the communion of local

12. *Report of the General Meeting of the Catholic Bishops' Conference of India, Goa, April 1986* (New Delhi: CBCI Centre, 1986), pp. 145-146.

theologies. Once theologising is seen as reflection on faith lived in context, no single theology can any longer claim validity for all times and places. Here too the principle of unity in diversity, that is of communion, needs to be applied.

What follows is a brief account of the local, contextual theology which has arisen in India in the post-conciliar years in response to the challenge of "Indianness" and which continues to develop today. However, the vastness of the subject makes it impossible to account for the personal contribution of individual theologians; we must be content to follow the collective reflection of Indian theologians as embodied in widely representative assemblies, conferences and seminars.[13] Moreover, the intimate connection between the three components of "Indianness" notwithstanding, space allows only for two sections devoted to inculturation and inter-religious dialogue respectively; human liberation will be touched upon only indirectly, in relation to the other concerns.

The Inculturation of the Liturgy and Sharing Worship

The term "inculturation" appeared for the first time in an official Church document with the Message of the Synod of Bishops in Rome on Catechetics in 1977; it was taken up by Pope John Paul II in the ensuing apostolic exhortation *Catechesi*

13. The documents published by the Catholic Bishops' Conference of India (CBCI) will not be considered here. The following may be mentioned. In 1977 the CBCI Commission for Dialogue published *Guidelines for Inter-Religious Dialogue* (Varanasi: 1977); a second, revised edition of the same appeared recently: CBCI Commission for Dialogue and Ecumenism, *Guidelines for Inter-Religious Dialogue* (New Delhi: CBCI Centre, 1989.) Among documents published by CBCI General Meetings treating the topics under consideration here the following can be listed: The Communication from the CBCI to the Synod of Bishops in Rome (1974) in *Report of the General Meeting of the Catholic Bishops' Conference of India (Calcutta, January 1974)* (New Delhi: CBCI Centre, 1974) 124-143; Statement on "The Church's Response to the Urgent Needs of the Country" in *Report of the General Meeting of the Catholic Bishops' Conference of India (Mangalore, January 1978)* (New Delhi: CBCI Centre, 1978); Statement on "The Church's Response to the Challenges of Contemporary Society with Special Reference to the Role of the Laity" in *Report of the General Meeting of the CBCI (Nagpur, February 1984)* (New Delhi: CBCI Centre, 1984) 75-84.

Tradendae (1979). The Council Vatican II had used the term "adaptation," first in the Constitution on the Sacred Liturgy *Sacrosanctum Concilium* (1963) and later in the Decree on the Church's Missionary Activity *Ad Gentes* (1965). There is no need to explain why "inculturation" has been substituted for "adaptation." Suffice it to recall that adaptation seemed to intend only the extrinsic accomodation of accidental elements to an unchanged substance; such a process remained somewhat superficial. "Inculturation," on the contrary, implies more. It may be thought that the Council laid the foundation for "inculturation" — though the term was not yet used — when in the Decree *Ad Gentes* it described the process by which, "rooted in Christ and built on the foundation of the apostles, the young Churches assume into a marvellous exchange (*in admirabile commercium assumunt*) all the riches of the nations which have been given to Christ as an inheritance" (AG, 22). The Decree explains: "They (the young Churches) borrow from the customs, traditions, wisdom, teaching, arts and sciences of their people everything that can be used to praise the glory of the Creator, manifest the grace of the savior, and contribute to the right ordering of Christian life" (*ibid.*). Surely, more is involved here than superficial adaptation.

Where the liturgy is concerned *Sacrosanctum Concilium* foresaw that, "mostly in the missions," a process of adaptation to the genius of the different peoples would be required; it set forth norms to be observed in such a process (SC, 37-40), while characteristically stipulating that "the substantial unity of the Roman Rite" needs to be preserved (SC, 38).

Soon after the Council the liturgical commission of the episcopal conference of India, with a large body of experts and consultants, set to work towards the adaptation of the liturgy of the Roman Rite to the Indian context. The first fruit of this work was the adoption in the liturgy of external elements from other religious traditions, such as postures, implements and symbols (1969). But the commission work reached far beyond such immediate results. A "Eucharistic Prayer for India" was composed (1971), soon followed by an entire "Ordinary of the Mass" (1973). Three volumes of "alternate" second readings for the Office of Reading in the Liturgy of the Hours (1973) which borrowed largely from the Sacred Books of Indian religions, were also written.[14]

There is no need to enter into the intricate reasons why all this work, though existing in print[15] and used unofficially, has not been officially approved at the highest level. More important is to examine the problems, pastoral and theological, which such far-reaching liturgical adaptation did not fail to encounter and to review the in-depth study that followed of the issues involved as well as the theological solutions which were arrived at.

Some difficulties had to do with procedure and the pastoral approach. The work had been done by a body of experts at the national level and by a national organism. This meant that it came from above, not from below, and was the result of academic study rather than the spontaneous expression of faith lived at the grass-roots. The inverse procedure seemed to be desired, that would proceed from life, not from the academy, and operate at the local, not the national level. While it was legitimate to speak of one Indian culture since there existed cultural elements common to the various regions, Indian cultures were nevertheless many. There was need, therefore, not for one Indian model of liturgical adaptation, but for several, in keeping with the diverse cultural contexts.

Diverse were, moreover, the religious contexts in which the liturgy was to be inculturated: Hindu, Muslim, tribal, and so forth. A liturgy adapted to the Hindu religious culture would not *per se* be applicable to a Muslim setting, and vice versa. The multi-religious context called for plurality in liturgical adaptation. As for concern for the poor and human liberation, it did not yet figure prominently in this early stage of post-Vatican II liturgical reform. Rather than emerge from the masses and speak to them, the reform emerged from the academy and spoke to the elite. Again, the process needed to be reversed and a "from below" approach to be adopted: the social dimension would emerge

14. A detailed account of that work and of the role taken in it by the National Biblical Catechetical and Liturgical Centre, Bangalore, and its director D.S Amalorpavadass, is found in J.A.G. Gerwin van Leeuwen, *Fully Indian - Authentically Christian* (Kamper: Kok, 1990) 63-97.

15. *New Orders of the Mass for India*, Bangalore: NBCLC, 1974; *Text for the Office of Readings*, 3 vols (Bangalore: NBCLC, 1973-1974.)

naturally if only the liturgy were allowed to reflect and give spontaneous expression to people's concerns. This, it may be affirmed, is one of the reasons why in more recent years more spontaneous liturgies have been given preference over stereotyped forms.

On the theological level, liturgical adaptation raised the problem of Indianisation vs "Hinduisation." While the Indianisation of the liturgy seemed, at least in theory, acceptable, was not its "Hinduisation" to be rejected a priori? Yet, given the close link in the majority religious community of India between culture and religion, was inculturation in a Hindu context possible without some degree of "Hinduisation"? Were there not, moreover, some religious elements and values in Hinduism which could be integrated in Christian liturgy, even though such assimilation called for discernment? Fundamental questions were, therefore, asked which concerned the relationship between the Hindu religious tradition, with its sacred books and liturgical rites, its doctrines and practices, on the one hand, and the mystery of Jesus Christ and Christianity, on the other.

This lead to a "Research Seminar on non-Biblical Scriptures" which was held in Bangalore (December 1974).[16] The immediate purpose of the seminar was to establish theologically the legitimacy of the process of liturgical inculturation which was taking root in the country, in particular the use of non-biblical Sacred Scriptures in the Christian liturgy at various levels, including the proclamation of those Scriptures in the liturgy of the word of the eucharistic celebration. Was such a practice theologically defendable? Could those Scrptures be considered as "seeds of the word"? And, if so, was there room in the liturgy of the word for the proclamation of these "seeds"? More specifically, could it be thought that the non-biblical Sacred Scriptures have in the Indian context a function similar to that of the Jewish Bible? Such questions lead the seminar to develop a theology of the word of God in its various forms and of the relationship of God's revelation in the history of the nations to the fullness of his revelation in Jesus Christ. The official "Statement" of the semi-

16. See D.S. Amalorpavadass (ed.), *Research Seminar on non-Biblical Scriptures* (Bangalore: NBCLC, 1974.)

nar[17] recognises unambiguously the unique significance for Christians of the New Testament as the official record of God's decisive revelation of himself in Jesus Christ(52). It states that the Old Testament too has special meaning and authority as the record of the historical preparation in Israel for the fulness of God's revelation in Christ (53). This notwithstanding, "the Holy Spirit is operative" also in the Sacred Scriptures of other religious traditions; they too manifest "in diverse ways the one mystery of God" and "reflect the experiences of these communities" with him (54). As such, they find their rightful place in the proclamation which the Church makes of God's dealings with humankind through the history of salvation.[18] The liturgy of the word, however, must culminate in the Gospel, as proclamation of the Good News of Jesus Christ, who is the fullness of revelation (58-62).[19]

Related to the question of non-Biblical Scriptures in Christian worship is the broader issue of mutual sharing in worship between Christians and the members of other religious traditions. A more recent Research Seminar, held at NBCLC, Bangalore (January 1988), studied this problem under its different aspects.[20] Its Final Statement[21] cannot be analysed here in details. Let it suffice to note the following: The document speaks of an emerging new consciousness, "not a break with the past but a mutation in self-understanding," of Christians in India (12), who see in their multi-religious challenging situation a *locus theologicus* (9): "The Christian identity and the ecclesial reality have to relate

17. See *Ibid.*, pp.681-695.

18. We may note that in an intervention at the Synod of Bishops in Rome on the Evangelisation of the Modern World (October 1974), Cardinal Joseph Parecattil, Archbishop of Cochin, had declared: "Theoretically speaking,... the introduction of readings from non-Christian Scriptures into the Divine Office and even in the liturgy of the word is not in itself objectionable. But the time may not be ripe for that, because the faithful are not yet prepared for such an innovation...". See D.S. Amalorpavadass, *Evangelisation of the Modern World* (Bangalore: NBCLC, 1975) 137.

19. Another Research Seminar on "God's Word in the Emerging India-2000" took place in Bangalore in March 1991 the proceedings of which were not yet available at the time of writing.

20. See Paul Puthanangady (ed.), *Sharing in Worship* (Bangalore: NBCLC, 1988.)

21. *Ibid.*, pp. 784-801.

afresh and respond adequately to the new exigencies and challenges of the pluri-cultural, pluri-religious and unjust human situation in India by new and creative forms of open, wider and inclusive fellowship" (15). The other religions are "authentic expressions of the God-experience of men and women throughout the centuries": Our awareness of the presence in them of the living God and of his Spirit is "the foundation and starting-point of 'sharing worship,'" for "all symbols and rituals are related to the ONE Sacrament of humanity, Jesus Christ" (16). Sharing worship consists first in mutual sharing of Sacred Scriptures or equivalent sources of religious experience in unwritten traditions (18). "Through the rays of the one Truth found in them, we (Christians) are lead to a progressively fuller realisation of the mystery of God and to a deepening of our Christian faith blossoming into new dimensions and perspectives" (23).

Sharing worship consists also in sharing sacraments and symbolic structures (24). In this matter, given the multi-religious experience of India, the attitude should neither be total acceptance nor total rejection, but "creative interaction" (26). "As Catholics inceasingly acknowledge that Christ manifests himself through his Spirit in the signs, symbols, rituals and sacraments of other religious traditions of humankind, they can also experience this through their participation in the official worship of these religions" (32). Are given as examples: sharing worship on the occasion of socio-religious feasts, in specifically religious festivals, in visits to shrines of other faiths (33). The "principle of reciprocity" can, however, be observed more freely in shared prayer than in other forms of shared worship (34), for which distinct situations need to be taken into account. Examples are: inter-religious rite for inter-faith marriage, sharing the eucharist with people of other faiths. For these and others, the circumstances need to be examined in each case.

Theology of Religious Pluralism and Inter-Faith Dialogue

What has been said above shows that in questions of liturgical inculturation and sharing worship a theology of religions and a praxis of inter-religious dialogue are already involved. It is to those two issues that we now turn our attention directly. We do so in the sequence just indicated, for the praxis of inter-religious dialogue needs to be grounded in a theology of religious pluralism. The development of Indian theological thinking on these issues will again be considered in its collective expression through important, broadly representative meetings and seminars devoted to them.

An international theological conference on Mission Theology and Dialogue took place at Nagpur in October 1971.[22] The Declaration of the Conference devotes a section to "The Theological Understanding of the Religious Traditions of Mankind."[23] It says:

> An ineffable mystery, the center and ground of reality and human life, is in different forms and manners active among all peoples of the world and gives ultimate meaning to human existence and aspirations. This mystery, which is called by different names, but which no name can adequately represent, is definitively disclosed and communicated in Jesus of Nazareth (13).

This means that "the self-communication of God is not confined to the Judeo-Christian tradition, but extends to the whole of mankind in different ways and degrees within the one divine economy" (14). Where individual persons are concerned, the human being who is a pilgrim on earth can only reach fulfilment through a positive response to the divine mystery (15); but, since the human is a social being, "concrete religious traditions provide the usual context in which he strives for his ultimate goal. Therefore the religious traditions of the world can be, in various degrees, expressions of a divine manifestation and can be conducive to salvation" (16); yet, "this in no way undermines the uniqueness of the Christian economy, to which has been entrusted the decisive word spoken by Christ to the world and the means of salvation instituted by him" (16).

It was necessary to quote at length this important and carefully

22. There exist two editions of the proceedings of the conference: Mariasusai Dhavamony (ed.), *Evangelisation, Dialogue and Development*, Documenta Missionalia 5 (Roma: Università Gregoriana Editrice, 1972); Joseph Pathrapankal (ed.), *Service and Salvation: Nagpur Theological Conference on Evangelisation* (Bangalore: Theological Publications in India, 1973.)

23. See Dhavamony edition, pp.1-15; Pathrapankal edition, pp. 1-16.

worded statement. It sets aside every theory which, while admitting the possibility of salvation in Jesus Christ for the members of other religious traditions, would deny that the sincere practice of those traditions might contribute positively to their salvation. It displaces the "fulfilment theory" propounded in the West by J. Daniélou, H. de Lubac and H. Urs von Balthasar and in the East by J. Farquhar and P. Johanns, in favor of that of the "presence of Christ" in the other religions, of which the main protagonists have been in the West Karl Rahner and in India Raimundo Panikkar. According to this theory the members of other religions are not saved by Jesus Christ without their respective traditions or in spite of them, but in the sincere practice of, and in a certain sense, through these traditions. The religious traditions of the world mediate salvation for their members — though in a manner which it is difficult to define — because the mystery of Jesus Christ is present and operative in them.[24] Their Sacred Scriptures and ritual practices can, therefore, be viewed as means of salvation, though not independently from, but in relation to the mystery of Jesus Christ, the universal Saviour.

This "theological understanding" of the religious traditions of the world has deep implications for inter-religious dialogue. The Nagpur Declaration devotes a section to this topic. It notes that "by its very nature dialogue... tends towards the ultimate vision of a perfect unification of all men which can be discerned in the convergent aspirations of the various religious traditions" (26); adding: "Dialogue... is good in itself, because it fosters mutual communion and edification" (26). In effect, from the "fraternal exchange of religious experience" there results a "mutual spiritual enrichment. This enrichment comes from the fact that in dialogue each partner listens to God speaking in the self-communication and questioning of... fellow-believers. It leads to a spiritual growth and therefore to a kind of deeper *metanoia* or conversion to God" (27). However, mutual sharing of religious experiences is not the only form of inter-religious dialogue; for dialogue exists

---

24. I have tried to elucidate how this can be understood theologically in a recent book, *Jésus-Christ à la rencontre des religions*, Jésus et Jésus-Christ, 39 (Paris: Desclée, 1989.) English translation: *Jesus Christ at the Encounter of World Religions* (Maryknoll, N.Y.: Orbis Books, 1991.)

wherever, "as religiously committed persons," "with their ultimate commitments and religious outlook," Christians and others
— no matter how different their religious persuasions may be —
engage together and collaborate in matters of common human
interest (24).

That "dialogue is good in itself" means that it cannot be
reduced to a means useful in the measure in which it conduces to
another activity which would have its own justification; the
deeper conversion of the partners of dialogue towards the God
who speaks to them through each other is an end in itself. Can it
be said then that for Christians inter-faith dialogue is an integral
part of the Church's evangelizing mission? Or even that in inter-
religious dialogue Christians and others evangelize each other? If
the Nagpur Declaration does not reach such a conclusion, the
reason is that its notion of evangelization remains a narrow one.
Evangelization is identified with the Christian proclamation of
Jesus Christ aimed at inviting others to become his disciples in
the Church community through baptism (19).[25] Many theologians today would disagree on this point with the Nagpur Declaration. For my own part, I have shown elsewhere that the notion
of evangelization has been much broadened in recent years to
include not only Christian witness and the proclamation of Jesus
Christ, but also such activities of the Church as the promotion of
justice and the work of human liberation, as well as inter-religious dialogue.[26]

A document published by the Vatican Secretariat for non-
Christians, entitled "The Attitude of the Church towards the
Followers of Other Religions: Reflections and Orientation on
Dialogue and Mission" (Pentecost 1984), goes in the same direc-
tion. It views the overall evangelizing mission of the Church as "a
single but complex and articulated reality," of which, without

25. This narrow notion of evangelization is even more evident at the Nagpur
Conference in the "Report of the Special Committee on Evangelisation, Dialogue
and Development." See M. Dhavamony (ed.), op. cit., pp. 17-20.

26. See J. Dupuis, "Le dialogue inter-religieux dans la mission évangélisatrice
de l'Eglise," in René Latourelle (ed.), Vatican II: Bilan et perspectives. Vingt-cinq
ans après (1962-1965), vol. 3 (Paris: Cerf et Montréal: Bellarmin, 1988), pp. 237-
262. The article has been included in revised, updated form, in Jésus-Christ à la
rencontre des religions (note 24), pp. 269-297.

pretending to be exhaustive, it enumerates some of the "principal
elements" (13). They are the following: presence and witness;
"the concrete commitment to the service of humankind and all
forms of activity for social development and for the struggle
against poverty and the structures which produce it"; liturgical
life, prayer and contemplation; "dialogue in which Christians
meet the followers of other religious traditions in order to walk
together towards truth and to work together in projects of
common concern"; "finally there is announcement and catechesis
in which the Good News of the Gospel is proclaimed and its
consequences for life and culture are analysed." "The totality of
Christian mission," the document concludes, "embraces all these
elements" (13).[27]

More is involved here than a question of words. To recognize
that inter-religious dialogue is, in its own right, an integral part of
the Church's evangelising mission, even while it does not aim at
the conversion of others to Christianity, has far-reaching consequences for the theology of dialogue as well as of mission.
Indeed, in a context of religious pluralism such as Asia offers,
dialogue becomes a privileged expression of mission, and as such
an apostolic priority. There exist concrete situations in which it
may be the principal way, or even the only way in which the
Church is able to fulfil her mission.

Not surprisingly then the Indian Theological Association chose
as topic for its 12th and 13th annual meetings (December 1988
and 1989) the theology of religions and of religious pluralism.
Two Statements have been published, entitled "Towards a Theology of Religions: An Indian Christian Perspective" (1988),[28] and
"Towards an Indian Christian Theology of Religious Pluralism:
An Ongoing Search" (1989),[29] respectively. Note must be taken
of the fact that since the 1971 Conference in Nagpur much work
has been done by theologians in India on the theology of
religions. The views which may have seemed somewhat new to

27. The text of the document is found in *Bulletin. Secretariatus pro non
Christianis*, n. 59; 19 (1984/4) 126-141.
28. The 1988 Statement is found in *Jeevadhara* n. 19; 109 (1989) 72-83; also in
Indian Theological Studies 26 (1989) 71-83.
29. The 1989 Statement is published in *Vidyajyoti* 54 (1990) 209-217. The
proceedings of both meetings have not yet been published at the time of writing.

many at that time are commmonly held today: Religions are viewed as means of salvation inasmuch as it is in the concrete circumstances of their life and in the sincere practice of their tradition that their members respond to God's offer of grace in Jesus Christ. On this foundation, the theological issue has recently taken a new focus: how must the reality of religious pluralism be interpreted theologically as part of God's salvific design for humankind? In the variegated reality of the Indian multi-religious context this question is a central one.

The 1988 Statement remarks from the outset that, though "religious pluralism has always been in India," "its recent manifestation calls for urgent attention" (1). "Is a convergence perhaps of the world's cultures and religions beginning to happen in our days?" (6). "We find ourselves in a new situation," "particularly signalled and shaped by the development of inter-religious dialogue, of inculturation and of the liberation of oppressed peoples" (7). This new situation calls for "a new theology of religions," "a new horizon of meaning" (8). Such a new theology "will emerge via theologies of dialogue, of cultural incarnation and liberation" (8). Thus, the conviction is expressed that the three factors that constitute "Indianness" must be held together in devising a theology of religions that would meet the present situation.

The document goes on to formulate searching questions, such as: whether religious pluralism can be viewed as the expression of the infinite riches of the Absolute, which no particular event or tradition can adequately represent or exhaust; whether the faith-experience behind the different symbols of the various religions is identical or different in, and specific to, each; whether dialogue can be authentic without the partner being accepted as equal on the religious level; whether a theology of religions acceptable to all traditions is possible without compromise with truth and without diluting respective convictions (9). The document does not, however, attempt to answer these or other intricate questions; what it does instead is to review the three main positions in the present debate on the Christian theology of religions: the ecclesiocentric, the Christocentric, and the theocentric; or, equivalently, the exclusive, the inclusive, and the "pluralistic" models. "Theocentrism," it is said, is "an attempt to find a common

theological platform in dialogue with adherents of other faiths."
It is based on the fact that God is the source and author of all
salvation, as also that "Jesus himself (was) centered on his
Father. He proclaimed himself as the way to the Father." Therefore, "the mystery of Jesus Christ cannot be interpreted except
theocentrically" (19).

It may be observed that this undeniable truth is in no way
contradicted by the Christocentric model; for, as that model
insists, if Jesus Christ is at the center of the mystery of salvation,
the reason is that God has placed him there as the universal
mediator and the one way to salvation for all people. But by the
same token theocentrism and Christocentrism, far from being
opposed to ech other, are mutually inclusive: Christian theology
is theocentric by being Christocentric, and vice versa.[30] In the
present theological debate, however, theocentrism stands for the
position — with John Hick as its main protagonist — according
to which Christianity ought to give up its traditional claim to
uniqueness for Jesus Christ, and recognise that the various religions represent distinct modes of God's self-manifestation to
different peoples, none of which has a distinct and singular title to
uniqueness. Such a non-Christocentric theocentrism is clearly
incompatible with the traditional self-understanding of Christian
faith.[31]

The Indian statement does not enter into the debate at this
point; it chooses instead to suggest another model which it calls
"anthropocentric" (20). This approach would consist in viewing
dialogue, liberation and inculturation, the three factors of
"Indianness," as the "new *locus theologicus*" (20). All three
elements are intimately related and their mutual connections need
to be highlighted.

To begin with, personal and social life and religion are dia-
logically structured (21); in dialogue, therefore, the partners are
challenged to refashion their own and their society's life and
activities (22), to liberate their respective communities from
various forms of alienation and inhumanity (23). Dialogue does

---

30. I have explained this reciprocal relationship between theocentrism and
Christocentrism in *Jésus-Christ à la rencontre des religions* (note 24) 133-141.
    31. See J. Dupuis, *Jésus-Christ à la rencontre des religions*, pp. 137-140.

not stop at sharing religious experience and intellectual reflection; "it is a process of liberation" (24).

Every religion, moreover, tends to the liberation of the human being — a liberation which is not only spiritual but has socio-political implications. In India this liberation cannot be successfully achieved by one community in isolation; the various communities must work together for the transformation of society and the betterment of persons. That is to say, liberation implies dialogue and on the part of each community a critical attitude towards its own tradition in order that it may sincerely enter into the common liberative process (25). Liberation has also a cultural task to play. The holistic approach to reality, characteristic of the "cosmocentric" culture of India, sees the Divine, the human and nature in continuity; this culture needs to be freed from the pitfalls of the dominating Western culture (26) and from the present threat to ecology (27). Such total liberation must engage the cooperation of all communities.

Finally, since culture is an integral part of a person's individual and social life, with religion as its core and heart, "inculturation is a dynamic process affecting every society and every individual" (28). In the Christian context, it cannot be narrowed down to the critical assimilation of certain elements of a particular culture; it implies "entry into the total religiousness or ethos of the people" — a process which demands from Christians "a reinterpretation of their self-identity," "at-one-ness" with different subcultures and groups, the shedding of what is foreign and alienating. In sum, "inculturation demands from each religious community a thorough reflection on its religious specificity as well as its particular sharing in a common culture" (29). This, again, is a common endeavor.

It is while speaking of the "Christian theological task" that the Statement returns to the question of Christocentrism and theocentrism. In Christian theology, it says, rather than excluding each other, both must go hand in hand. Theocentrism allows us to understand other religions "as ways offered by the common author of life and salvation" to various peoples, each with their own specificity; it does not, however, by itself "articulate a universal theology of religions." In the Christian understanding Christocentrism is required to highlight the "common ground

and inter-relationship" between religions (31). "A Christian is...
conscious that he can theologize only as a Christian who finds his
commitment to God, humankind and nature in Jesus Christ, in
whom he finds his specificity. That is why he is simultaneously
Christocentric and theocentric, as far as the transcendent pole of
religion is concerned" (32).

The question, however, needs to be asked whether the Statement binds Christocentrism and theocentrism closely enough to
each other. In the integral Christian perspective God's action
among peoples cannot be severed from the mystery of Jesus
Christ and its universal presence in history. An integrated theo-
Christocentric perspective is required in order to establish both
the salvific value of other religions and the specificity of the
Christian way.

On its part the document insists that to the theo-Christocentric
approach — which accounts for the "transcendent pole" of
religion — the "anthropocentric" one needs to be added; for
"man is the other pole of religion" (32). While the Christian is
convinced that "Jesus Christ and his life, especially his death and
resurrection, have a universal significance for the total liberation
of man," this does not prevent the Christian from recognizing
that the dialogue partners "have encountered God through other
mediations." In fact, their testimony can lead one "to glimpse
more and more the depth and intensity of the mystery of God
manifested in Christ" (32). Having thus pointed to some of the
benefits Christians can derive from dialogue, the document ends
by calling on them to "enter into a creative relationship" with
people of other faiths. This calls for a "recognition of others as
others," for a "culture of togetherness, even in matters religious."
Christians and others are made to discern that their respective
world-views, values and perceptions can correct each other and
are mutually complementary. But, it is stressed once more, inter-
religious dialogue may not be isolated from the overall reality of
the Indian context; it is within "the inter-religious praxis of
dialogue, liberative action and inculturation" that "a genuine
Christian theology of religions" will emerge (36-37).

The close analysis of the 1988 Statement of the Indian Theological Association — which has been interspersed here with

some critical observations — allows us to review the 1989 Statement more rapidly. Building up on its predecessor, the new
statement tries to offer a Christian theology of religious pluralism. The question for such a theology is: What is the meaning of
the plurality of religions in the world from within the perspective
of Christian faith? (8-9). While speaking about other faiths "with
integrity and total respect" (9), Christians cannot but ask this
question from the point of view of their faith (10), leaving it to
other believers to reflect on the same from the perspective of their
own faith (10).

Linked with the previous statement, the present one expresses
the conviction that in the Indian context a theology of religious
pluralism must be based on the threefold praxis of liberative
action, religious dialogue and inculturation. It expatiates on the
contribution which each of these three elements must make to
such a theology.

To begin with, the common struggle of people of different
faiths for human liberation potentially leads to a transformed
understanding of religion (12). It calls for a critique of religious
traditions inso far as often they have been obstacles to liberation
(13), and for a rediscovery of their liberative potential (14). "A
liberative hermeneutic of religions," the Statement declares,
"opens up towards a liberative ecumenism of religions," freeing
religions from their exclusivism and bringing them closer together
in mutual acceptance and relatedness (15).

On the other hand, inter-religious dialogue is the necessary
foundation for a theology of religious pluralism. No religion can
any longer define itself in isolation from the others; rather, every
religion must "evolve its own self-understanding in its manifold
forms of relatedness to other religions" (16). True dialogue takes
place between persons "in the specificity of their own faith"; it
"demands loyalty to one's own faith, and readiness to share it
with members of other faith-traditions and to listen to them with
reverence and appreciation." While holding to the specificity of
their faith, Christians must transcend its "inherent limitations" in
their orientation to the ineffable mystery of God; they must be
disposed for "further exploration" of their own faith-experience
through dialogue. This sense of the transcendence of God and of
the limitations inherent in the articulation of their faith will lead

them to "a new approach to a theology of religions" (18). While they adhere in all fidelity to the reality of Christ and "its all-pervading role in shaping (their) life," "openness to the inexhaustible mystery of the divine self-manifestation" will also make them realise "the inherent limitations of God's self-communication through Jesus Christ." Speaking now in the first person, the Statement goes on to say: "We... do not claim any kind of ultimacy for any of the articulations of our own faith-experience," but, "keeping our hearts attached to the Christ-event... and at the same time throwing our minds open to the vast and ineffable mystery of God communicated to us through Christ," we allow ourselves to "get transformed as we enter deeper and deeper into the hidden mysteries of our own faith-experience, where the specificity of our faith opens up and leads us to a wider and more universal experience of God, who is the Savior of all and who alone knows the ultimate mystery of salvation of all people" (19). Christians, therefore, should see themselves as "pilgrims in Christ," but at the same time co-pilgrims with others towards the fulness of truth (19).

As for inculturation, the Statement understands it as the "mutual fecundation" or "natural symbiosis" which takes place through the "creative encounter" between two religions and cultures in the dialogal experience of pluralism (21). It arises from the practice of sincere togetherness, that is, of entering into human community and fellowship with each other (22). Such "inter-culturation" implies not only adopting some external features of each other's tradition, but accepting its *mythos* in a "cultural symbiosis." Through it both partners are invited to "a new self-understanding which is a continuous process of reinterpretation" (23). Thus, inter-culturation has profound theological implications: It requires genuine dialogue, implies common sharing in a liberative praxis, and leads to a mutual fecundation of ideas and a new community of praxis (24).

The last section of the Statement is entitled "Our Vision of Christ and the Theology of Religious Pluralism." It is explicitly devoted to what for every Christian theology of religions constitutes the decisive question, the Christological question. The vision proposed here is that of a kenotic Christ, whose kenosis led him to the death on the cross, which in turn is "consecrated by the resurrection and symbolised in the eucharist" (26). The kenotic Christ belongs to the whole of humanity and is present in every human vicissitude, leading people to their self-realisation. "His is a liberative action which makes the person(s) whole (and) transforms the cultures it encounters" (27).

At this point the Statement cannot avoid the problem raised by the traditional Christian claim to uniqueness for Jesus Christ in relation to similar claims to uniqueness on the part of other religions. To construe a dilemma between theocentrism and Christocentrism is not the answer, the Statement says (28). A "different perspective" is suggested, capable of holding them together. Christ "is constitutively the way to the Father and as such he is theocentric. But to the one who is on the way, the way is also the goal" (28). This Christ, turned to the Father, "is with the members of all religions in their journey towards the Absolute" (29), as he also is with the masses in their struggle for liberation (30). From Christians, discipleship of such a Christ demands a *metanoia*, by way of a greater openness to all humanity for the building up of one community of hope (31).

There follows an important statement on uniqueness and specificity, diversity and dialogue:

Every religion is unique and through their uniqueness religions enrich each other. In their specificity, they manifest different phases of (the) supreme Mystery which is never exhausted. In their diversity they enable us to experience the richness of the One more profoundly (32).

When, therefore, religions encounter each other in dialogue, "they build up a community in which differences become complementarities and divergences are changed into pointers to communion" (32).

If some observations need to be made on this christological section, they must deal with kenosis and uniqueness. The vision of the kenotic Christ is helpful on more than one count. It enables us to find him present in people, especially the poor and the oppressed, and in their struggle for liberation and fulfilment. It, moreover, sets the model which the Church ought to reproduce in her own life. However, while the Church remains a pilgrim on earth, the Lord himself has passed from kenosis to glory. It is the risen Jesus whom God has established as the Christ, the Lord and universal Savior. It is he who through his Spirit is now present and operative not only among Christians but also among the members of other religious traditions and in their traditions themselves. Again, it is he, dead but risen and alive for ever, that Christian faith professes to be unique and of decisive significance for the salvation of people and peoples.

In conclusion the Statement affirms once more that a true theology of religions "can emerge only from a healthy interaction which involves both sharing of experiences and the critique of expressions" (33). Since "no religious language can adequately express the mystery," "cultivation of a deep-seated respect for religious expressions other than our own" is called for (34), as well as a positive acceptance of other religions. This "does not necessarily mean an intellectual agreement but ... manifests itself in a shared praxis" and constant listening to each other (35). "In a pluralistic society like (India's), genuine religion essentially entails a relationship with other religions.... In short, to be religious is to be inter-religious" (36). The Christian community must, therefore, find its identity in relatedness to the rest of the human community. It will then be able to discover "the One in the midst of the many" who illumines and unfolds the ineffable riches of the religious heritage with which the Spirit of the Lord has endowed India(37).

Conclusion

The above survey, though incomplete, suffices to show that much theological work has been done in India during the last two decades on the subject of inculturation and inter-religious dialogue. The intention has been to allow the theological community in India to speak for itself through various seminars and assemblies.[32]

Following the present trend in Indian theological thinking,

32. I may also refer to an article on inter-religious dialogue in India. See J. Dupuis, "Le dialogue avec l'hindouisme dans la mission de l'Eglise en Inde," *Bulletin. Pontificium Consilium pro dialogo inter religiones*, n. 71; 24 (1989/2) 257-269; repris dans *La documentation catholique*, n. 2006; 72 (1990) 516-521.

stress has been laid on holding together the three factors that together constitute "Indianness": cultural and religious pluralism, and the poverty of the masses. There follows the need for theology to combine the three concerns of the local Church for inculturation, inter-religious dialogue and a liberative praxis, keeping sight of their mutual relatedness and interaction. Only the first two of these concerns have been dealt with explicitly here, while the third could only be treated indirectly.[33] This should not be understood as a sign of lesser interest or importance as the insistence on holding the three together suffices to show.[34]

At the end of this survey, it may be said that the theological community in India is responding creatively and responsibly to the need, increasingly being felt today, for a theology at once local and contextualised. Such a theology, to be sure, is destined to do an important service to the mission of the Church in India; it will also contribute its share to the theology and mission of other Churches and to their communion.

33. I may refer to two articles on the present role of the Churches of Asia, and in particular of the Church in India, in the socio-economic problems of today. See J. Dupuis, "Un decennio di riflessione nelle chiese dell'Asia: Il mutato ruolo della chiesa nei problemi socio-economici," *La Civiltà Cattolica*, n. 3262; 137 (1986) 326-339; id., "Il ruolo della chiesa nei problemi socio-economici secondo la riflessione teologica asiatica," *La Civiltà Cattolica*, n. 3293; 138 (1987) 355-368.

34. Among the many assemblies of theologians in India dealing with human development and liberation and the role of the Church, the following may be mentioned: the International Theological Conference of Nagpur (October 1971) (see note 22); the Research Seminar on the Indian Church in the Struggle for a New Society (October 1981): see D.S. Amalorpavadass (ed.), *The Indian Church in the Struggle for a New Society* (Bangalore: NBCLC, 1981); the ninth annual meeting of the Indian Theological Association on an Indian Theology of Liberation (December 1985): see Paul Puthanangady (ed.), *Towards an Indian Theology of Liberation* (Bangalore: NBCLC, 1986); the tenth annual meeting of the Indian Theological Association on Socio-Cultural Analysis in Theologising (December 1986): see Kuncheria Pathil (ed.), *Socio-Cultural Analysis in Theologising* (Bangalore: Indian Theological Association, 1987); the eleventh annual meeting of the Indian Theological Association on *Communalism in India*: see S. Arulsamy (ed.), *Communalism in India: A Challenge to Theologising* (Bangalore: Clarentian Publications, 1988.)

INCULTURATION IN JAPAN

Jan Van Bragt

Permit me to begin by two preliminary remarks. First, my work as a missionary in Japan has been mostly in the line of the interreligious dialogue rather than direct pastoral activity, and I am not sure whether that puts me in an advantageous or on the contrary in a disadvantageous position to talk about inculturation. Secondly, my contribution, rather than a report on the achievements of the Catholic Church in Japan in the line of inculturation, will mostly consist of some reflections on inculturation in the light of the Japanese social and cultural situation. That it could not very well be a mere report on achievements is due to the simple fact that achievements in this line are rather rare in Japan, although not non-existant. This verdict is laid down eloquently, for instance, in this text by a Japanese priest-writer, who is sometimes called a "truly Japanese priest," with the implication that this is a rarity, if not a freak.

> "In the manner of evangelizing during the hundred odd years since the Meiji Restoration (1868), the tendency to cut the Japanese converts off from the mainstream of Japanese culture, to Europeanize them, and to set up a bridge head of Western Christian culture has been far too strong.
>
> Indeed, in the Meiji era, the Japanese adopted all kinds of cultural elements from the West, without thereby becoming Westerners. They took it all in in a Japanese way, and in many cases were not even aware how much they transformed these elements in the process. This kind of "adapting adoption" was made possible by the fact that Western thought entered Japan through the filter of Chinese characters.
>
> However, Christianity, and Christianity alone, entered Japan without this mediation by Chinese characters. It was brought in by missionaries, i.e., living people that had the Western way of thinking and the history of Western culture in their very blood. As a result, it was only Christianity that did not permit itself to be received *à la japonaise*, but obliged the Japanese to take it in the

form wherein the Europeans had modeled it. Herein lies the main reason for the fact that the Japanese, while gladly taking in all kinds of Western things, have obstinately kept refusing to accept Christianity. Instead of planting a seedling, Christians since the Meiji time — Catholics as well as Protestants — have tried to plant into the Japanese soil the full-grown tree of Christianity as it had grown in European soil."[1]

Excuse the length of the quotation but it appears to convey the message, in a much more striking way than I could ever do in my own words, that Christianity does not spread in Japan because it is not inculturated. It is precisely about this message that my paper wants to be a meditation.

Let us open the vista a bit wider and add that Japan is a typical part of Asia, that continent where the missionary effort of the Church clearly appears to have failed. Or, to say it in the words of the Anglican canon, Max Warren: "We have marched around the alien Jerichos the requisite number of times. We have sounded the trumpets. And the walls have not collapsed."[2] This failure in Asia invites comparison, of course, with Africa and South America where mission appears to have been more of a success. That might become a topic for tomorrow's discussions, but for now I prefer to approach it from a different angle.

Speaking of "failure" invites reflection on the reasons for that failure and, maybe more fundamentally still, on the meaning itself of the "failure of evangelization." Speaking of failure implies an image of what should have been accomplished. Thus, evangelization in Asia is a failure indeed when measured by the original intention of bringing all (or at the least the greater part) of the Asian people into the fold of the Church. The weak figure of the Church in Asia is beautifully presented in the address, "For all the Peoples of Asia," made by the Asian bishops in their 1970 meeting: "Our brothers in Asia, we are small in number with little of human resources; with little, even, of human wisdom and power; with almost no influence, in our great continent, on the councils of the nations." This image reminds one of the situation

1. Inoue Yoji, *Nippon to Iesu no kao* (Japan and the Face of Jesus) (Tokyo: Hokuyosha, 1976), p. 64. My own translation.

2. As quoted in Wilfred C. Smith, *The Faith of Other Men* (New York: Harper, 1972), p. 120.

of the early Christians in the Roman empire, as reflected, for instance, in the words of Saint Paul to the Corinthians: "Now remember what you were, my brothers, when God called you. From the human point of view few of you were wise or powerful or of high social standing." (1 Cor 1:26) This parallelism may be one of the reasons why, far from experiencing this weak figure of the Asian Church merely as a downright deplorable one, I find something eminently fitting and, why not, providential in it. Still, also this cannot be the whole truth.

There is one last consideration to be addressed before entering the main body of my essay. We, missionaries in Japan are often challenged by the question: "What are you people doing in Japan? After 130 years of missionary work, you can come up with only one million Christians (of whom 400,000 Catholics) in a population of 123 million, while in the neighboring country, South Korea, already some 10 million people, or about one fourth of the population, have become Christians." Indeed, even within the same Asian continent, the Church in Japan can be called a failure. Speaking of Korea brings back to me a memory which I want to share with you. Some eight years ago (1982) I was invited to give a talk at a university in Pusan and thus got my first chance visit to Korea. I remember vividly how a bus ride through the Korean countryside (from Pusan to the old capital, Kyongjung, I believe) provoked in me a real "culture shock." Used as I was to the Japanese countryside where every village and turn of the road shows up signs of Japan's traditional religiosity — the big roofs of Buddhist temples, the gates (*torii*) and sacred woods of Shinto, and so on —, I was deeply perturbed by the fact that I could not discover any sign of religion in the Korean villages, except perhaps two or three Western-style steeples of Christian churches. I had to ask myself: Why does that sight not make me, who am after all a missionary? I could tell myself initially that the many churches in a single village is an all too visible sign of the inner division of Christianity, and that, true enough, those Western-style steeples do not harmonize with the environment. In the end I had to admit to myself that what really disturbed me was something else and that, deep down, I missed the visible presence of Korean traditional religiosity. I am convinced that this memory is very relevant to what I am trying to

say here tonight. So, I may have to come back to this, but one
obvious lesson I was taught there can be mentioned immediately:
The difference in success between the Church in Korea and the
Church in Japan cannot be explained by saying that the Church
in Korea is inculturated — in the sense of being adapted to the
traditional culture — while in Japan it is not.

At this point, we may be ready to ask the big questions:
1) Why the failure of the Christian mission in Japan (and Asia)?
2) Why do we want the Church in Japan to become inculturated,
to become a Japanese Christianity?
3) What would real inculturation of Christianity in the Japanese
reality mean and entail?

Why the "Failure" of the Christian Mission in Japan (and Asia)?

I believe that we cannot avoid looking at this question in the
face, since the reasoning often goes: "Christianity does not spread
in Japan because it is not inculturated." When we provisionally
apply the traditional yardstick whereby failure and success of the
mission are measured, namely the number of conversions, I
would indeed think that the lack of inculturation is one of the
reasons for the small number of registered Christians in Japan. I
then want immediately to add that there is another, and more
decisive, reason for the paucity of Christians in Japan, and in
Asia. It is the fact that, as a world religion, Christianity did not
arrive second in most parts of Asia, but third or fourth.
Let me explain that cryptic sentence a bit. The so-called "world
religions" are never the first kind of religiosity in place in a
people. They are always second-comers, on top of and partially in
opposition to the native religiosity of a people, that has found its
first expression in native or tribal religions. This might set us
thinking again about what an expression like *anima naturaliter
christiana* could mean, but more to the point, herein may lie the
deepest reason why these world religions have to undergo a
process of inculturation. If they do not succeed in striking roots
in the natural religiosity of a people, they will never touch the
lives and hearts of that people. At best they will a veneer over

totally heterogeneous elements or may become part of the make-up of a social elite that wants to distance itself from the common plebs. Christianity in the West, Budhism in the East, Islam in the Middle East (and parts of Africa and Asia) apparently succeeded in growing such roots. [3]

In Asia, however, Christianity — with the exception of some tribal societies, like the greater part of the Philippines — nowhere appeared on the scene as the first world religion; found the place occupied, as it were, by another world religion, mainly Buddhism and/or a highly reflected native religious philosophy, like Confucianism and Taoism in China. On the other hand, world history seems to evince an iron rule, according to which a second world religion does not succeed in supplanting the world religion already in possession. Applied to Japan, this would mean: Even if duly inculturated, Christianity would not have, and will not, become the dominant religion in Japan by supplanting Buddhism. To go back a moment to the reason for the "success" of Christianity in Korea, in the same line of thinking, the following historical fact may emerge as an important explanatory factor. For many centuries, Confucianist pressure kept Buddhism away from most of the people, who in many cases had no popular religion except for a primitive shamanism, so that, for all practical purposes, Christianity could appear to them as the first world religion on the scene.

Why Inculturation of Christianity in Japan, and Asia?

In the Hibbert Lecture of 1989, the Benedictine monk, Bede Griffiths, successor of Fathers Monchanin and Le Saux in the ashram of Shantivanam, stressed the necessity of inculturation of Christiaity in Asia as follows:

"A serious challenge is now facing us: That of rethinking our religion, not any more in the light of Western, but in the light of Eastern thought, and thereby discovering another dimension of

3. I do not really know where to put Hinduism in this scheme. Could it be classified as a native religion that gradually — and mainly under the influence of Buddhism and Jainism? — took on some traits of a world religion?

Christianity. This could be as decisive for Christianity today as it was for the primitive Church when it passed from its original Jewish matrix into the Greco-Roman world. We have to remind ourselves that today two thirds of humanity live in Asia and that, for more than 90% of these people Christianity is a totally foreign religion."[4]

Japan, with its handful of Christians in a population equal to that of the greater part of Western Europe, is as good a place as any to become fully aware of that fact. As to the necessity of inculturation, I agree, of course, wholeheartedly with the tenor of Bede Griffith's declaration, but I am primarily concerned with the "quality" of that necessity: that it not be interpreted, in the prolongation of a "conquest theology," as a so-called "strategic necessity" for Christianity: Our mission is to supplant all other religions and to bring all people on the face of the earth into the Church, so that Christianity becomes the universal religion of all humanity. This cannot be done, we now came to realize, without inculturating Christianity profoundly into the cultures of the different peoples.

I would like to suggest that a genuine and fruitful reflection on the inculturation of Christianity in Japan needs as prerequisites a new picture of the religion of the future in the world at large, specifically in Japan; and a fresh look at the mission of the Church in our pluralist world, specifically at the desirable role of Christianity in Japan. It is clear enough that these big topics cannot be satisfactorily treated here, but still, before going any further, I want at least to try out some formulations.

At least theoretically speaking, the requirements of incultura- tion may be very different, depending on whether the aim is to become the only religion of a people — becoming the whole dough — or to become a leaven in the dough of a people and its religiosity. We cannot go into this, but I imagine that this could be most easily demonstrated in the realm of morality. There is, however, a tricky question involved here. It may be legitimate, and even mandatory, for Christianity to try to be a leaven in society — "the salt of the earth" — but not to become an "elite" in any social or even moral sense (a gathering of the righteous).

4. According to the French translation in the *Bulletin de l'A.M.I.* No. 49 (1990), p. 68. I translated back into English, because the Original English text was not available to me.

This might for instance imply that the inculturation efforts in Japan should not be primordially directed at Japanese classical culture, but perhaps even more at the deeply imbedded folk traditions and, anyway, the needs of the ordinary people.

Secondly, reflection on the inculturation into the Japanese reality must be done in the light of the real needs of the Church — both universal and local — and of Japan — both Japanese society and the individual Japanese. It starts from, and makes sense only through, the conviction that Christianity needs Japan, like it needs all other peoples and civilizations, in order to turn its universality *de jure* into a universality *de facto*, not in the sense of all-containing but of being really open to all. On the other hand, Japan needs Christianity — I would like to say "a strong dose of Christianity." The lack of enthusiasm for the "foreign missions," as they used to be called, in West European Christianity during the last thirty years seems to suggest that this second conviction may have been largely lost in a Europe turned in on itself after the period of "world-conquest," and its formulation may therefore be offensive to some ears. Every missionary could tell of unpleasant memories in that regard during their periods of furlough in the home country. Fortunately, things look differently from inside the mission, and I for one have another memory that easily counterbalances these other ones. Keiji Nishitani, Japan's leading religious thinker during the last twenty-five years (he died in November 1990 at the age of 90), himself a convinced and practising Buddhist, with whom I happened to be on very good terms, once scolded me outright saying: "What are you Christians doing in Japan? Why don't you make more fervent efforts to gain more converts?" And he made it clear that, in his view, a strong Christian influence is a necessity for Japan, and Christianity's present strength is not sufficient to insure that influence. I am not sure of all the points on which Nishitani wanted that Christian influence to bear, but from my point of view I can see the role of Christianity in Japan at least in the following terms, and I want to suggest that the need for inculturation and the modalities of the inculturation will have to be weighed against these and similar factors.

I offer you now my short list of possible positive contributions of Christianity to Japan, without being able, in the short space at my disposal, to sufficiently explain why these contributions are particularly needed in Japan. First of all, and negatively speaking, this looks like the right moment to say expressly that I do not believe that it is the role of Christianity in Japan to do away with and to supplant or even absorb the established religions: Shinto, the Buddhist sects, and let us add Confucianism (although this is not a formal religion in Japan). This would not be a positive contribution to, but rather an impoverishment of Japan, and should thus not be aimed at with inculturation as a strategic means.

Positively, the following contributions of Christianity seem indicated — each corresponding to a need of Japanese society. As one formulation has it, "A Church is inculturated when it answers the real needs of society and individuals."

There is first of all the universal role of representing, embodying, and making influential in society the spirit of Jesus Christ. I think here especially of concern for justice and of active and universal love. Do the Japanese not know love? Of course they do, but they tend to be satisfied with benevolent feelings and certainly to restrict their love to people of their in-group, finally to their fellow Japanese. The moment when I have felt most proud of our little Japanese Church was not when Pope John Paul visited Japan (1981) and, together with the Catholic Church in Japan, got an enormous lot of coverage in the Japanese media, but when the Vietnamese boat people started drifting to the Japanese shores and the Catholic Church was absolutely the first (soon followed by Protestant Churches) to effectively help them by lodging them in church buildings and offering them all kinds of services. A little later that example was followed by some non-Christian religious organizations. We could then see the leaven at work in the dough; it was an absolutely Christian act and, at the same time, exactly what Japan stood in need of at that moment. There is much talk nowadays of "internationalization" in Japan (exchanging the "island mentality" that thinks of Japan only for a more global outlook), but I heard it said some twenty years ago that "there are only two real agents of internationalization in Japan, namely Communism and Christianity." I think that this stays true today, although by now Communism has lost much of its salt.

A second role of the Church in Japan is to offer individual Japanese a real chance for a personal encounter with Jesus Christ. There is no need, I believe, to enlarge on this, but we could put it in a larger context. I believe that a personal encounter with Christ is a *nec plus ultra*, but I also believe that a real encounter with the Buddha is very beneficial. Anyway, what most Japanese lack in this totally economy-and-consumption oriented society is a "spiritual path": A chance for the individual to discover his/her true self, the deeper dimension of the human. A few Japanese find this opportunity, mainly in Zen halls, and the Catholic Church offers its faithful retreats and so on, but I believe that the time has come for the Church to appeal to the other religions to collaborate in multiplying these occasions, and not only for the own members. If the Church would decide to open, say, retreats to non-members, it would naturally be induced to incorporate therein Japanese traditional forms of prayer and meditation.

Further, Christianity can and must instigate the religions of Japan to discover in their own religiosity motivation for social and ecological action or, at the least, to open their religiosity toward this kind of concern. The consciousness that social concern is an integral part of a religious attitude may be relatively new in Christianity, but it is certainly absent from Japan's traditional religions. If it is true, however, that the present situation of planet earth demands a general mobilization of the so-called "forces for good," this could be called a providential role for Christianity. Again, this would require an adapted reexamination of the question in the light of, and together with, the other religions — in the course of which the influence will of course not be all from one side, but an inculturation will naturally go on.

My next point is, in fact, related to this. Christianity in Japan has the role of offering individuals and groups, including other religions, a standpoint from where to take a critical stance towards the state or the politico-industrial powers that be. This would call for a longer examination of the traditional stance of Japanese religions towards the state, something we cannot think of offering here. Suffice it to say that religions in Japan, according to the motto, "religion for the well-being of the state," have traditionally seen themselves in the service of law and order

("harmony"), and that Japanese Buddhism has habitually forsaken the transcendence of the religious principle and spoken of
Buddha law and King's law as identical or as the two wings of a
bird. It is here that our Christian (Semitic) stress on the transcendence of God over all things of this World ("*Allah akbar*" —
God is greater), states and emperors included, is indispensible.

As my last point I want to mention the service Christianity can
render Japanese individuals by offering them a religious system
that is more present in all the aspects of their lives — lucky as
well as unlucky occasions, material as well as spiritual needs —
than any other Japanese religion by itself. Here again my explanation cannot be anything but rudimentary. Shinto is geared to
the celebration of life in the agricultural cycle of the year and in
the rites of passage of the individual. Buddhism in Japan special-
izes in sacralizing the deaths in the family and the relations with
the souls of the deceased ancestors. Most Japanese avail themselves of both those services, but even then, no Japanese religion
offers any religious support, for example, when the individual
faces death. Here again the suggestion could be made that, if
Christianity could convince the "clergy" of the other religions to
put care for the dying on their agenda, it would certainly render a
great service to the Japanese, and might thereby itself come to a
really inculturated way of caring for the dying Japanese. Furthermore, Japanese established religions reduce salvation to the spiritual realm, while showing scorn for prayers for material benefits,
a realm which is then left to superstition-laden folk religion.

One conclusion that might possibly be drawn from my short
list of services which Christianity can render to Japan appears to
be that inculturation of Christianity would be rather a disservice
to Japan if it resulted in weakening these characteristics of
Christianity.

**What would real Inculturation of Christianity in the Japanese
Reality mean and entail?**

We come here to the third "chapter" and I am not even going
to try to be systematic in this somewhat more concrete treatment
of inculturation of Christianity in Japan, but I am simply going

to mention some points which may help us to see the problem in all its complexity.

Why so little Inculturation up to now?

Here we must go back to history and may remark that Japan has been unlucky in the historical periods wherein it received the gift of Christianity. Japan first heard of Jesus Christ from Francis Xavier, at the time of the counter-reformation, wherein the adagium *extra ecclesiam nulla salus* appears to have been taken rather literally and all other religions were seen as the work of the devil. (Witness the answer given to the concerned question of the new converts where their ancestors would be: "In hell"). It heard of Christ a second time, in the middle of the 19th century, from French missionaries, carriers of a rather Jansenistic Catholicism, and from American missionaries, representatives of "a Protestantism still so influenced by what we may call the 'Puritan mentality' that there was no room for compromise with regard to 'heathen rituals.'" [5] In both cases one was miles away from a basic trust in the native religiosity of the people — a trust which would only reject these elements that are clearly contrary to the Gospel.

The other decisive factor was undoubtedly the fact that the young converts, in their situation as a tiny minority, felt the psychological need for a strongly marked personal identity "over and against" the religions from which they came, and found this sense in the imported exterior forms of Christianity, so totally different from the ones they were used to. For many of them some imported incidentals — let us say, the devotion to our Lady of Lourdes — became "personal symbols of their original choice." [6] (The same phenomenon can be seen in the Western converts to Tibetan or Japanese Buddhism).

Inculturation and Language

Inculturation is sometimes defined as "putting the Good News into words and symbols that can be understood." I doubt whether these words can cover the whole process of inculturation but

5. David Reid, *New Wine* (unpublished manuscript), p. 122.
6. Sean Dwan in *The Missionary Bulletin*, Vol. 41/4 (1987), p. 224.

they express at least two things: That translation is an important factor of inculturation and that a literal translation is not good enough. We must admit that, on the point of translation of the Bible and Christian technical terms, Christianity has been rather quick and bold. The rapid translation of the Bible, first into classical Japanese and somewhat later into the spoken tongue, contrasts strangely with the historical fact that Japanese Buddhism has been using the Buddhist Sutras in their Chinese translation for almost fourteen centuries — Chinese being the Latin and Greek of the Japanese intellectuals — and arranged for a Japanese translation only in modern times, while continuing the use of the Chinese versions in their liturgy even today. No wonder that an old bonze once told me: "I read the Gospel regularly; that I understand at least." Of the hazards of translating religious terms I can offer here only a single example. How was one going to call "*Deus*, God" in Japanese? In the earliest days (16th century) one opted for a moment for "Dainichi Nyorai," the name of the most highly exalted and most cosmic Buddha. This was indeed a bold move, but when the disadvantages thereof became clear, one went back to the untranslated *Deus* (pronounced *Daios*) till the end of the Kirishitan Era. In the second wave of evangelization, in the Meiji time (19th century) one borrowed the name of Confucian origin used in China for the Christian God, namely (in the Japanese pronunciation) "Tenshu" (Lord of Heaven); but afterwards, in the boldest move of all, the Protestants started using "kami," the word for the myriads of Shinto gods, notwithstanding the fact that it does not require much of a study to know that, conceptually, there is very little in common between those two. Some twenty-five years ago Catholics decided to follow that example, and now the word "kami" is in general use in Japanese Christianity. The result is rather surprising. When an average Japanese, say sixty years ago, used the word "kami," the image in his head was naturally that of the shinto gods, but it appears that today, when a Japanese uses the word, its content is at least half Christian. No wonder that I once heard a young and fervent Shinto priest-scholar accuse us Christians that we had "stolen the word." Another priest-scholar of our acquaintances maintains that, as a result, Shinto now needs to elaborate for the first time its own "theology" in order to catechize the people about what "kami" really means.

A recent counter-example can be found on the Buddhist side. In the English edition of the writings of the founder of the Shin sect of Pure Land Buddhism, Shinran, the translators keep the central Japanese term, "shinjin," and refuse to translate it into the English word, "faith," because its content would differ too much from the Christian notion of faith.

The Inculturation which Japan expects from Christianity

The inculturation demanded by Japanese culture — in other words, the conditions under which Christianity could be fully accepted in Japan and undoubtedly gain many more converts — could be summarily described as follows. *Primo*, to subordinate itself to, and put itself into the service of, the state or, if you want, of Japan, the "land of the gods." *Secundo*, not to pretend to be a self-sufficient religion (and certainly not the only valid one), but instead to accept to fill a well-defined slot, to play a limited ritual role, within the totality of Japanese life, without stepping on the territories of the other religions.

This might be the central lesson to be learned from Japanese history. Not following these rules brought to the early Christianity of Japan one of the harshest persecutions in the history of Christianity. Following these rules has brought Buddhism in Japan success and prosperity. Buddhism has thereby acquiesced in a thorough Japanization and has been assigned as its main portion the, indeed important, realm of funerals and mortuary rites for the ancestors, wherein about every Japanese participates.

As a little intermezzo, I can tell you here that something in that line is factually happening to Christianity in Japan. The Japanese people, with a certain degree of connivance on the part of the Christian Churches, are little by little creating a special "niche" for Christianity in their polymorph religiosity. The Japanese in general have come to accept Christianity as the religion of Christmas and of marriage ceremonies or, to say it differently, they have come to accept Christmas and a church marriage as elements in their own diffuse religiosity. For most Japanese, Christmas has obtained a (modest) place in the yearly cycle of religious ceremonies, as it were as the "year-end party of the nuclear family." And in the life cycle of the individual, in the rites of passage, many Japanese have come to see a church marriage as

the best way to sacralize that important moment in their lives.
This constitutes, of course, a certain form of acceptance of
Christianity, but the tendency is clearly to encapsulate Chris-
tianity in these rather innocuous compartments.

To come back now to our basic argument, the crucial question
is, of course, whether Christianity could ever really subscribe to
the above rules and submit to this kind of inculturation without
giving up its own nature. I do not think Christianity could or
should do this, but this confronts us directly with the question of
how basic or fundamental Christianity's inculturation in Japan
could then possibly be. What is "basic inculturation"? To answer
this question, the distinctions often made between classical
culture and popular culture, traditional culture and modernizing
culture, culture and politico-economic realities, and so on do not
lead us very far. We probably need, here the notion of "basic
cultural codes" Eisenstadt speaks of. Eisenstadt holds the position
that all societies have basic "codes," which constitute the hidden or
deep structure of the social system, and which connect the broad
contours of institutional order with answers to the basic symbolic
and cultural problems of social existence. Basic inculturation could
then be defined as adaptation to that cultural code of a people,
wherein of course culture and religiosity are inextricably interwoven. I submit that, in the case of Japan, the just mentioned two
requirements are expressions of (one part of) Japan's basic cultural
code. These basic codes, by the way, appear to be very persistent
over time, and able to withstand all kinds of upheavals and
influences. "Although during periods of rapid change and tur-
bulence the codes are subject to dispute and uncertainty as to
their application and institutionalization as 'ground rules,' their
continuity even in postrevolutionary societies such as Russia and
China is apparent."[7]

Supposing then that this "basic" inculturation is not possible
for Christianity in Japan, and not even desirable for Japan itself,
can we then still speak of inculturation in a real, albeit more
limited, sense? I think so, and I would like to suggest that the
Japanese experience teaches us that it is sound to work, from the
start, with a consciously limited or, if you want, dialectical,

7. K. Peter Takayama, in *Journal of Church and State*, Vol. 32/3, p. 530.

notion of inculturation — somewhat in the line of Aylward Shorter's definition of inculturation as "the creative and dynamic relationship between the Christian message and a culture or cultures."[8]

The Inculturation of Buddhism in Japan

We have come across Buddhism already as the first-come world religion that makes it very difficult for the second-comer, Christianity, to spread in Japan and, thus, unwittingly, did us a great disservice. On the other hand, however, Buddhism can be of great service to us, provided we pay attention to, and draw the lessons from, the history of its encounter with (Chinese and) Japanese culture. Christianity may still be a dwarf in Japan but it sometimes gets the opportunity of climbing up the shoulders of that giant, Buddhism. I cannot dream of even sketching that history for you, so I shall offer only two reflections.

1. I have already indicated that Buddhism in Japan was assigned the realm or compartment of the dead. I can now add that it has identified itself so much with this role that it is often called a "Buddhism of funerals and mortuary rites," and indeed not only finds therein its means of subsistence, but devotes 90% of its energy to these ritual activities. What is more, a well-known Buddhist monk, Watanabe Shoko, after pointing out, in a best-selling book of his, that mortuary rites had no place in original Buddhism, speaks of these practices of Japanese Buddhism as "mortuary rites wherein a Buddhist veneer is spread over a folk-religious foundation," and asserts that, in this way, Buddhism "has become little more than a representative or mask of Japanese folk religion."[9] Indeed, when a Japanese hears the word *hotoke* (the Japanese translation of "Buddha"), he or she thinks first of all of the deceased (or even a corpse), and *butsudan*, which is translated as "Buddha altar" or "Buddhist family altar," has

8. Aylward Shorter, *Toward a Theology of Inculturation* (Maryknoll, N.Y.: Orbis Books, 1988), p. 11.; or, if you permit me to try out a definition of my own: a way of evangelization that meets the real needs of a people or society.

9. Watanabe Shoko, *Nihon no Bukkyo* (Japan's Buddhism) (Tokyo: Iwanami, 1958), pp. 117 and 112. A (bad) English translation of this work exists under the title: *Japanese Buddhism: A Critical Appraisal* (Tokyo: Kokusai Bunka Shinkokai, 1968.)

JAN VAN BRAGT

come to mean first of all the place for the mortuary tablets of the
ancestors. Even the ideal of Buddhism, *jobutsu* (attaining Bud-
dhahood or enlightenment) now evokes for most Japanese the
moment wherein the spirit of the deceased, originally unsettled
and a threat to the living, settles down as an ancestral spirit,
thanks to the mortuary rites offered by the descendants.

At our latest interreligious dialogue symposium, in 1989, this
triggered the question, addressed by a Protestant pastor to the
Shin Buddhist interlocutors: "When looking back on history, do
not you, Buddhists, think that you made a mistake in inculturating so deeply in Japanese ancestor worship?" — which first
provoked an embarassed silence and then the answer that Buddhism tried all the same to remove the superstitious elements
surrounding death and afterlife.

I fear that the judgment that Buddhism in Japan has become
little more than a veneer overlaying folk religion is bound to
draw fire from Professor Neckebrouck, who has accused writers
on South American Catholicism, who consider that 500 years of
evangelization there have only managed to brush a veneer of
Christianity over deep layers of paganism, of "acculturation,"
meaning "the refusal to accept as authentically Christian that
which is different from a particular cultural expression of Christianity, namely that of the West."[10] Indeed, I too believe that
Watanabe's picture is a bit one-sided and that, all in all, Buddhism has been a real support and, in some senses, an "uplifting
presence" in the lives of the Japanese people. It is also true that,
in the midst of the mass of "social Buddhism" and in a way
supported by it, pockets of pure Buddhist impulses and practices
survive.

2. A second reflection centers on an element to which the South
American liberation theology has recently sensitized us, namely,
the liberating role of religion — "liberating" then not only in a
personal but also in a social sense. To make a long story short, I
shall simply quote a kind of conclusion I had to come to recently
in an article on that point. "When taken in the stricter, more
sociological sense wherein we are taking them presently, it would

10. Valeer Neckebrouck, *La Tierce Église devant le problème de la culture*
(Immensee: Verein zur Förderung der Missionswissenschaft, 1987), pp. 34-36.

seem that most liberative elements present in original Buddhism... were not permitted to exert their influence, to any great
extent or for any considerable length of time, but were effectively
neutralized by the Japanese basic cultural code — which, in our
perspective, we could characterize...as a 'cosmological culture of
salvation.'"[11] Among Japan's great religionists we find a few
notable exceptions to this rule: people who maintained the transcendence of the Buddha law over the King's law and were thus
able to take a critical stance over and against the social injustices
of their times, but the ripples they stirred up on the pond of
Japanese society were soon smoothed out by forces from within
the Buddhist establishment. The past, however, is not necessarily
the future, and if Buddhism in Japan — maybe prompted thereto
by Christianity — could awaken to the liberating elements it
carries within itself, it would, by its rootedness in the Japanese
soil, have the power necessary to do something about it.

Inculturation actually happening in Japan

Until now I may have given the impression that nothing in the
line of inculturation has happened or is happening in the Christian Churches of Japan. To counteract that impression, I feel
bound to devote the space left to the, indeed still rather timid,
moves toward inculturation detectible there. We must distinguish
between spontaneous inculturation — adaptations which the
Japanese faithful make themselves, without even being conscious
of them, by simply following the Japanese life style and folk ways
also in their Christian practice — and deliberate attempts at
inculturation by clerics and intellectuals.

As to the first kind I shall be short and simply quote a few
examples. Personal relationships play an extraordinarily big role
in Japanese society and religion, to the point that the eminent
Japanese buddhologist, Nakamura Hajime, could write that Japanese religiosity does not transcend the "social nexus." It is not
surprising then that the link between the convert and his "guru,"
the priest that instructed and baptized him, is a stronger and
more enduring relationship than is generally found in Western

11. Jan Van Bragt, "Liberative Elements in Pure Land Buddhism". *Inter-
Religio*, No. 18 (1990), p. 55.

churches. This can create problems when the priest is moved to another parish or the convert himself moves to another part of Japan. A contiguous phenomenon is that of the strong "founder cult," which is a conspicuous trait of the Japanese religious world. This also finds its way spontaneously into the Christian Churches, so that a Protestant author could write: "In the world of Japanese Christian institutions, a founder is commonly accorded a degree of ritual respect that has, so far as I know, no counterpart in United States Protestantism."[12] Because obligatory periodical attendance at religious services has never been part of Japanese religious life, our Japanese Christians naturally tend to think lighter of the Sunday Mass obligation and, in general, the catalogue of routinely confessed sins is rather different from that in the West. "I have caused inconvenience to others" (even when it is none of their fault, for example in the case of sickness) and "I have scolded the children" are clear favorites in the Japanese confessional.

As for deliberate attempts at inculturation, let us first single out two areas wherein these attempts have been conspicuously absent. First, the area of ecclesial organization. An old Japanese bishop once confided to us priests: "Japan should have, not sixteen bishops, but one." He alluded to the fact that religions in Japan tend to have a strictly hierarchical organization under one single head, and to have one, mostly very imposing, headquarters. In contradistinction, the Church in Japan has no visible head, with the strange result that outsiders tend to treat the priest in charge of the, far from imposing, central bureau of the Japanese bishops' conference as the patriarch of the Catholic Church in Japan. A second neglected area is that of the very idea of a "follower of Christ" and of "conversion to Christ." In reality, there are in Japan three million people who declare themselves to be Christian when asked for their religion, while our statistics show only one million baptized and registered members. Still, the Churches continue working with a single model of a "follower of Christ": A baptized member of a Church. This problem is apparently not unique to Japan, since a Burmese priest recently wrote: "Our understanding of conversion to Christ must be broadened.... Are

12. David Reid, *New Wine*, p. 117.

there not also possibilities of confessing Christ in 'non-Christian' ways?"[13] And Marcello Zago, presently superior general of the Oblate Fathers, provides the necessary background when he writes: "[In Asia] religion is regarded rather as a way of experience and of life than as a monolithic whole, as a movement rather than as an obligatory structure. Buddhism, for example, admits an enormous number of degrees of adherence, within which groups of 'spirituals' or of monks provide the driving force."[14] This is evidently not simply a question on the level of theological abstraction, but could deeply influence the practical "strategies of evangelization"; and, anyway, serious theological reflection is needed (but non existent) on how far the Catholic Church in Asia could make that Buddhist paradigm its own.

When we then finally come to the positive attempts at inculturation that have taken and still take place in Japan, we cannot omit mentioning the name of the best-known Christian of Japan, Uchimura Kanzo. He is a Protestant Christian who, at the beginning of this century, in his desire for a truly Japanese Christianity, tried to combine his love for Christ with the spirit of the samurai, and started what he called the non-Church movement, because he wanted to sidestep clerical organization and imported external formalities that place an unnecessary burden upon believers of a different culture. To quote only a few sentences from his voluminous writings:

> "When a Japanese truly and independently believes in Christ, he is a Japanese Christian, and his Christianity is Japanese Christianity. It is all very simple.... A Japanese by becoming a Christian does not cease to be a Japanese. On the contrary, he becomes more Japanese by becoming a Christian.... Where are the missionaries who are broad enough and deep enough and courageous enough to work with us to make Japanese Christians and establish Japanese Christianity?"[15]

Uchimura's case seems to prove two things. First, that the need for inculturation has been felt in Japan for a long time already.

13. Khin Maung Din, in R.W. Rousseau (ed.), *Christianity and the Religions of the East* (Scranton: Ridge Row Press, 1982), p. 87.

14. Marcello Zago, in *Concilium* 144 (1978/4), p. 73.

15. Uchimura Kanzo, as quoted by Goro Mayeda in *Philosophical Studies of Japan* Vol. VII (1966), p. 104.

Secondly, the fact that Uchimura's program has been viewed with
suspicion by the official Churches of Japan illustrates once more
that thorough inculturation is hard to take for established
Church organizations. Still, we can agree with the estimate made
by another influential Japanese Christian: "Whether one is for or
against him, he [Uchimura] is the man who made Christianity
approachable for the Japanese in the widest and most enduring
way."[16]

A second point to be made here is that inculturation in Japan
has tended to concentrate on the realms of aesthetics and of
personal spirituality. As to aesthetics, many sporadic attempts are
being made, from church architecture, over the adoption of
Japanese calligraphy, all the way to the writing of Christian Noh
dramas. In view of the fact that traditionally religion and aesthetics are tied up in Japan in an extraordinarily intimate way, this
tendency itself can be called a typically Japanese one. On this
point, Christianity in Japan stands in sharp contrast with the
churches of neighboring Korea where, in Minjung Theology and
so on, inculturation is much more approached from the angle of
Christian action in accord with the concrete socio-political situation.

In this connection, we must also mention the nearly miracu-
lous fact that an abnormally great percentage of Japan's most
esteemed and popular novelists are Christians (and particularly
Catholics). The names of Endo Shusaku, Miura Shumon, Sono
Ayako, for instance, may ring a bell with you. If it is true, as
somebody wrote, that "artists (and not theologians) represent the
cutting edge of inculturation in any culture,"[17] inculturation in
Japan appears to have a promising future.

In the realm of personal spirituality there is, as you probably
know, the so-called "Catholic Zen" movement, with names such
as Enomiya-Lassalle, William Johnston, Kadowaki Kakichi,
Oshida Shigeto. This movement is still limited to a minority of
Catholics but cannot fail to have a lasting impact on Christian
spirituality in Japan. I can tell you, that these people did not take
very kindly to Cardinal Ratzinger's Letter to the Bishops on

16. Goro Mayeda, *ibid.*, p. 103.
17. Sean Dwan in *Inculturation* Vol. V/4 (1990), p. 24.

Some Aspects of Christian Prayer. I have spoken expressly of *personal* spirituality, because the official liturgy of the Catholic Church as yet shows very little evidence of inculturation beyond a literal translation of Roman texts.

Finally, I want to present to you, in a nutshell, three fields wherein the battle for inculturation is joined in earnest.

1. The Attitude of the Church towards State Shinto and Emperor Worship.

Before and during the Second World War Japanese Christians were often put in a delicate position, when they were obliged to participate in "worship" at Shinto shrines and, on other occasions, were asked privately by the *kenpeitai* or secret police: "Who is higher, the emperor or God?" Officially, of course, that period has ended with the surrender of Japan in 1945 and the new constitution that guarantees freedom of religion, but in fact — as you probably have gathered from the news bulletins around the funeral of Emperor Showa and the enthronement ceremonies for the present emperor — the government, in connivance with patriotic organizations (for the purpose of honoring the souls of the soldiers killed on WWII battle fields) and the Shinto establishment, are actively trying to push the clock back to the golden pre-war era. They consider themselves as the representatives of "the authentically Japanese," the traditional Japanese values, or — to say it in a terminology which I have already introduced — the "basic cultural code" of Japan. In their view, Japan and the emperor are and stay divine, and every Japanese, in order to be a real Japanese, is supposed to venerate these sacred realities in the way of Shinto — which is then declared to be not a religion but the national essence.

The Christian Churches are then caught between the clear duty of taking a stand against that movement, which threatens to reduce the Japanese people again to servitude and, on the other hand, the desire to dialogue with the Shinto religion and to inculturate into the authentic Japanese values represented by Shinto. To this little sketch I can only add that most Protestant Churches are vigorous in their protests, while the Catholic Church wavers between the two attitudes. These days, the leaders of some Buddhist sects take part in the protest movement but they do not succeed in drawing along their followers who, for too

long, have been motivated by these same leaders to unquestioning
obedience to the state.

2. Christianity and Ancestor Worship.

Ancestor worship is undoubtedly a central element of Japanese
native religiosity. In other words, the ancestors form an important part of "the sacred" in Japan as well as in China and Korea,
so that real inculturation cannot by-pass that element. The problem is already an old one, since, as you probably know, it
formed the core of the historical battle around the so-called
Chinese rites. In Japan, the battle has been joined anew some six
or seven years ago, at the occasion of a little booklet, published
by the Committee for Interreligious Dialogue of the Japanese
Bishops' Conference and suggesting very tolerant rules of conduct
for the Japanese Catholics. This booklet elicited at first harsh
criticism from some bishops and priests but, significantly enough,
got a good deal of, mostly favorable, attention from the other
religions and even in the secular press. Personally, I am convinced
that there is nothing contrary to Catholic doctrine in that so-
called "ancestor worship," but that nevertheless the Church must
be very careful to keep it in its rightful and subordinate place — a
bit like the veneration of the saints — lest Christianity too be
swallowed up by ancestor worship, the way Buddhism was.

3. The Case of Japanese Theology.

Looking at the theology taught at the theological faculties and
seminaries of Japan and the books published by the recognized
theologians, it appears that we can safely apply to the Japanese
scene, even today, the judgment reached in the document of the
CCA (Christian Conferences of Asia) Consultation, held at
Kandy, Sri Lanka, in 1965: "The Asian Churches, so far, and in
large measure, have not taken their theological task seriously
enough, for they have been largely content to accept the ready-
made answers of Western theology or confessions...."[18]

Fortunately, this is not the whole picture. There are in Japan,
at the same time, people — philosophers rather than theologians,
lay people rather than clerics — who try to do theology, rethink

18. As quoted in Richard W. Rousseau, *Christianity and the Religions of the
East*, pp. 129-130.

their faith, in the light of their Japanese heritage. Most of these people are actively engaged in the interreligious dialogue, especially with Buddhism, and try to "relate theologically to other Asian religions and religious traditions." One more source and incentive of that kind of theologizing is the *Auseinandersetzung* with the ideas of the so-called "Kyoto School philosophy," a philosophical tradition, which originated at the State University of Kyoto, is very religion-centered, and finds its inspiration in the Buddhist tradition, but explicitly relates all the time to Christianity. Recently, several of the main works of that school have appeared in English translation, with the result that some American theologians have joined the debate.

I would like to end with a pious wish: That we may see in the near future some Japanese saints, who embody in themselves to an eminent degree the most beautiful traits of Japanese native religiosity: a high sense of God's immanence in themselves, in other people and in nature (a beautiful Shinto trait); a radical and forever grateful recognition that one is what one is through others the Buddhist (*pratitya samutpada*); and a great capacity for silent, image-less contemplation.

M. L'ABBÉ FRANÇOIS BOURGADE (1806-1866) IN DIALOGUE WITH MUSLIMS AT CARTHAGE: A FORGOTTEN DISCUSSION ON THE UNIVERSAL MEANING OF JESUS BY A MAN WHO PASSED INTO OBLIVION

Arnulf Camps

The encounter between Islam and Christianity is the longest in the history of the meeting between Christianity and other world religions. Tracts of controversy have been written by both partners for more than thirteen centuries. Their number — in many cases not their quality — is impressive. During all these centuries they have been studied and commented upon.[1] Nevertheless, I have to add one more author to this long list of writers interested in discussion between both religions. This is Monsieur l'Abbé François Bourgade who lived during the last century in Northern Africa and who is never mentioned by scholars studying the history of this meeting. Paul Gabend in his short biography of Bourgade called him in 1905 "un oublié," "a man who passed into oblivion" and he was right.[2] In this essay I want to draw attention to Bourgade as he deserves particular attention.

It is not an easy matter to present the life of a forgotten person but I shall try to give some insight into the context in which he

---

1. Moritz Steinschneider, *Polemische und apologetische Literatur in arabischer Sprache zwischen Muslimen, Christen und Juden, nebst Anhängen verwandten Inhalts* (Leipzig, 1877 (reprint: Hildesheim Georg Olms, 1966)); Gustav Pfannmüller, *Handbuch der Islam-Literatur* (Berlin-Leipzig: Walter De Gruyter, 1923 (reprint 1974)); Johann Fück, *Die arabischen Studien in Europa bis in den Anfang des 20. Jahrhunderts* (Leipzig: Otto Harrassowitz, 1955); Adel-Théodore Khoury, *Polémique Byzantine contre l'Islam (VIIIᵉ-XIIIᵉ s.)* (Leiden: Brill, E.J., 1972².) J.-M. Gaudeul, *Encounters and Clashes, Islam and Christianity in history*, 2 volumes (Rome: PISAI, 1984); Klaus Hock, *Der Islam im Spiegel westlicher Theologie* (Köln-Wien: Böhlau Verlag, 1986.)

2. Paul Gabend, *Un oublié: L'Abbé Bourgade, Missionnaire Apostolique, premier Aumônier de la Chapelle Royale de Saint - Louis de Carthage (1806-1866)*. Auch, Imprimerie centrale, 1905.

lived and in which he played an important role. Further, I shall
describe the outstanding features of his dialogue with his Muslim
friends at Carthage. Finally, I shall ask whether Bourgade's
approach is still a valid contribution to current Islamo-Christian
discussion on the universal meaning of Jesus.

The Life of Monsieur L'Abbé François Bourgade

He was born in 1806 in France and soon after his ordination to
the priesthood he arrived (towards the end of 1837) in Algeria.
He was appointed spiritual director of the Sisters of Saint Joseph
who had arrived in 1835 and were active in hospitals, sanatoria,
schools, houses of refuge and orphanages. Bourgade is described
as a man who appeared reserved and rigorous but possessed of
great zeal and charity. He was a good adviser and a resolute
guide.[3] In 1837 the diocese of Algiers was established and Monsieur l'Abbé Dupuch was appointed the first bishop. In the
beginning the bishop was very favourably disposed to the Sisters
of Saint Joseph who were engaged in many charitable works at
Algiers, Bône and Constantine among Muslims, Jews and Christians. However, soon he asked the Sisters to become a diocesan
institute and he suspected that l'Abbé Bourgade, their director,
did not advise them to be flexible. The bishop deprived Bourgade
of all his powers and finally forced him to leave the diocese.
Bishop Dupuch caused many more difficulties and was removed
from the diocese in 1845.[4]

Bourgade left Algiers in 1840 and took refuge in Rome. He
discussed his problem with members of the Roman Curia and —
after having obtained the title of an Apostolic Missionary — was
appointed extraordinary confessor of the Sisters. The Sisters and
their foundress, Mother de Vialar, had left Algeria and settled in
Tunisia. Bourgade joined them in the beginning of January 1841.
He acted as their spiritual and temporal director and soon
emerged as the chaplain of the French and the French speaking
population. Tunisia was an Apostolic Prefecture served by Italian

3. A. Pons, *La nouvelle Église d'Afrique ou le Catholicisme en Algérie, en
Tunisie et au Maroc depuis 1830* (Tunis, 1930) 11.
4. *Ibid.*, 18-19, 53-56, 58-61.

Lazarists and Capuchins. Bourgade was its first French priest. He assisted at the blessing of the Royal Chapel of Saint Louis, the king who had died at Carthage in 1270. In 1843 Bourgade was chosen to be the royal chaplain of this sanctuary. In the same year the Prefecture was raised to the status of Apostolic Vicariate and Bishops Sutter, a Capuchin friar became the first bishop (1843-1880). Bourgade was succeful in making the Royal Chapel a center of French culture. Next to the building a small home for the French consul and for Bourgade was erected and the compound was changed into a beautiful park. Bourgade received many guests from France and built a museum for the many Roman and early Christian relics of Carthage. He gathered a large group of Muslim friends who were religious and secular scholars, officials at the court of the ruler, Bey Ahmad Pascha, and others. With them he held many theological discussions; in which he proved to possess a deep knowledge of the Arabic language and culture as also of the Holy Book of the Muslims, the Koran, and Islamic law and exegesis. He published these dialogues in three books: *Soirées de Carthage* (Paris 1847), *La Clef du Coran* (Paris 1852), and: *Passage du Coran à l'Évangile* (Paris 1855). These 611 pages are of extraordinary quality but never mentioned by scholars. Bourgade established a French hospital, a college for Muslims they are Jews and Catholics, a house of refuge and a hostel. Up country, where he passed most of his time, Bourgade took many other initiatives. His College of Saint Louis was entrusted to the Capuchin friars. The other institutions were managed by the Sisters of Saint Joseph and by the Christian Brothers. [5]

Again Bourgade experienced difficulties, with which some authors deal briefly. In 1848 there was a revolution in France and his benefactress, Queen Marie-Amélie, could no longer support him financially. The Italian Capuchin friars considered the activities of this French priest to be too intrusive and his influence on the Sisters of Saint Joseph too exclusive. For them Bourgade's canonical position was out of all proportions. Moreover, some French consuls complained that Bourgade was not flexible enough. It is certain that Bourgade was rigorous — he never smiled —

5. *Ibid.*, 222-231.

fervant and possessing an open intelligence. The Vicar Apostolic,
Bishop Sutter, dismissed him as chaplain of the Royal Chapel of
Saint Louis, his one and only official post. A liver disease was the
decisive factor for his return to France in 1858. He went to Paris.
In 1861 he edited a bilingual review in French and Arabic:
L'Aigle de Paris; in 1863 he was the director of Birgis in Arabic;
in 1864 he published a brochure of 200 pages: *Lettre à M. Ernest
Renan* and in 1865 another one: *Association de Saint-Louis ou
Croisade Pacifique*. He translated some Arabic novels into
French. On March 20, 1866 he died, left on his own and most
probably in reduced circumstances.[6] We may find in comfort
some the knowledge that the future archbishop of Tunis or
Carthage, Cardinal cavigerie, gave financial support to and
exchanged letters with the Sisters of Saint Joseph and with l'Abbé
Bourgade from 1856 to 1858. At that time Lavigerie was living at
Paris and was in charge of the *Oeuvres d'Orient*. Bourgade met
Lavigerie after 1858 in Paris and interested him in his college at
Tunis and in his project of fostering closer ties between Muslims
and Christians.[7]

Tunesia from the years 1841 to 1858

Tunesia did not fall into the hands of the Turks. The country
was ruled by a person called the Bey. Most of the inhabitants had
changed their nomadic existence for life in the urban centers. In
the countryside the cultivation of olives was an important source
of income. Owing to its central position on the southern shores of
the Mediterrenean Sea, Tunesia had become a seagoing nation
and had admitted quite a number of French and Italian settlers.
Both France and Italy showed a great interest in maintaining
economic and political ties. As soon as Algiers was taken by the
French in 1830, the influence of France was more strongly felt in
Tunesia. The Bey, Husain Pascha, immediately took action by

6. *Ibid.*, 231-232. *Mgr. Baunard, Le Cardinal Lavigerie*, First tome (Paris:
Ancienne Librairie Poussielgue, 1912) 493-494. Cfr. P. Gabend, *Un oublié: l'Abbé
Bourgade*, 37-41.
7. A. Pons, *La nouvelle Église d'Afrique ou le Catholicisme en Algérie*, pp. 236-
238.

offering his favors to the French Catholic community in his country. He defended them against antichristian manifestations and donated to the king of France a piece of land at Carthage to erect a monument in honor of Saint Louis who had died on that site. In 1833 the ancient hospital of the Trinitarians was given to the Catholic Church to start a place of worship and in 1837 the Church of the Holy Cross was dedicated. The number of Catholics increased and in 1834 the following statistics were given: 6000 Catholics, 300 Greek-Orthodox, 100 Protestants in the city of Tunis, 150 Catholics in Bardo, 500 Catholics in La Goulette, 250 in Sousse, 50 in Monastir, 60 in Mahdia, 600 at Sfax and Djerba, 60 in Bizerta; a total of 8,070 Christians of whom 7,670 were Catholics.[8] The relations between the Bey, Husain Pascha, and France were excellent. On the occasion of his visit to France he observed: "Others have aspired after the title: pilgrim of Mecca, I wish to have no other than pilgrim of France, that is, pilgrim of the European civilization."[9] This may prove that the elite or the high society was keen on building up contacts with European culture and especially with French Catholics. The times were favourable for the dialogues Abbé Bourgade undertook and described in his three works.

A few words may be added concerning the history of the Catholic Church in Tunisia. By the end of the first century Christianity was implanted there. Saint Augustine an Saint Monica were not the least of the Christians. In 180 the church suffered the first of many persecutions. In the fourth century the Donatist schism disturbed the faith of the Christians. In the seventh century Islam spread all over the country. The loss of Christians was enormous as also was the emigration to Europe. The Church continued to exist, nonetheless, for another three centuries. The last contact between a Roman pope and the bishop of Carthage was in 1076. By the end of the thirteenth century Franciscans and Dominicans started a new venture, as did the Capuchins and Lazarists in the seventeenth century. A perfecture was erected in 1650 and this was elevated to an Apostolic Vicariate in 1843. The first Vicar Apostolic was Bishop Fidelis of

8. *Ibid.*, 206-209.
9. Thomas William M. Marschall, *Les Missions Chrétiennes*, 1 (Paris, ed. Ambroise Bray, 1865), p. 484.

Ferrara, former provincial of the Capuchin Province of Bologna.
He arrived by boat at La Goulette accompanied by two Italian
Capuchins. As he yet was not a consecrated bishop, the French
consuls, the Bey and his ministers were rather disappointed.
Through the intervention of the consul general Pope Gregory
XVI amended the situation and on October 29, 1844 Fidelis was
consecrated bishop in Rome and called himself Bishop Fidelis
Sutter. He was again received at La Goulette, this time with great
pomp and joy. He and his confreres enjoyed the admiration and
many favors from the Bey and from the people, who considered
them to be as worthy of veneration as their cadis or marabouts. [10]
This climate of friendship and understanding was favorable for
the apostolate of Abbé Bourgade. He could use his many talents
in creating new institutions and by gathering around himself
friends from intellectual and Muslim circles. [11]

Outstanding features of the dialogue between Bourgade and his Muslim friends

It is an endless task to give a survey of a dialogue of 611 pages!
Moreover, in the next section ample attention will be paid to
Bourgade's opinion on the universal meaning of Jesus Christ.
Here we intend to give a description of the quality and the main
topics of this dialogue in order to make the later reflection more
understandable.

Bourgade himself was very conscious of the unusual character
of his dialogue. In the introduction to his first volume he wrote:
"As far as the core of the questions is regarded, we less pretend
to deal with it than to help others to hit on the idea of dealing
with it. The field is large and the Muslim is more accessible to
reason than one often is accustomed to think. One must only pay
attention — when speaking to him — to do away with any

10. David B. Barett, *World Christian Encyclopedia* (Nairobi: Oxford University
Press, 1982) 677-679. I. Malkin (ed.), *La France et la Méditerranée, vingt-sept
siècles d'interdépendence* (Leiden: Brill, E.J., 1990.)
11. A. Pons, *La nouvelle Église d'Afrique ou le Catholicisme en Algérie*, pp. 206-
219.

appearance of proselytism; one of the first prescriptions of the Koran is indeed to flee those who speak against the religion. This explains the not very normal procedure in these dialogues. No serious question will be treated in a serious way. What should be put forward as a principle is left open-ended with regard to a conclusion and that conclusion is left to guesswork."[12] This is the Socratic method and — indeed — quite exceptional in the history of the encounter between Islam and Christianity. No wonder that the French minister of the Navy asked Father François Libermann for his advise in 1847. Libermann judged the work as being somehow simplistic a — theoretical piece which did not agree with the reality faced by the missionaries.[13] Bishop Pavy, bishop of the diocese of Algeria from 1846 till 1866, was more positive in stating that the three works of Bourgade contained a simple talk, ingenuous and friendly. He observed that there was no controversy in them, as such an attitude was forbidden by the Koran to its believers. Cardinal Lavigerie, archbishop in the North of Africa from 1867 till 1892, did not use the Socratic method of Bourgade as he preferred to commit himself to works of charity in the name of Jesus and to wait till Muslims would understand this call.[14]

A second quality of Bourgade's dialogue is that he is fully at ease within the Muslim and Korawic context. He knows all the Muslim expressions, such as: "By the Prophet, wisdom is with you!," "Praise be to God, I do not belong to the number of the obstinates!," "God is knowing," and "May peace accompany you!." The interlocutors are members of the Tunesian society in all its variety: cadi (jurist), mufi (judge), a secretary, a dervish, a jiri (a wealthy intellectual from Algeria possessing good contacts with European culture), three dignitaries, a black African servant-family, an Italian gardener, and so forth. On the Christian side a

---

12. M. L'Abbé Bourgade, *Soirées de Carthage* (Paris, 1847) 5.
13. Paule Brasseur, *Les religions traditionnelles et l'Islam vus par les premiers missionnaires français à la côte d'Afrique (1815-1880)*, in *Les Réveils Missionnaires en France du Moyen-Âge à nos jours (XIIᵉ-XXᵉ siècle)* (Paris: Beaudresne, 1984) 358. Paul Coulon, Paule Brasseur etc., *Libermann 1802-1852* (Paris: Du Cerf, 1988). There is no mention of this matter in the latter study.
14. Georges Goyau, *Un Grand Missionnaire, Le Cardinal Lavigerie* (Paris: Plou, 1925) 256.

priest and a religious Sister are prominent. The text is full of quotations from the Koran and the Holy Scripture. The Koran is quoted by using the Koranic titles of the chapters or suras. Bourgade had a good knowledge of the Arabic language, as well as of Christian and Muslim exegesis. Finally, all the dialogues take place in Tunesian surroundings, in the houses of the inter-locutors. There is no doubt that they really took place and that they are not an invention.

It is interesting to read that the priest taking part in the dialogue at the end of the first volume takes leave of his com-panions since he has to start out on a long journey of several months' duration. He leaves at the point at which the cadi states that from Abraham through Ismael and Isaac two great rivers have originated, that flow through different countries without loosing sight completely of one another and that one day — not far away — if it pleases God — the two rivers will join and become one. Both the mufti and the priest acclaim: May it please God! Apparently, the interlocutors have reached the stage of understanding the importance of Abraham for all three faiths claiming descendence from him. The months of absence of the priest gives the other interlocutors plenty of time to meditate on this insight.

A similar situation is to be found during long passages of the second half of the second volume: the priest seems to be absent. This time the absence has another reason. The tension between the jiri and his secretary becomes stronger and stronger. The secretary is well versed in the Koranic doctrine but he is not open-minded and rather conservative. The jiri, however, who joined the discussion only at the beginning of the second volume and who had invited the interlocutors to his up-country mansion, evolves from openmindedness and eagerness to learn towards scepticism and doubt. On page 146 of the second volume the jiri arrives at a point where he is willing to dismiss his secretary by saying: "The mufti has spoken with that kind of wisdom which distinguishes him; the cadi has forsaken neither his talent nor his sagacity. As far as my secretary is regarded, up till today I thought to have a man of merit; I now see that I have an imbecile. From now onward I no longer rely upon his service." This clash does not have as a consequence that the secretary

leaves the scene. Continues to take part in the discussions, but his
role has been changed from assistant to the jiri into an independent interlocutor. He does so on his own competence since he is a
doctor, the son of a doctor and educated among doctors.[15] Up to
the end of the dialogue the secretary continues to defend the
straight line of the truth — that is, in his own words the system of
Islam — and he does not agree with the jiri — nor with the cadi
and the mufti — who move from doubt concerning this system to
an experience of liberation by discovering that a scientific and
historical study of many passages of both the Koran and the
Gospel is helpful in understanding how the leaves, mother of the
book, have come down in the field of the Gospel and how they —
transplanted like exotique plants — have remained sterile. Both
the jiri, cadi and mufti agree that these leaves must return to their
original home and that they will find their full development by
doing this.[16] The cadi expresses this new conviction in a myste-
rious and oriental way: "The hand which wrote the passage of
the Koran has sopped the reed in the inkpot of the Evangelist,
but without taking enough ink. He did not want to sop twice."[17]
At the end of the third dialogue the change in the mind of the jiri,
the mufti and the cadi, who at this part of the discussion are
called the Arabs, becomes explicit. They ask the priest to recite
his own prayers "which — if it will please God — will soon be
our prayers."[18] The priest recites the Apostles' Creed, the Ten
Commandments, given by God to Moses and perfected by the
Messiah, the Our Father, taught by Jesus, and the Hail Mary,
which starts with the salutation addressed by the angel to Mary
as it is to be found both in the Koran and in the Gospel. After
each recitation the Arabs answer: "Amin."[19]

   At point in our essay it is good to ask the question whether
Bourgade remained faithful to his intended Socratic method.
Most certainly, Bourgade raises a lot of questions. One may say
that all the questions treated in the numerous oral and written controversies between Christians and Muslims and between

   15. M. L'Abbé Bourgade, *Passage du Coran à l'Évangile* (Paris, 1855), p. 219.
   16. *Ibid.*, pp. 227, 121, 181.
   17. *Ibid.*, p. 135.
   18. *Ibid.*, 228.
   19. *Ibid.*, 228-230.

Muslims and Christians during the centuries after the death of the prophet Mohammed return somewhere on the 611 pages of his three volumes. However, Bourgade did not become a polemist or a controversialist. When the priest is taking part in the conversation one can discover the real attitude of Bourgade. The priest raises questions by quoting both the Koran and the Old and the New Testament, by quoting Fathers of the Church and Christian theologians, statements of Christian Councils, passages of the Sunna, Islamic theologians, and Muslim authorities, and by referring to sayings of Muslim and Christian leaders. Having done this, he patiently waits for commentaries from his interlocutors. Quite often the result is that an agreement is reached. On some occasions this approach leads to a dispute between the interlocutors, al though at the end of the third dialogue it is only the secretary who continues the dispute whereas the jiri, the cadi and the mufti start agreeing with the priest. The role of the priest is limited to insisting on the importance of historical facts and scientific conclusions. He never becomes aggressive, insulting or hasty. He is waiting for the moment in which the inner light and conviction of others break through. He never gives in to the temptation to be victorious in his words or deeds. Time and again he states that he is a humble servant of God and of all human beings. He is a facilitator! Truth should be born; it should be given a chance to become fertile. The priest acts as a midwife in the process of giving birth. He is not a proselytiser.

The priest is very much impressed by humanitarianism and is critical with regard to certain Islamic customs. True humanism is one of the main criteria to discover truth in religion. This humanism is not Western; it is universal. According to Bourgade it is to be found in the most perfect way in the teachings of Jesus. Jesus Christ perfects all that is good in human nature. Jesus did not come to destroy but to bring perfection! The priest — or Bourgade — stresses the point that every human being has been created as an image of God. This is the reason why all human beings are equal and capable of meeting and learning from each other. In all honesty we may state that Bourgade remained faithful to his Socratic method and that he deserves a place of honour in the history of the encounter between Islam and Christianity. He reminds me of a modern dialogue between Mohammed Talbi and Olivier Clément which was published two years ago. Talbi (1920), a Tunesian and historian of international fame, wrote: "To everyone his own characteristics and physiogonomy. To everyone to accept oneself in accordance with the free will given by God. Our respect of the choice of our brother in Adam and Eve is not different from the respect we owe to the plan the creator has made for each of his creatures."[20]

Bourgade and the Universal Meaning of Jesus

Bourgade divided his work three parts: Evenings at Carthage, The Key of the Koran, and the Passage from the Koran to the Gospel. The logic of this division is clear. The first part is rather traditional as the main points of difference between Islam and Christianity are listed without any attempt to solve them. It is an inventory of the problems but also a proof of the stalemate existing for centuries. At the end of this part copies of the Bible and the Koran are exchanged. This is done as the discussion made clear that an objective study of both Holy Scripture is the only way for a new approach. After this the priest takes his leave for a long absence.

In the second part the partners in the dialogue start searching for a key to open the closed door. The question is how to deal with sacred texts that are not in all respects in agreement with each other? They key is to be found through a study of learned scholars and of the Koran. In other words the key is provided by historical and scientific studies and approaches. It is through the application of this key that a division of mind becomes evident. The jiri, cadi and mufti are willing to accept the results of this search, but the learned secretary shows no freedom of mind. The key or the new method is applied to several problems raised by comparing the Bible and the Koran.

The third part starts with a crisis. The jiri has been so impressed by the study of the Sunna and the Hadith and by a close study of the Koran that he said to have passed from doubt to

20. Mohammed Talbi et Olivier Clément, *Un respect têtu* (Paris:Nouvelle Cité, 1989) 100.

incredulity. He has discovered during the dialogues in the second part that many facts and miracles mentionned in them are not correct. They are pious inventions and he has come to the conclusion that even the Koran is only a word of a human being. He is disturbed by this conclusion and not in a position to take supper with his interlocutors. He is also disturbed by the attitude of his secretary. He passes the night by studying his books and by dictating notes and proposals to the secretary. The secretary cannot stand this any longer and starts a heavy discussion. But the jiri sticks to his conviction that the Koran is the work of a human being and not a divine book. For him it is evident that the religion of Abraham has been lost since that religion has been corrupted in the hands of both Jews and Christians. He wants to stay in his situation of doubt and is inclined to stop discussions on religious matters.[21]

It is at this juncture that the priest makes an important observation. He tells the jiri that he has mistakenly identified the religion of Abraham with the Koran. Moreover, historical research is able to understand the situation of Mohammad and the position taken by the Koran. It was a great thing that Mohammed converted from polytheism to monotheism and he deserves praise for this. He had to deal with many Jews and he tried to understand their doctrine. The same is true for Christianity which he received through not so orthodox Christians. It is not necessary to do away with the whole of the Koran. It is enough to complete some passages by means of the Gospel. In this way these dead passages will receive a new meaning. In principle most Christian doctrines and even the sacraments are included in the Koran. The virtues of the Koran can be brought to perfection by means of the virtues of the Gospel.

I quote a long passage from Bourgade:

"Moses was sent to give a preparatory law; Jesus to perfect that law. The son of Abdallah (Mohammad) came 1215 years after Moses, 573 years after Jesus. He met a people not ready for the law of the Gospel and possessing the ignorance and hardheadedness of the Jewish people during the time of Moses and also the obstinacy in error, a wound sometimes worse than idolatry. The new lawgiver

21. M. L'Abbé Bourgade, *Passage du Coran à l'Evangile*, 5-24.

gave to his people a law containing preparatory elements taken
from the law of Moses and seeds and elements of the evangelical
law. It looks as if he left it to God and to the right time when the
passage from the preparatory elements to the full truth would take
place. Thus it happened that Mohammad, later in time than Moses
and Jesus, placed himself — in the order of ideas — as a contemporary of Moses and a precursor of Jesus: the second proof of
wisdom. Mohammed has reestablished the unity between the Bible
and the Gospel, unity broken by the Jews. The Koran has even —
due to the true elements in it — more relationship those two books
than certain parts of the Koran have among themselves."[22]

In this way Bourgade — or the priest — clears the way for a
fruitful continuation of the dialogue. For him the contradictions,
the historical, astronomical, physical and other assorted errors of
the Koran should not prevent scholars from considering the
Koran to be a book worthy of attention. It is a preface to the
Gospel. The Koran may not be a book directly written by God.
It has a human author, but this does not have as a consequence
that nothing in the Koran is divine. The priest tells his interlocutors that they must go the way of emancipation and he extends to
them the hand of a friend. After that the interlocutors keep
silence and look intensively at each other. The mufti and the cadi
seem to be full of hope and the secretary knocked down; the jiri
has a serious and impassible face,[23] but the jiri is willing to
continue the discussion.

The rehabilitation of the Koran, proposed by the priest, is now
applied to the doctrine of the Trinity and to the divinity of Jesus.
With regard to the divinity of Jesus, we find a very profound and
learned discussion of the expression, Word of God, found both in
the Koran and in the Gospel. It is explained that God has no
body and that the Word of God is the essence of God. It is also
proved that human nature is sinful and needs redemption
through God becoming man. The crucifion of Jesus and his
resurrection are discussed at length, since the Koranic view on
these facts is rather ambiguous. Time and again the priest stresses
the point that his intention is not to contradict the Koran; it is
rather to discover the full meaning of the Koranic texts through

22. *Ibid.*, pp. 27-28.
23. *Ibid.*, p. 34.

the method of historical exegesis of both the Koran and the Gospel. This is done with great delicacy. In this way the universal meaning of Jesus is made clear to Muslims without doing injustice to the value of the Koran. For the priest it is no a matter of rejecting the Koran and accepting the Gospel. On the contrary, Muslims cannot arrive at the fulness of salvation in Jesus without using the preparatory path of the Koran. This is Bourgade's main argument.

Many details of the discussions have been passed over: Old Testament prophecies concerning the coming, life, death and resurrection of Jesus, the Spirit Paraclete, the faith of Saint Paul and his conversion, the example of the early martyrs of the Church and the spread of the Gospel compared to the spread of Islam. Negative points have not been put aside. Never has the fundamental principle of the Gospel and Jesus bringing the Koran and Mohammad to perfection been given up. Bourgade did not give his interlocutors an abstract and theoretical view on the universal meaning of Jesus. He definitively was not a dogmatic theologian. He was a scholar in Arabic language, in Koranic doctrines, in Muslim history and exegesis, and also in Biblical studies and Christian history. He used these sciences in a then very uncommon way.

Bourgade must have been an extraordinary man in his day. He initiated a new approach in an old and rather unfruitful controversy between Christianity and Islam. He did so in a country where for centuries a friendly meeting between the two religions had been impossible. He could profit from the new political situation due to the influence of France in the region of Northern Africa and to the favourable attitude of the ruler of the country, the Bey of Tunisia. Yet he did not use this new climate as a kind of instrument to convert Muslims. He preferred dialogue above aggressive missionary methods. For him mission was dialogue, a meeting between religious persons and human beings trying to accept each other as children of the same Creator and as pilgrims on the same way to salvation. The uniqueness of Jesus was, for him, not an argument to do away with the prophet of Islam, Mohammed. He tried to give both their due place in God's dealings with humankind.

Bourgade was really an exceptional person. That may have

been the reason why he got into difficulty and why he had to leave his beloved Carthage. Thus he became a forgotten man. His method was not considered to be prudent. We may, nonetheless, ask ourselves what would have been the situation of Christians in Northern Africa if Cardinal Lavigerie would have adopted Bourgade's approach?

ENCOUNTER: AN OROMO VIEW OF CHRIST

Lambert Bartels

When, quite unexpectedly, I received an invitation from the Faculty of Theology of this university to participate in this colloquium on 'The Universality of Christianity' I was rather surprised, since I am not a professional theologian. Then I read I that I had been invited as "a man of practice" because of my work as a missionary-anthropologist in Africa, more specifically, in Ethiopia, and — to be still more specific — among the most numerous people of that country, the Oromo perhaps twenty million in all, and, as such, the most numerous people of East Africa.

When we hear the term "Man of Practice," we expect facts, data based on experience, knowledge born from daily life rather than theory, or a rationally elaborated system, for example, in this case, an Oromo Christian theology. Out of my very practice grew a need for study of the latter: the study of Catholic theology, of Christian theology at large, and of the human sciences, not only anthropology, but also comparative religion, psychology, parapsychology, biology and linguistics.

Various Methods of Evangelization

A missionary, even a missionary-anthropologist, is by definition a man or woman with a message. In my case it was quite natural that the message was the form of Christianity passed on to me half a century ago, a message time- and culture-bound but, despite all this, immensely rich.

There are missionaries who continue to bring this message of the beginning of their career until the end of their lives. There are others who adapt their original message to their experience as a missionary, and often very aptly so. Others who, at a certain moment in their missionary life, feel compelled to make a complete changeover. They stop speaking to the people as messengers and begin to listen to them. Such was the case with the great Belgian missionary, Placide Tempels, who, after ten years of addressing the people onesidedly, decided to tell them: "Please, tell me first, what God has told you; after this I'll tell you what he has said to us."

Such has been my own approach from the very beginning — though I hasten to say that I did not begin my missionary career until after I was fifty years old. So I had got ample time to grow — thanks to the example of some enlightened missionaries, some studies in comparative religion and cultural anthropology and a short stay with an Indian tribe in the Amazon forest which, in retrospect, has proved to be a good preparation for the understanding of the cosmic worldview which I met in Ethiopia during my twenty years stay with the Oromo.

In his book *La Tièrce Église devant le problème de la culture* [The Third Church faced by the problem of other cultures']. Valeer Neckebrouck has called my approach to this problem *Explicitation*. He has devoted a whole chapter of his book to my work and has shown that he has understood it very well. He presents my work among the Oromo as a new approach. He writes:

> This method of evangelization opposes to a Christ, prisoner of a Church which tries to monopolize him, a Christ who transcends all institutional cadres, all religious and cultural categories familiar to western Christians only, Christ as a presence universally accessible, one for sure with the historical Jesus, but not exhausted by him — a Christ who precedes the missionary everywhere, a Christ who is present in the culture of every people and every nation. In other words, the "limits" of the Christ-event do not fully coincide with those of the Jesus-event. If there is only one single Jesus, there are several, even many different, manifestations of Christ among various peoples and cultures (...). The missionary problem, then, does not consist in bringing Christ to those cultures, but in exploring, with immense respect, the features of his face among them and make them visible.[1]

1. V. Neckebrouck, *La Tierce Église devant le problème de la culture* (Immensee: Verein zur Forderung der Missionswissenschaft, 1987) pp. 105-106.

Or, as my Oromo assistants like to phrase it: "We are in search of the place Christ has given himself in our people from the very beginning, long before Jesus of Nazareth was born."

My Oromo Assistants

My closest partners in this encounter were grandchildren of the last traditional "highpriest" (Abba Bokku, Holder of the Staff) in the area. This suggests that their family had a deeply traditional education. They belonged to the borana-clan which traces its genealogy back to the Borana-tribe in the East, from where their people emigrated westwards some four centuries ago. My partners were Gammachu Magarsa (Magarsa being his father's name), his brother Qajeela, and their youngest sister Aagitu. When I met them for the first time (1980), Gammachu and Aagitu were studying in the University of Addis Abba.

After three years of working with me, Gammachu left the country in order to study anthropology in Kenya and Qajeela took his place at my side. The three of them had been educated in Christianity, in various degrees, first by the Presbyterians and then by the Adventists (both of them American missionaries). Their education in mission-schools proved to be an asset rather than a set-back in our encounter. In addition, all three were gifted and articulate. The two brothers were highly inspired poets.

Gammachu

During our joint work on my book *Oromo Religion*,[2] we naturally came to talk about his Christian faith.

It did not take a long time before he told me:

> Abba, I never met a priest like you. With you I can speak on equal terms. The Presbyterians and Adventists (he had still good friends among the latter) used to speak to us as if they had God in their pocket. You want us to tell you what God has said to us, Oromo. It is he who has brought you to us and me to you. The Presbyterians

---

2. L. Bartels, *Oromo Religion. Myths and Rites of the Western Oromo of Ethiopia. An Attempt to Understand* (Berlin, 1983.)

and Adventists used to baptize people in the name of Jesus Christ as our "personal saviour." They separated us from our ancestors who are still in us. We feel as if we are only half baptized. Of the catholic priests I do not know much but, as it seems to me, they, too, came to us with a message only, without realizing that we had a message for them as well. You came in order to listen to us first.

Later on he articulated even more sharp what all this meant to him:

You know that I always have thought in terms of what other educated Oromo would say of it (he refers mainly to his Adventist and Protestant friends) because education for us meant not feeling our God through ourselves. They brainwashed us and tried to make sure that our link with Him was never direct.

Qajeela

"He has more of a priest than I have," Gammachu said of him. As articulate and gifted as is his brother, he is rather a mystic and, as it is with such people, to a great extent self-forgetting. He could say, after giving me some precious new insights: "Abba, don't mention my name when you write about these things. I am the voice of my people." Yet, he too, no less than his brother, is typically Oromo in both his outspokenness and his extreme sensitiveness with regard to our exchange of thoughts "on equal terms." One word of his I will never forget: "Abba, if from time to time we can not grow angry with each other, we are not one." Once, when I had asked him to write down his feelings about a subject, he suddenly interrupted his work saying: "O Abba, I am so happy that you leave me one hundred percent free. Thanks to you, my ancestors have matured in me." Thus pointing at his newly found Christian faith as an Oromo.

Aagitu

Her partnership in our encounter was extremely welcome, not to say indispensable. For us, he represented the women's world in her people, marked by a greater attachment to tradition, openness to other aspects of reality and values than men, and another experience of the divine. In addition — and this was very important — she proved to be as good an interviewer as her brothers. To her I owe insights and personal experiences which I never would have heard from them.

From "Research" to "Encounter"

This lecture has been presented under the title "Encounter: An Oromo View of Christ." The main word in this title is "encounter."

I wrote my book *Oromo Religion* as a missionary anthropologist. An anthropologist carries out "research" as it is commonly called. Within the limits of his craft he reports, as objectively as possible, about certain aspects of a people's culture. My position is different. Initially I thought it was well formulated in this way: "An exchange of thought on equal terms between a western Catholic priest and some young gifted Oromo people of various Christian denominations about their religious experience in two different thought-worlds." As was to be expected, however, it soon turned out that our contacts were to become much more than a mere exchange of thoughts. Personal values and personal religious experiences made for mutual enrichment, a deeper understanding of our own spiritual heritage, and, surprisingly, an equally deep awareness of the many things we shared in common long before we came to know each other.

This emerges from a talk I had with Qajeela:

Q. Abba, through this work with you my eyes were opened.
A. So were mine, thanks to you
Q. Brother Gammachu once told me that at times you could better express in words what we think than we ourselves can.
A. Here, too, I could say the same to you.
Q. Shall I tell you something? (his eyes started twinkling) It was less by going to church than by working with you that I got to love Jesus Christ.

His younger sister phrased it this way:

Abba, you have changed us; we have changed you. Thus it should be.

Finally, the word "encounter" was chosen. By the way, the same word was also chosen by Placide Tempels as the title of one of his books, *Rencontre*.

The Name Waaqa

The word *waaqa* has a double meaning. The first is "vault of heaven." The second approximates what is meant by the English word "God." [3]

As we will see, however, *waaqa* comprises more than "the Supreme Being, creator and ruler of the universe, regarded as eternal, infinite, all powerful and all-knowing" in the sense that Webster's dictionary gives it. It comprises more, since it also includes countless particular manifestations of Waaqa in this world, refractions of his all-comprising creative activity, all of them so many aspects of the divine.

An Immanent God

In other words: To the Oromo God is one and many at the same time. All the refractions of his creative activity are God in a way, since — and this is essential to understand — in their eyes creation is an ongoing process. It implies God's permanent active presence in every creature. The Oromo have a special name for these refractions: *ayyaana*.

To which comes Qajeela's great idea that it is God himself as our own creator, God as he is in us, who makes us see himself in all other creatures as their creator.

To the Oromo the divine is immanent in this universe. The divine, as has been is not thought of as detached from this universe in time or space. It is not, however, a static immanence; it is an endless gigantic display of creativity encompassing all creatures, keeping them the way the divine wants them to be,

3. In our western languages we still find some remnants of a former use of the word "heaven" for "God." In English expressions such as "Heaven beware" and "For Heaven's sake" — in French the saying "Aide toi le Ciel t'aidera" — "Help yourself and Heaven will help you" — in Dutch the exclamation "Lieve Hemel — Dear Heaven."

guiding them, ruling them. To the Oromo Chesterton's remark that it could well be that God says to the sun every morning: "OK do so: rise once more!" comes most near to the way they see things. So the Newtonian view of the universe as a mechanism detached from its maker but working perfectly according to in-built "laws of nature" simply lies beyond the horizon of the Oromo thought-world.

As a result of this it is not surprising that the biblical story of creation is not highly regarded. Qajeela:

> Every time I read there that God, after creating something, looked at his work and "saw that it was good," I ask myself: "Why does he need to test his work? Why must he *see* whether it was good or bad? He is living in the very things he creates. And why should he take rest after he had finished his work? It was not finished at all: it was bound to go on. To us, Oromo, all things God creates existed in him without beginning and they will continue doing so world without end. God is not something. He is also not nothing. He is himself. You leave it to your heart and keep quiet. This is some-thing divine, something of an almighty mystery. Do not give it to your ear, to your eyes, to your tongue, to your brains, but only to your heart, to your very own self."

However, as we will see more clearly later on, to the Oromo God is immanent in his very transcendence. All the Creator's refractions in this universe remain one with him and he himself is more than all his refractions together. As the Oromo phrase it:

> He is at the same time in all *ayyaana* and behind all *ayyaana*.

Unsearchable Mystery

> There is a boundary of Waaqa no man can pass. If we would know him the way he is in himself, we would be like him; we would not be men anymore. (Gammachu)

To which his younger brother Qajeela made this perceptive remark:

> "However, that boundary of Waaqa is only on our side. Waaqa himself sees us and is *in* us and knows us better than we know ourselves.

> You westerners always want to look at Waaqa directly as he is in himself. As for us, we look at our children, our cattle, the trees, the clouds, the stars, and see him there. (Qajeela)

Here follow some words of Gammachu which would well deserve to be written above each page of this essay:

> Whenever we are speaking of Waaqa (God) we are bound to say truth and untruth at the same time. For all this we think Waaqa likes us to speak of him, even if it is in such an imperfect way, and he blesses us when we do so. Whatever we say of him, we trust Waaqa himself will give meaning to our words.

Waaqa, Source of Life

> If somebody asks me: "How many children do you have?" I reply: "You want to know how many children *Waaqa* has given to me? Waaqa has given me three children." I would not say: "I *have* three children." Nor will I say so in regard to my cattle and chickens. We do not count whatever has life. People can ask us: "How much do you have" where money, chairs or containers are concerned, but not when the things concerned have life." (Assistant Asafa Disaasa)

They have a feeling, indeed, that all life belongs to God and that people are not free to dispose of it. In one of his best talks with me Gammachu went deeper:

> Wherever there is life there is Waaqa. Waaqa *is* life. Life never dies: it only takes another shape.

In the Oromo view unanimated matter does not exist.

Holy Scriptures

> We, Oromo, do not have holy books such as the Bible of the Christians, but if we had written our own Bible, it would have been better than the other one. (An old man)

From the mouth of the still pre-Christian and anti-Islam Oromo in the Far East, we heard this statement:

Christians and Muslims say that their holy books have been written by Waaqa himself... This is not true: they were written by people with the help of Waaqa.

To Oromo God reveals himself, or, the as they put it, "God speaks to them through the 'book of creation.'" This is not a name coined by them. In fact it gradually came to be used by me and my assistants.

The "Book of Creation"

It is the sole "book" Waaqa has really written with his own hands, he alone, and he is still writing it. In this book every creature is a word of Waaqa to us and it can be read by all people, black and white and in between, literate or not, and thus it was done by our ancestors and by the whole of mankind, long before the first script was invented. — and they read it well. (Qajeela)

Indeed, to every people, each in its own way, the Book of Creation became the foundation of their man-made laws which are no more than applications of this fundamental law in the frame work of their own way of life, adapted to their own needs, their own character as a people, their ideals and also their weaknesses, their pride and their egoism.[4]

We find an eloquent illustration of this in the ritual by which the Oromo proclaimed their laws every eight years when a new set of people took over general responsibility for the well-being of the people as a whole. In this ritual those who are about to assume power, kneeling and lifting their hands in prayer, first accept the fundamental law of the book of creation from Waaqa's hands. It is the law of mutual respect and support between mother and daughter, father and son, master and ser-

---

4. Cf. A Pieris S.J., *'Love Meets Wisdom'* — *A Christian Experience of Buddhism* (Maryknoll: Orbis, 1987) p. 98. "When trying to understand the primordial truths as taught in various traditions, one must learn to distinguish between the various founders' *basic intuitions* (which often converge) and their immediate *transmissions* within the conceptual framework of various cultures wherein different religions originate. They again should be further distinguished from the doctrinal elaborations that logically flow out of them."

vant, small and great, a relationship that also required that
everyone should live up to his/her own place in society. Animals,
too, were included... plants even, and ordinary water (in contrast
with mineral water). While accepting this law, the ritual leaders
were kept in their hands a special kind of grass, symbolizing both
distance and harmony between people, *tehokorsa*. This law is
called *safuu*. After this the leaders rise up and start proclaiming
anew their human laws, ancient ones and new ones, but not with
grass but with a whip in their hands.

> While saying Waaqa's safuu they kneel down. While beating the
> law of man they keep standing. This safuu is like a prayer: while
> pronouncing it they pay honor to Waaqa by kneeling down. (Sha-
> gerdi Bukko, ritual expert)

A Cosmic Morality

So the foundation of Oromo morality is not a set of commandments given from above by which people have to abide, but this
very cosmic order in which God goes on speaking to them. Every
being is given a place within this cosmic order and must live up to
this place and its own identity. It has both a duty and a right to
do so. As long as it abides by this, all others have to respect it
and to help it to be (that is, to become) what its creator intends it
to be.

In the Oromo view this holds good not only for humans but
also for animals, plants and insects. The Oromo consider all of
them as endowed to a certain extent with freedom.

As far as people are concerned, every word or deed that hurts a
fellow-creature and above all a fellow-human is sin. All sin has a
cosmic dimension. It is always something against Waaqa as he
lives and works in his creation. It always harms the cosmos in one
way or another. In Oromo view it is the cosmos itself which
reacts to this, that is, the divine in every creature, "its ayyaana,"
reacts to it, defends itself, takes revenge. This is the deepest
background of many so called "superstitions," such as this, for
instance. While speaking of a pond of mineral water (a holy pond
in their eyes) which had fallen dry, an old Oromo told me: "Once

somebody soiled this pond by bathing in it while he was impure. Since that day the pond has refused to give us water."

So the idea that God punishes or rewards, so to say, from above, from outside this creation, is alien to Oromo. True, they do speak of God as "punishing" them, but this God is immanent in his creation and he always acts, as it were, "horizontally," or better "innerworldly."

A Covenant

To Oromo Waaqa has a covenant (*wadda*) with the whole of creation (but especially with humans). It is, we could say, "creation-oriented." This reminds me of Gammachu's words, while we were speaking of the plight of his people, threatened with the extinction of their cultural-religious identity. His words sounded like a cry of despair:

> If Waaqa does not like us, why does he go on giving us children?!

A young Borana, too, spoke of the number of their children as a proof that things were still well between them and Waaqa.

Indeed, their covenant with their Creator is like the "covenant without words" between parents and children. It endures, even when a child goes astray.

> I like that story of Jesus about the lost son and his father. This is our Waaqa. I also like Jesus' words that his father in heaven goes on causing his sun to rise on bad men as well as good, and his rain to fall on honest and dishonest men alike. Thus it is with our covenant with him as well.
>
> So God continues to create out of love.
>
> Waaqa only creates what he likes, and he only likes things in which he sees himself. (Gammachu)

In the Oromo's eyes every people, yea every creature has its own covenant with Waaqa as their own creator. In my talks with my assistants about Christian ideas of God they said at times: "This I do not like; this is not *our* Waaqa."

Openess to Other Religions

Indeed, the Oromo are well aware of the fact that "their Waaqa" is not absolute and universal. They like the image of all peoples sitting around God, each of them on their own stool, from where they see God in a way which certainly has much in common with others, but at the same time is never wholly shared by them. Their may even be blatantly contradictory elements — which, however, are believed to complement one another in some way beyond our present understanding. Consequently, in the relationship between people of various religions respect is needed for things we do not understand, things we cannot combine with our own limited experience of God's unsearchable mystery. Religions are, moreover, called to enrich each other as much as possible.

> If western Christians really want to know God and themselves and the world, and even grow in this knowledge, they should also look at the different faces of God with other peoples, and these peoples should do the same with regard to western Christians. (Gammachu)

So in the Oromo view the variety of religious experience is willed by God.

Note:

Throughout the previous pages I have allowed the Oromo to speak for themselves as much as possible (explicitation). In the light of what follows, it may be useful to draw the reader's attention to the fact that throughout our encounter we were confronted with the difference between two different patterns of thought or modes of consciousness: the Oromo one and the scientific one of the West.

In western thought a distinction is made between objective and subjective. This is a result of Greek philosophy which is also in the heart of our theology. To the Oromo such a distinction does not exist. To them things are always at the same time what they are in themselves and what they are to us. To them both aspects are part and parcel of the same reality. By their very nature all beings cannot but influence each other. All creatures with which we come in contact are called to influence us for better or worse and vice-versa, whether we are conscious of it or not. If we are conscious of it, they become a "you" to us. They are no longer a neutral "it." We address them and we feel addressed by them. To put it in western terms, they are "personalized." To the Oromo the whole cosmos is potentially personalized in this sense. Qajeela, being a technician, speaks of a magnetic field in this context.

For him as to his fellow Oromo, this psychic relationship is most intimately connected with a religious one. To him all beings have something of the divine in them, their ayyaana, the active presence of their creator in them, who is also his own creator. To which we could add an even deeper word of his: "To tell you the whole truth as I feel it, it is our own creator in us who makes us see himself in things outside of us."

Such then is Qajeela's experience of reality which pervades all his words when he is speaking about this world as he sees it; all things are a "you" to him and the very divine in them is always a "Thou." This is what makes him and his people reluctant to define things rationally, be it God, ayyaana, a human or even a cow — though God knows how much his people (traditionally pastoralists) know of cattle.

This is also the reason why the reader can not find clearcut definitions in this essay. Whenever my Oromo assistants are speaking, there are symbols and comparisons. We do not define what is a "you" to us. This also accounts for their accepting contradictions in man's speaking about the divine — contradictions which are not tolerated in our western conceptual way of thought.

We saw that the name "Waaqa" evokes not only the idea of "Supreme Being, creator of heaven and earth," but also countless particular manifestations or refractions of God's creative activity in this universe. For these countless manifestations or refractions of his on-going and all-comprising creative activity in every creature Oromo have a special name: "ayyaana."

Here we touch the specifically Oromo appreciation of God's immanence in this world.

Because of special constraints and the many aspects of the world of ayyaana, I will cite here only those aspects which are most pertinent to the subject matter of this volume.

Everything has a twofold nature: one part we see with our eyes, the other part we do not see with our eyes but with our heart. This invisible part of them is the most real. We call it "ayyaana." You will never understand us, unless you realize that we see everything in this way. (Gammachu)

Some Statement about Ayyaana Taken at Random

All creatures — people, animals, plants, stars, stones have their own ayyaana. Every person has his own ayyaana. Every clan and also our people as a whole have their own ayyaana, and also mankind has its own ayyaana, the ayyaana of humanhood. Even this universe as a whole has its own ayyaana.

These ayyaana rule our lives. They make us the way we are.

Ayyaana — Something of Waaqa

Waaqa is one but the ayyaana, too, are Waaqa in a way. It is therefore that I do not like it when you call the ayyaana "superhuman." Are they merely superhuman? They are much more: they are something of Waaqa. It is in the many ayyaana that Waaqa himself comes close to us and that we are united with him. (Gammachu)

When once I asked a Catholic Oromo priest what ayyaana was, he literally repeated Gammachu's words: "Ayyaana is Waaqa in a way."

Gammachu continues:

For all this, no Oromo will ever say: "Waaqa *is* ayyaana" no more than I will say that you yourself and your hand are one and the same thing. When you give me your hand, do I call then your hand merely a link between you and me? No, your hand is you yourself in a way. If I kiss your hand, I kiss you, and if I pray to my father's ayyaana, I pray Waaqa.

Even less we will ever say that man is "something of Waaqa" because Waaqa's ayyaana is in us. To tell you the full truth — O, my tongue is growing heavy now — we see the ayyaana as flowing out of Waaqa in a way, filling the whole of creation, both inside and outside. However, the ayyaana remain invisible. What is visible in man is not his ayyaana. This visible aspect of man is rather formed and conditioned by his ayyaana; his ayyaana manifests itself in it.

While speaking in this fashion Gammachu also intends to say that in this universe God Creator is present *only* in his refractions, the ayyaana. As his brother confirmed:

In this world God *is* ayyaana.

At the same time both the oneness of the Creator with his refractions and the distinction between them is maintained in words, rituals and prayers. The greatest ritual expert in our area, Shagerdi Bukko, put it this way:

Ayyaana is Waaqa-God but Waaqa is not ayyaana.

Other sayings are:

Waaqa is the source of all ayyaana.
Waaqa is more than all ayyaana together.
Waaqa is behind all ayyaana

Indeed, he is more than all his refractions together. Once Aagitu formulated all these things magnificently in this way:

While thinking of Waaqa and ayyaana I like most this comparison. Waaqa is like a source and the ayyaana are the streamlets that flow from this source. Out of the streamlets other streamlets are flowing, endlessly. These streamlets are not the source: they are one with the source, they are something of the source; but they are not the source itself.

Ayyaanticha

Gammachu gives the final touch:

As the source of all ayyaana in this universe I would like most to call him "Ayyaanticha." "Ayyaantichicha" would be even better; it is a word we coined ourselves, but it is a word coined entirely according to the rules of our language. It better expresses that this "Ayyaanticha" is absolutely the primeval source. However, in daily speech we mostly say "Ayyaanticha." It is this "Ayyaanticha" or better "Ayyaantichicha" which is the best Oromo name for Christ.

The Oromo View of Christ

When I met them for the first time, my assistants were already Christians. They never lost their appreciation for what the foreign missionaries had done for them.

For all this they were still deeply rooted in their people's past. They could still say with Qajeela: "I am more my ancestors than I am myself."

They never came to accept the image of a God detached from his creation, a God not immanent in this world, a God who had not revealed himself to their ancestors as well, a non-cosmic God as they found him in the Bible and the Gospels.

It was in fact through me that for the first time they heard from the mouth of a Christian priest that Christ had been living in their people from the very beginning.

If Christ then was really the Son of God, why shouldn't he be as cosmic and as immanent in this world as the Waaqa of their fathers? Why then could their people's covenant with this Waaqa not persist within christianity as well?

So their new Christian credo became:

> As the source of all ayyaana in this world we call Waaqa "Ayyaan-ticha" and this Ayyaanticha is Christ to us.

It is in this sense that they read the first chapter of the letter to the christians of Colossae where the author speaks of Christ as the one through whom and in whom all things have been created and who holds all things together as one single whole — a Christ who incarnates in all creatures but eminently so, for us christians, in Jesus of Nazareth.

This then has been the outcome of what Qajeela repeated again and again to me:

> Abba, the great problem for you is the way we see Jesus Christ.

Gammachu's Comment:

> While speaking of Jesus Christ I make a great distinction between Jesus of Nazareth and Christ. I believe they are one but, at the same time, they are distinct from one another. Christ is Waaqa as the source of all ayyaana in this world. Through whom the whole of creation came into existence and is kept in existence ongoingly. He

fills everything in this universe and the highest of all things in this universe is Man (and the highest of all men is Jesus of Nazareth in whom he took a human shape).

If western Christians tell me that Jesus was born from a human mother and lived as a righteous man, anointed and blessed by Waaqa above all men, I am glad to hear this. Indeed, Jesus was the greatest and most holy man ever to exist. He died for the highest good of mankind. He became "the man, the human being by excellence," the man after whose image all men are made and with whom all men are equal. All men should try to be like him.

However, I do not see him as a man only, I also see him as one with the source of all ayyaana and as such we, Oromo, like to call him "ayyaanticha." This ayyaanticha in him and one with him, is Christ to me. He is one with the man Jesus but also more. Ayyaanticha in himself has no human shape. He was with us already before Jesus of Nazareth was born, filling this whole universe with his creative power through millions of minor ayyaana who flew out of him. It was only afterwards that this Ayyaanticha whom we now call "Christ" took a human shape in the Son of Mary. So this Christ is not only to be found, as some Christians seem to say, in Jesus of Nazareth, though he showed himself in him most perfectly. In him he showed us most what Waaqa wants us to be.

As far as we Oromo are concerned we call this Christ "Boraanticha," a name which, like the name "Christ" means "the Anointed one." He is the source of the common ayyaana of our people. All peoples have their own ayyaana, their own "Anointed one," and in him their own covenant with God.

From old the Oromo have said prayers, brought sacrifices and poured out libations to their Boraanticha, and they are still doing so throughout Oromoland and even in this town of Addis Abba in the month of Gimbot.

It is this Boraanticha whom we, Christian Oromo, identify with the Christ-with-them, present in their midst from the very morning of our people.

Qajeela's Comment:

While thinking of our Boraanticha I think of Jesus of Nazareth and while thinking of Jesus of Nazareth I think of our Boraanticha. Yet I do not imagine Jesus then the way he is presented in the pictures we see of him. All these features of his disappear for me, he becomes light, only light but in a human shape. He becomes immediately international to me.

Abba, did you not tell me once that the very name "Christ" was given to Jesus of Nazareth after his death by Greek speaking people and that it meant "the Anointed One?" We Oromo have our own name for him: we call Christ as far as he is the common ayyaana of our people as a whole "Boraanticha" and this name means the "Anointed One" as well.

I like Jesus words to his friends: "Nobody can ever see the Father unless through me. When you see me, you see the Father, too." Do you know what I think out of my own ayyaana? I think in heaven we will continue seeing the Father only in Jesus, Son of Man. To me what Christians call "heaven" means being with Jesus-Christ, living with him, knowing him as he really is. And I cannot but imagine this heaven unless within the universe of Christ-Ayyaan-ticha.

A final talk with Qajeela

Before I had this talk with Qajeela I wanted to make sure that he would speak as an Oromo only, perfectly free from any influence of Christianity as he had got to know it from the Presbyterian and the Adventist missionaries.

Q. You want me to speak about Jesus of Nazareth as an Oromo only?

A. Yes, I would like you to speak out of the depths of your own ayyaana only. Think of your grand-grandfather Kurra Hedde who never was a Christian. He is now with his ancestors in the place of righteousness (iddo dhugaa), he has fullness of life now, he is with Jesus Christ up there, and his ayyaana is also in you. Pray him to tell you what he would say to you, his grand-grandson, as you are now: a christian. Speak with him about your belief that Waaqa as he is in this world — you call him Ayyaanticha, the source of all ayyaana — has become a man, born from a human mother, Jesus of Nazareth. It is you Qajeela, who should pray him, since you are one with him, much, much more than I am.

The next week he came back. I asked him if he had prayed.

Q. Yes, I have prayed, and this is what Kurra-Hedde told me.

'My grand-grandson, the reason why the Christ-Ayyaanticha became a man in Joshua of Nazareth, a man like us, a man among us, and why he suffered and died in this world is this: he wanted to show his people that he loves them. He himself, being Waaqa-in-this-world, is Fedha Bullo (the One who only acts according to his own will, wholly independent on all created powers and on whatever we human beings call good or bad). He kills and nobody can kill him. He can do whatever he likes. He is the law-giver, but he himself is above all laws.

In Joshua of Nazareth he wanted to show his people that he also loves them. He wanted to go under all the laws he had given them, living with us in this imperfect world (*iddo hirruu*) as our brother, a man like us, born from a human mother like we are. [5] He also wanted us to see in him how we should live and to hear him speaking to us with a human voice. You, my grand-grandson should know this already. Were you not with the Borana and did not you ask them 'Tell me, why did Waaqa send you your first qalu (highpriest) from heaven that he might speak to you? Why did he not speak to you himself?' they answered you: 'How could he possibly have done so? We would not have understood one single word of his. He had to speak to us with a human mouth.'

If you say: 'Waaqa came on this earth, suffered and died,' our people do not understand it. 'How could Waaqa die?' they will say. But if you say: 'Our Waaqa as he is with us in this world, the source of all ayyaana, sent out the highest ayyaana to take a shape in Joshua of Nazareth, born from a human mother, to live and suffer with us, then they will understand. For Joshua there was laughing and weeping, eating and drinking, joy and suffering, life and death. He did not rejoice himself alone, nor did he suffer alone. When we are happy, he is happy; when we are suffering, he suffers.

We can say: 'Waaqa loves us' but we cannot say: 'O Waaqa I love you. If we say: 'Waaqa. I love you,' it is against *safuu* (against the distance and respect we owe Waaqa). Such things we say to men like us. Our love of Waaqa is doing his will. However, to Joshua we can say: 'I love you.' In him we can deal with Waaqa as a man." [6]

5. In the Oromo's eyes, indeed, merely assuming a human body would not have made him a real man. A human birth is essential.
6. Later on Gammachu wrote in the margin near these words: "Wonderful"!

This is what my grand-grandfather told me and he made me feel
that he was glad that he had matured in me.

A Prayer

Better, however than all talks and comments, my assistants
have shown what all this means to them in their prayers, prayers
in the form of poems, such as the following one of Gammachu, in
which both Christ-Boraanticha and Jesus of Nazareth are prayed
to together:

O my Boraanticha
creator of my people,
for all things you did for us
what can I pay you back?

O my Boraanticha
root of all ayyaana,
you are the firstborn of mankind
it is through you that our great Waaqa rules.

The greatest gift Waaqa has given us
it is you, our Boraanticha.
It is through you that we experience Waaqa
it is through you that we came to know him.

You are both father and mother;
you begot us and brought us up.
Firstborn by excellence
source of both father- and motherhood.

O bright full moon,
it is through your ayyaana
that stars appear at night.
O, be to us both morninglight and sun.

O Boraanticha,
unfathomable mystery of heaven and earth
guard us with your shepherd-staff
and we will sleep in peace.

You who defeated death,
who became our *galla* throughout life[7]

7. *Galla*: provisions for a journey.

take our hands and lead us
and we will follow you.

O ruler, arm of Waaqa,
anointed by Waaqa himself
our eyes are blind:
open the way for us.

Whenever we are speaking of Waaqa, we are bound to say both truth and untruth at the same time. For all this, we think Waaqa likes us to speak of Him, even if it is in such an imperfect way, and we feel He blesses us when we do so. Whatever we say of Him, we trust He Himself will give meaning to our clumsy words. May it be so.

Some Final Remarks

Not all the results and aspects of our encounter have been given here.[8] Nothing has been said about my partners' idea of the Trinity which in their eyes is revealed to us within this very universe of ours. Nothing has been said about their comments on afterlife, judgement and hell. Nothing has been said about this world as a place of evil, suffering, oppression and exploitation of people by people. Not enough has been said about my Oromo partners' other thoughtworld - a thoughtworld they share with the great civilizations of India and China and most peoples of the Third World up to the present. I am hopeful of making up for these deficiences in a book to come.

I would like to thank my Oromo partners for the pains they have taken to make their views and feelings clear to "their brothers and sisters in the West" by discussing them with me, so

8. Many aspects of our encounter needed to be omitted in this article. Indeed, nothing has been said about my assistants' idea of the Trinity, which in their eyes is revealed to man within this very universe as they see it.

Nothing has been said about their comments on afterlife, judgement and hell.

Nothing has been said about the fall as they see it and their view of this world as a place of evil, suffering, oppression and exploitation of man by man and, at the same time, a place of righteousness, wonderful beauty and genuine love and self-sacrifice.

I am hopeful of publishing a book about all this very soon.

to say, on two quite different wavelengths at the same time. May their willingness to do so meet with appreciation and understanding.

On their part they ask their brothers and sisters in Christ to give them time to grow in their own way of experiencing "their Christ" as he has been living in them from their very birth as people. "This is a work of fifty years," Gammachu once assured me, and he thought this to be a long time. Mediterranean Christianity was given centuries to grow towards its present form and its present richness. Oromo Christianity will not be that fortunate. Yet their confidence in the future of their newly found Christian faith is rooted in their deep conviction that God is faithful to his own ways. They voiced this confidence as follows: "We do not want to be Christians "in a cage." We want to be one with all other Christians. We do know that for the sake of unity and in order to express this unity certain compromises will be unavoidable. No man or woman in this world of ours can be exclusively oneself. The same holds true for peoples. We only want to remain the way Waaqa has made us and to continue seeing and experiencing him the way he has revealed himself to us and is still doing so up to the present. We like your Pope when we see him kissing the earth of every country he pays a visit to. We like to see him blesing all people who come to welcome him, regardless of their being Christians or not." It reminds one of the words once spoken in Uganda by Pope Paul VI: "My children, I want you to be good children *and* good Africans."

CULTURAL ANALYSIS AND INCULTURATION IN THE LOWLAND FILIPINO CONTEXT

José M. de Mesa

Much has been written about inculturation since the Second Vatican Council (1962-65). The scope of the literature ranges from general introductions or overviews on the subject, and broad suggestions of theological approach to specific guidelines related to methodology and to very particular points regarding a cultural element or an aspect of the Gospel. Thanks to these studies awareness as to what the inculturation process requires has increased. Such awareness, however, particularly for the Philippines, is but the beginning. Knowing what needs to be done is not yet doing what is to be accomplished.

Awareness of the Importance of Cultural Analysis

Among the things which have been identified as particularly necessary and urgent for the realization of inculturation in the Philippines is an increased attention to cultural analysis. [1]

Early attempts at re-rooting the Gospel culturally have indeed exhibited the awareness and conviction that culture needs to be

---

1. Cf., for instance, Reynaldo Ileto, *Pasyon and Revolution: Popular Movements in the Philippines, 1840-1910* (Quezon City: Ateneo de Manila University Press, 1979); Benigno Beltran, *Christology of the Inarticulate: An Inquiry into the Filipino Understanding of Jesus Christ* (Manila: Divine Word Publications, 1987); Dionisio Miranda, *Pagkamakatao: Reflections on the Theological Virtues in the Philippine Context* (Manila: Divine Word Publications, 1987) and *Loob: The Filipino Within* (Manila: Divine Word Publications, 1989); Albert Alejo, *Tao Pol Tuloy!* (Quezon City: Ateneo de Manila University, 1990); José M. de Mesa, *In Solidarity with the Culture: Studies in Theological Re-rooting. Maryhill Studies 4* (Quezon City: Maryhill School of Theology, 1987) and *Kapag Namayani Ang Kagandahang-Loob ng Diyos* (Quezon City: Claretian Publications, 1990).

analyzed consciously and carefully.[2] But little has been done to explore issues related to the analysis itself.

The question of approach, for instance, needs singular attention. Bearing in mind that cultural analysis here is utilized for the purpose of bringing the Gospel and the culture into mutual interaction for a desired integration, how is culture to be dealt with? Does inculturation, because it aims at embodying the Gospel in an imperfect culture, have to favor a hermeneutics of suspicion in order to purify the ambiguity present in cultural elements deemed appropriate for expressing the Gospel? Or must it prefer a hermeneutics of appreciation in order to discover and recover the positive, life-giving aspects of the culture? Or should it, perhaps, be more realistic and balanced by discerning both the positive and the negative aspects of the culture so that it can promote the former and eliminate the latter?[3] Are the answers to these questions to be given on the basis of theoretical advantages and disadvantages, or should the choice of approach not rather depend on the concrete situation in which the local Church finds itself?

Cultural Analysis as Thematic Cultural Exegesis

There are many ways of dealing with issues connected with

2. See, for example, Douglas Elwood and Patricia Magdamo, *Christ in Philippine Context* (Quezon City: New Day Publishers, 1971); Vitaliano Gorospe and Richard Deats, eds., *The Filipino in the Seventies* (Quezon City: New Day Publishers, 1973); Leonardo Mercado, *Elements of Filipino Theology* (Tacloban City: Divine Word University Publications, 1975) and Leonardo Mercado, ed., *Filipino Religious Psychology* (Tacloban City: Divine Word University Publications, 1977); the issue on the International Colloquium on Contextual Theology in *Philippiniana Sacra* XIV: 40 (January-April, 1979); Anscar J. Chupungco, ed., *Liturgical Renewal in the Philippines: Maryhill Liturgical Consultations. Maryhill Studies*, 3 (Quezon City: Maryhill School of Theology, 1980).

3. For an example of a hermeneutics of suspicion, see Juan Luis Segundo, *The Liberation of Theology* (Maryknoll: Orbis, 1976); a hermeneutics of appreciation, cf. J.J. Mueller, *Faith and Appreciative Awareness: The Cultural Theology of Bernard E. Meland* (Washington, DC: University Press of America, 1981); for a so-called balanced approach, cf. Patricia Licuanan, "*A Moral Recovery Program: Building a People — Building a Nation,*" A study submitted to the Senate Committees on Education, Arts & Culture and on Social Justice, Welfare & Development (9 May, 1988).

cultural analysis; this is only one of them. The purpose of this essay is to put forward a preliminary and, therefore, tentative study on cultural analysis itself in view of its importance for inculturation. We shall discuss cultural analysis here as a "*thematic cultural exegesis*"[4] understood in the following manner: a systematic process of bringing into explicit awareness and orderly categorization (i.e., to thematize) the implicit cultural meanings arising from a tradition of experiences which are embodied in specific cultural elements or aspects within the framework of culture as an integrated system for the purpose of proclaiming the Gospel. This way of dealing with cultural analysis suggests three important areas to be considered: culture, exegesis and themes. Realizing that we cannot possibly tackle all related issues or discuss those we do examine exhaustively, we will only deal here with the most relevant for the Filipino situation.

Culture

Awareness of Our Being Inextricably Cultural

One of the first things which must be realized in the task of inculturation is the pervasive influence of culture in our lives. It is not something limited only to some areas of life. Human beings are totally and inextricably immersed in culture, their society's design for living.[5] The assimilation and interiorization of the culture is so successful in general that an individual's thoughts, feelings and actions seldom really conflict with those of his or her society. The connection between nature and culture is so intimate that culture becomes a kind of "second nature."

Our culture shapes both our acting and thinking. It provides the model(s) of reality that governs our perceptions, although we are likely to be unaware of its influence on us. For the way we understand things seems to us to be "just natural." Experience,

4. For the use of this phrase, see Miranda, *Loob, passim*; cf. also Robert Schreiter, *Constructing Local Theologies* (Maryknoll: Orbis, 1985) 41.

5. An accepted culture covers everything in human life. See the treatment of culture, for instance, in Paul Hiebert, *Anthropological Insights for Missionaries* (Grand Rapids, MI: Baker, 1985) 30-52 and L. Robert Kohls, *Survival Kit for Overseas Living* (Yarmouth: Intercultural, 1984) 17-20.

whether we recognize it or not, is very much cultural; that is, interpreted from a specific cultural frame of reference. Thus, to understand ourselves as Filipinos, our experience and situations, there is a genuine need to fathom our culture in a conscious manner. Failure to do so will prevent us from probing deeply into it.

"Feel" for Culture as Resource

The realization that we are inextricably cultural is, in itself, of considerable usefulness in undertaking cultural exegesis. For indigenous theologians this means that their very persons are a resource in knowing the culture better. They can draw from their deep and personal experiences of their culture to illumine, verify, criticize or correct data coming from outside their personal selves.

The "feel" for one's culture need not be considered an obstacle to a so-called "objective" analysis. On the contrary, it is an aid in comprehension. Bernard Meland's theological approach to culture, for instance, recognizes the importance of feeling as part of thinking and thinking as part of feeling.[6] He gives the example of the way a mother knows the presence of her love for her child but is unable to explain it. Or the way two lovers both know that something is wrong between them by subtle and unspoken communications in silence and eye contact. For both the mother and the lovers trusting the feeling is important in understanding the prevailing situation.

The method, then, suggests that participants of the culture should take into account their feelings about their culture in the effort to understand it. In fact, one may say that feelings about the culture is, to some extent, a privileged way of understanding it. There is, after all, a kind of knowledge which only comes from sensitivity and love. Nevertheless, such feeling must ultimately be subjected to scrutiny. Cultural data earlier grasped intuitively has to be consciously examined.

6. Cf. J.J. Mueller, *What Are They Saying About Theological Method?* (New York: Paulist, 1984), pp. 49-50.

A Multi-cultural Situation

A third point regarding culture which we ought to bear in mind in the Filipino situation is the fact that there is more than one culture in the Philippines. The country's situation is one that is multi-cultural. The designation "Filipino," therefore, is not simply a culture. Rather, it represents cultures. "Filipino" is much more descriptive of citizenship in the nation-state which is the Philippines. There is no doubt that lowland Filipinos compose the majority; nine out of ten Filipinos are lowlanders. Hence, one can understand why lowland Filipino became virtually synonymous with Filipino. This, however, tends to obscure the presence of a plurality of cultures in the nation. Besides the lowland culture, there are also the cultures of the mountain peoples, the Muslims as well as those of the different tribal groups. [7]

The process of inculturation must respect this plurality of cultures in the country. In other words, if this endeavor is to proceed properly, cultural analysis needs to be done within each cultural context (cf. *Ad Gentes* 22). Needless to say, this kind of effort will not only enrich cultural understanding within each cultural group (a task worthwhile pursuing on its own), it will also promote cross-cultural relationships through the revelation of commonalities linking these cultures. After all, whether a Filipino is of the mountians, lowlands or Muslim or a member of a tribal group, there is a basic Malay stratum underlying his or her culture. [8]

The Advent of the Industrial and Technological Society

The advent and development of the industrial and technological society is also an important issue related to culture. Social change must be reckoned with if culture is to develop. This makes it imperative for people to become aware of their own culture,

7. Cf. N. Vreeland, G. Hurwitz, P. Just, P. Moeller and R. Shinn, *Area Handbook for the Philippines* (Washington, DC: American University, 1976), pp. 75-98.

8. See *And God Said, "Bahala Na!": The Theme of Providence in the Lowland Filipino Context. Maryhill Studies 2* (Quezon City: Maryhill School of Theology, 1979), pp. 1-3.

especially if they wish to preserve what they consider valuable in their way of life. A closed society easily regards its customs, mores and symbols as absolutes. Where there are changes in living conditions and contact with others is made possible, thanks to the technology behind mass media and means of travel, society this sort will come to realize the relativity of its own beliefs, values and customs.

People need to assess which elements or aspects of their culture they should strengthen, modify, transform or even abandon in the face of new situations they find themselves in. Uncritical knowledge of their own culture may lead to the setting aside or forgetting of worthwhile traditions just because "modernization" brings something new and attractive.[9] It would be a pity if a people lost valuable cultural elements for want of awareness of these very elements.

Exegesis

"Exegesis" is an interpretative activity. As cultural analysis, it explicitly intends to make sense of the implicit cultural meanings arising from a tradition of experiences which are embodied in specific cultural elements or aspects. The culture is, as it were, a text which has been written by previous generations of people in a given society and which needs to be read and interpreted by the present one. In the context of inculturation in the Filipino setting, exegesis of the culture has to seriously consider questions related to perspective and approach utilized.

Perspectives Underlying the Exegesis

Understanding is always understanding from a particular standpoint. This means, first of all, that the examination of any aspect of the culture is not done in an a-historical manner. We look at culture in relation to what is going on in our society. This indicates that cultural exegesis should focus on those elements or aspects which have a bearing on relevant issues, concerns or

9. Antoine Vergote, "Folk Catholicism: Its Significance, Value and Ambiguities," *Philippine Studies* 30 (1982) 15-16.

questions. Indeed, if we are sensitive to the culture and to what is presently going on, certain facets of the culture will suggest themselves as in need of attention. In any case, we must make sure that what is being analyzed in the culture ought to have an important connection to the present-day experience of people. Otherwise, our cultural exegesis will be irrelevant because it insists on doing its examination of the culture in isolation from what is currently going on in the lives of people.

The exegesis of culture, secondly, is the drawing out of the implicit meanings for the purpose of "bringing the Good News into all the strata of humanity, and through its influence transforming humanity from within and making it new" (*Evangelii Nuntiandi* 18). It is, perhaps, this connection between cultural analysis and evangelization that can justify our use of the term "exegesis." Rather than simply being descriptive in its understanding of the culture, this kind of analysis is also prescriptive from an evangelical perspective. Particular attention is, therefore, given to those elements which have a potential for expressing, first of all, the heart of the Gospel in a culturally intelligible and situationally relevant manner.

The Insider's Point of View

A third element in this exegesis is the adoption of "the insider's point of view" vis-à-vis the culture. As an aid towards a respectful, and even appreciative, understanding of the culture, the analysis spoken of here is one which is carried out by the native participants of the culture. It represents the participants' spontaneous grasp and analysis of their own culture in contrast to an "outsider's" perspective of the foreigner. Theologians are beginning to make use of the emic-etic understanding of the culture in anthropology.[10] Insight into a culture is better achieved, according to this distinction, if the perception from "the inside" is complemented by an understanding from the "outside." The converse is, of course, also true. I am inclined to think, however, that any self-definition of the culture must first come from its native participants.

10. Cf. Robert Schreiter, *Constructing Local Theologies* (Maryknoll: Orbis, 1985) 41, 161; Charles Kraft, *Christianity in Culture* (Maryknoll: Orbis, 1979), pp. 36, 293.

Yet, it is precisely this approach which has been wanting in the Philippine scene. In general the culture has not been examined "from within" and "in its own terms," even when the study was undertaken by native Filipinos. This neglect is very evident in the area of cultural research and popular discussion. Attempting to pin down, as it were, the Filipino identity through its value-system, scholars and commentators of the Philippine scene scrutinized indigenous ideal and actual values of the natives. Unwittingly, they displayed in their writings a perspective not truly sympathetic to the Filipino culture because it was foreign. The view was that of "outsiders" considering their outlook as superior to the standpoint of the culture they were observing. In the comparison, the Filipino culture lost out. This is not meant to deny or disparage the contribution that outsiders can and do render to the understanding of the culture. This does not even suggest that translations from one culture into another are completely unnecessary. Insisting on an approach from within is just the taking of responsibility of insiders for the growth and appreciation of their own culture. Besides, the discovery of concepts and theories significant to Philippine society and culture is more important than blind translations of western ideas, no matter how faithful one is to the original.

Reviewing the body of literature written on the self-identity of the Filipino with this approach, Francis Gustilo was surprised to discover that negative or disparaging traits predominate in many of these writings. [11] It was as if Filipinos were primarily a bundle of problems for which a variety of remedies had to be prescribed. The result of this way of approaching the indigenous culture was, to say the least, unsatisfactory. It was also clear that among its unverbalized methodological assumptions was the cultural superiority of the Euro-North American West. This did not go unchallenged.

The early seventies, for example, witnessed a strong and collective protest against both the colonial character and the uncritical acceptance of American psychological models. [12] The move made

11. Francis Gustilo, "*Towards the Inculturation of the Salesian Family Spirit in the Filipino Context*" (Unpublished Doctoral Dissertation. Salesian Pontifical University, 1989) pp. 51-58.

12. *Ibid.* Other recent manifestations motivated by nationalism were the

Filipinos aware of the American orientation of psychology in a country which used the English language in teaching and research. Because language was seen as an embodiment and expression of the culture, one of its major complaints was that psychology graduates who got accustomed to and have become dependent on American theories and methods were prevented from thinking in Filipino and from formulating theories based on Filipino experiences. Studies made from such a perspective failed to see local values in terms of the Filipino worldview and experience and, in that sense, presented a distorted picture of them.

The uneasiness with studies which relied uncritically on a borrowed language, inapplicable categories of analysis and token use of local language and culture brought about an alternative approach to the local culture in which language became the key issue. Advocates of this method believe that language is a rich resource for understanding culture from within. It "is not merely a tool for communication nor is it a neutral system of signs and symbols. Each language is partisan to the values, perspectives and rules of cognition of a particular class or society. For this reason, one's faith in language leads to the belief that meaningful concepts in understanding society and human behavior are probably most identifiable in the language." Proponents of this new approach are, therefore, trying to remedy "an imbalance in the situation where the Filipino is primarily characterized by the judgmental and impressionistic point of view of foreigners." They are accomplishing this through an intensive pursuit of developing the indigenous national culture and through a program of using the indigenous language in their research and publications.[13]

Accent on the Positive: a Methodological Option

In a certain sense, the exegesis which I am advocating is not simply the same as an emic analysis of the culture where the native participants of the culture become cognizant of both the

demand of activists for the end of American imperialism, the break of Filipino music with Western melodies and lyrics, the widespread use of the vernacular terms in government and in the restaurant business and the advocacy of universities for the use of Filipino instead of English for instruction.

13. See *ibid.*, pp. 56-57.

positive and the negative in their inherited way of life as a people. No doubt, an awareness of this sort may readily be called "balanced." It provides a knowledge of the pluses/strengths as well as the minuses/weaknesses of the culture. While this is necessary for a wholistic grasp of the culture (in so far as this is possible, naturally), it is not necessarily advantageous or called for *at this particular juncture of the history of the country*.[14] Still less can we benefit from a reading of the culture which harps on what is wrong with it.[15] What is sorely needed is a hermeneutics of appreciation which highlights the positive in the culture. While anthropological and theological reasons are part of the underlying motive for stating this, the most compelling in the present-day context of the Philippines is our experience of colonization.

Colonization had led, among other things, to the depreciation of the native culture and consequently of its dignity. Culturally speaking, the situation is better characterized as "imbalanced" rather than normal. It is in order to remedy the imbalance that we need to undertake a cultural analysis which is methodologically tendentious and emphasizes the positive. Our purpose in doing so is to regain an appreciation of the culture and recover a healthy sense of cultural identity as a people.

The promotion of cultural identity and integrity should be seen for what it really is, a soteriological issue. Cultural dignity is one of the essential dimensions of our humanity and sense of wholeness. We become human persons through culture (cf. *Gaudium et Spes* 53); it continues to nourish us by providing us with an experience-based and time-tested design for living. Although ambiguity is undeniably present in our indigenous way of life, the beliefs, values, customs and institutions which our people have developed through many generations are fundamentally directed

14. Cf. Licuanan, "*A Moral Recovery Program: Building a People — Building a Nation.*"

15. Cf. Gustilo, "*Towards the Inculturation of the Salesian Family Spirit in the Filipino Context,*" pp. 52-53; A Dutch anthropologist remarks in a study of lowland Filipino culture that high school and college texts compare Filipino habits with those of the Japanese, Germans and Americans. The latter are always presented as superior at the same time that the presumed Filipino qualities and values are criticized and degraded. See Niels Mulder, "Appreciating Lowland Christian Filipino Culture," *Working Paper 141,* (September, 1990), Sociology of Development Research Center, University of Bielefeld, Germany, 15.

towards the humanization of our world. The basic thrust of culture, at least in intent, is positive and life-giving.

Colonial experience under Spain and the United States had eroded our sense of pride in our own indigenous lowland culture (Mountain and Muslim Filipinos were never colonized!). There is really no need to belabor the point of what colonization did to the self-image and, consequently, self-esteem of the natives. This has been amply documented in other works.[16] What Dr. José Rizal, the country's national hero, wrote regarding the effects of the colonial experience suffices as a summary of what happened to the way people thought about themselves and their cultures:

> Then began a new era for the Filipinos; little by little they lost their old traditions, the mementos of their past; they gave up their writing, their songs, their poems, their laws in order to learn by rote other doctrines which they did not understand, another morality, another aesthetics different from those inspired by their climate and manner of thinking. Then they declined, degrading themselves in their own eyes; they became ashamed of what was their own; they began to admire and praise whatever was foreign and incomprehensible; their spirit was dismayed and it surrendered.[17]

No wonder colonialism, together with its continuation in neo-colonialism, is regarded as a social malady. Not only have they compelled people to reject themselves and to lose their identity, they have also persuaded the local people to want what their Western counterparts want. Not having acquired a self-identity in the past, thrown they are today into a technological and industrial maze whose meanings they have not sorted out for themselves.[18] One can, therefore, ask whether this lack of cultural identity is responsible for the "crisis of faith in each other" of Filipinos.

---

16. For a summary treatment of as well as published references about colonization and its effects, cf. Jose M. de Mesa, *"Providence as God's Concern for His People in the Lowland Filipino Context: An Attempt at Theological Re-rooting of a Gospel Theme"* (Doctoral Dissertation. Katholieke Universiteit te Leuven, 1978), pp. 4-35.

17. Teodoro Agoncillo and Milagros Guerrero, *History of the Filipino People* (4th ed.; Quezon City: R.P. Garcia, 1973), pp. 112-113.

18. Mina Ramirez, *Communication From the Ground Up* (Manila: Asian Social Institute, 1990), pp. 20-24.

For this reason, I find a presentation of a so-called "balanced" analysis of the culture *untimely*. It is, of course, true that we should be aware of our strengths and weaknesses as a people. I do not, in any way, deny the ultimate need for this. In ideal conditions where people have a strong sense of cultural identity, it would be foolish to object to such an analysis, but those ideal conditions are not present.

Perhaps, an analogy will help. The Filipino search for cultural identity and integrity is like that of persons who need to redevelop self-identity and regain self-respect after a personal psychological tragedy. During the phase of recovery, it is necessary to emphasize what is positive in these persons, precisely so that they can regain lost self-esteem. Conversely, it is not the moment to impress on them what their strengths are, on the one hand, and what their weaknesses are, on the other. It is not the time to make sure that they have a balanced image of self. These people are not able to handle that at the moment. Later, when they regain self-confidence and self-respect in their own eyes, they can look at themselves more critically from a position of strength. There is, after all, a time for everything.

Similarly, the Filipino corporate cultural personality, as it were, is still in the stage of rebuilding identity and restoring respectability in its own eyes. It is not difficult to ascertain why. The Philippines have undergone two major colonial experiences. While undeniably, there have been some benefits derived from the Spanish and American regimes, it is equally certain that colonization has had a tragic effect on the sense of cultural pride. Thus, cultural analysis has a very specific agenda in the lowland Philippines today.

Any form of analysis is done within a particular context and from a definite perspective and theoretical framework. The development of a cultural exegesis *for now* should be aimed at the retrieval of the wisdom and genius of the lowland Filipino culture. Such retrieval, the rediscovery and recovery of the many positive elements and aspects of the culture, is a worthwhile undertaking. Furthermore, there is something to build on. Culturally founded upon the fundamentally positive thrust of culture as a whole and theologically based on the Christian conviction that divine presence graces the way of life of a people, we can consider cultural exegesis done for this purpose as a form of discernment of God's living presence within culture. Did Vatican II not speak of "spiritual treasures" in every culture which ought to be recognized (cf. *Gaudium et Spes* 58; *Ad Gentes* 11)?

A cultural exegesis which promotes an "appreciative awareness" is not blind to the danger of romanticizing culture. It is aware of cultural ambivalence. Moreover, it makes us conscious of the pitfall connected with the critical dimension of the Gospel-culture dialogue. This danger is that of being overly critical at the expense of seeing the beauty and strength of the culture. The theological priority of God's offer of life and love in the faith relationship reminds us that "original blessing" rather than "original sin" is at the beginning of human existence in the world. Should this not serve as a guide in our approach to culture? And are we not well-advised in following the suggestion of Bishop Kenneth Cragg who says that "our first task in approaching another people, another culture, another religion, is to take off our shoes for the place we are approaching is holy. Else we may find ourselves treading on (people's) dreams. More seriously still, we may forget that God was there before our arrival?"[19]

Ultimately, the intention of such an examination is to empower people; that is, to enable people to regain their sense of pride over their way of life so that they would take their destiny as a people into their own hands. A step towards this is the regaining of confidence and pride in their culture. A concrete move to realize the step is a cultural exegesis in the spirit of appreciative awareness. One is reminded at this juncture of the truth of the statement that the Church "by the very fulfilment of her own mission... stimulates and advances human and civic culture" (*Gaudium et Spes* 58).

Thematization

The richness of the lowland Filipino culture calls for a *focusing* to draw out particular aspects or dimensions of cultural elements related to the issue, concern or question requiring a Christian

19. Source unknown.

response. Without this, one would be overwhelmed by an abundance of data and fail to make sense of them. A fruitful way of organizing such data is by way of themes, where related ideas converge into a cluster, throw light on one another, and form distinct yet integrated wholes.

Thematizing, to be sure, is limiting. But it does provide a feasible way of understanding and appreciating the culture. At any rate, any manner of looking at cultural reality (or any reality for that matter) is necessarily a limited way of looking at it. Interpretation, which is an intrinsic part of experience, in one way or another selects, limits, and demarcates our grasp of reality. Besides, comprehensive analysis is not really necessary for the theological task to move ahead. Rightly has it been said that "our contemporary world of experience must be reflected in theology but not necessarily in the form of a comprehensive economic, political, sociological or philosophic analysis, but rather as a recurrent theme touching upon our contemporary experience and sense of life and current concern."[20]

Themes, which provide starting points for cultural analysis, can be drawn either from the culture itself or from the Gospel. Themes from the culture may revolve around important aspects of the indigenous worldview. Hence, key dimensions as well as elements involved in those dimensions[21] or key ideas around which other ideas cluster can be the springboard of the investigation. Bear in mind that it is the issue, concern or question which guides us to a particular theme or even a set of themes. It sensitizes or alerts us to the relevant cultural themes which must be analyzed. Naturally, the better the analysis of such themes, the more usefulness they can offer.

Likewise, such issue, concern or question may indicate for us which theme in the Gospel is relevant. The usefulness of this manner of proceeding arises from the fact that there are times or occasions when we (at least, initially) are more familiar with the Gospel theme related to the human situation than with a cultural

20. Hans Küng, "Toward a New Consensus in Catholic (and Ecumenical) Theology," *Journal of Ecumenical Studies* 17: 1 (1980), p. 15.

21. The "anthropological constants" suggested by E. Schillebeeckx may be a good guide in discovering key concepts in the culture. Cf. *Christ: The Experience of Jesus as Lord* (New York: Crossroad, 1983), pp. 731-743.

one. In this case, we let the Gospel theme sensitize us, in turn, to one that is cultural. This evangelical theme alerts or leads us inevitably to a cultural one because reality is culturally interpreted if we remember how inextricably cultural we all are.[22]

Doing this sort of exegesis for the purpose of inculturation does not start by arbitrarily selecting any theme which a theologian might fancy. The necessary rootedness of theological reflection does not permit us to forget that a recognizable reference to the lived experiences of people is the basic condition in the interpretation of the faith. Hence, the primary importance of the human situation, context or experience in terms of issues, concerns or questions.

Because the whole process of the thematic cultural exegesis is done precisely for the sake of evangelization, local theologians undertaking this task have constantly to bear in mind the dialogical relationship between the Gospel and their culture. Since these two poles are in constant mutual interaction, it is possible to draw themes from either source to start the exegetical process. The importance of "love" in the Judaeo-Christian Tradition, for instance, may be regarded as a major category by which exegesis of the culture may start. In this case, beliefs, values, customs, institutions illustrative of "love" in the culture are subjected to analysis to see if common elements or characteristics emerge. On the other hand, we can begin with one of the most important values in the Philippines, *kagandahang-loob*, and then check out which cultural beliefs, values, customs and institutions embody and express this value.

Starting, needless to say, is not continuing or finishing. The theme used as a starting point is precisely that: a *starting point*. Further analysis may reveal something else: a new theme, combinations of themes, further elaboration or correction within the theme or even abandonment of it in favor of another one. There will always be a need for further checking whether the theme which one started with is still an adequate instrument for further analysis. Thematic cultural exegesis is, for sure, an on-going task within the inculturation process.

22. The four structural elements proposed by E. Schillebeeckx may be helpful in this connection. See *ibid.*, pp. 638-643.

JESUS, CHILD AND LORD:
THE UNIQUENESS OF CHRIST
IN THE FILIPINO CONTEXT

Jimmy A. Belita

Introduction

The *Santo Nino* or Holy Child is one of the most popular images (*imagen*) in Filipino popular Catholicism today. A nation-wide survey made several years ago found out that thirty seven percent chose the *Santo Nino* as their favorite image of Christ, compared to the forty three percent that chose the Crucified Christ.[1] In one of the latest surveys made in Metro Manila, the *Santo Nino* again is next to the Sacred Heart as the preferred image and that most home altars are those of the *Santo Nino*.[2] It was through this image that the native Filipinos encountered for the first time the Christian religion and the Catholic world of symbols, when a statue of the Child Jesus was given as a gift to the wife of the chieftain on the occasion of her baptism. When the invaders left in defeat, they left the *Santo Nino* behind which the natives subsequently venerated. The Spaniards learned about that practice of veneration when they returned with Legaspi almost half a century later. It can be said that a Catholic devotional practive endured without the Church's official and hierarchical sanction; Catholic life was a priestless. That the *Santo Nino* made an impact on the native's life could be read from Hiligaynon (Western Visayan natives) poetry showing references to the Santo Nino, amidst the spirits of the native world.[3]

1. Benigno P. Beltran, SVD, *The Christology of the Inarticulate. An Inquiry into the Filipino Understanding of Jesus the Christ* (Manila: Divine Word Publications, 1987) p. 57.
2. Carmen R. Gaerlan. "An Initial Study on Selected Religious Beliefs and Practices of Filipino Popular Catholicism." Unpublished Work, 1990.
3. Lucilla Hosillos. *Originality As Vengeance in Philippine Literature* (Quezon City: New Day Publishers, 1984.) See also Jimmy Belita, "The *Nono* and the *Nino*:

The easy manner with which the animistic natives accepted the *Santo Nino* without the Church's formal structures leads us to the problem of the uniqueness of Christ. For if Christ were already perceived as unique, which necessarily became an issue of lordship, Christianity must clash with the deeply rooted religiosity of animism. If the *Santo Nino* had commonality with animistic practices,[4] the element of uniqueness would not be there. The fact is that the Santo Nino became the popular image of Christ and this must have affected the concept of uniqueness. This paper will show that the theology of Christ's uniqueness was linked to the ideology of power of the dominant class in the West and that, in the process of inculturation among the indigenous people of the Philippine islands, these natives adopted the religious cult with originality, but *originality as a vengeance.*[5] The two "vengeances" are the Santo Nino of the Cross, and the Santo Nino of the Fiesta. But, first, there is a need to describe briefly the animistic world of the Filipinos; this will be followed by a similar description of the uniqueness and lordship of Christ.

The Animistic World of the Filipinos

This writer is a participant observer of the animistic world, born and raised by parents who believed in its beings and ways, behaved according to its taboos and formulas, and lived with those who share the same beliefs. This animistic world can best be described by means of the corresponding behavioral patterns of

A Development of Folk Catholicism As Seen in a Hiligaynon Poetry," Unpublished Article, p. 10. The *Santo Nino* and the *Santo Cristo Crucificado* are said to be "vengeances" to a rationale unwittingly introduced for the white domination. Instead of simply accepting the lordship of Christ (a fitting model of Christianity as a dominant class), the dominated Filipinos accept Him as the Lord Infant Jesus, but more infant and crucified than Lord, with all the weaknesses and powerlessness that the images suggest.

4. In religions like Buddhism, Taoism, and Confucianism, which have a bias for the world of spirits, there is no category or phenomenon classified as idolatry just as there is no theology of adoration here, either. See William Thompson, "Jesus" Unsurpassable Uniqueness: A Theological Note." *Horizons* (1989) 101-115, p. 107.

5. Hosillos, *Originality As Vengeance in Philippine Literature*, p. 39.

its believers, like ourselves. We looked at the open spaces and woods as dwellings of the *nonos*, regarded as "tutelary or guardian spirits."[6] In going through a forest, passing by a tree, fording a stream, or doing any similar activity we were to say *Panabitabi* ("please, move aside, we are going through"). The invocation would usually be followed by: *maagi ang hari* ("the king is passing by"). This was said perfunctorily as a request not directly addressed to any one spirit.

Permission was needed to pick a flower or a fruit or help oneself to the trees for fuel.[7] Similar to the use of the word *hari* (king), the flower- or fruit-picker or the woodgatherer invoked the word *pari* (priest), to tell the spirit that it was the priest's will and not the picker's that ordered the act.[8] In sicknesses attributed to the *nonos*, the relatives or family of the sick made offerings of food wrapped and suspended in nearby trees, hoping that the sick would get well again. In activities like these, there generally were people, usually old and female, who did the supervision with apparent skill and know-how. It was always important that the "priestess" establish the patient's non-responsibility for what might have caused the affliction.

These *nonos* could not be said to be "persons" or personal deities. They were believed to be more like "indeterminate auras" as Rafael[9] neatly phrases it, "emanating from certain objects in nature- trees, rocks, rivers, fields, even crocodiles." Offerings made were not meant as signs of veneration, as Christian theology would interpret it, but as appeasement. No personal relationship could be made with them, for they did not even have fixed names,[10] unlike the God or the angels of Jews and Christians. Whereas among the believers of the religions of the book (Judaism, Christianity, Islam, Hinduism, Buddhism) which have

6. Vicente L. Rafael, *Contracting Colonialism, Translation and Christian Conversion in Tagalog Society under Early Spanish Rule* (Quezon City: Ateneo de Manila University Press, 1988) pp. 110-115.

7. P. Ortiz Tomas, *Practica del Ministerio Que Siguen Los Religiosos Del Orden de N.S. Augustin en Filipinas* (Manila: Convento de Nuestra Senora de los Angeles, 1731.) Quoted by Rafael, *Contracting Colonialism*, pp. 111-112.

8. *Ibid.*

9. Rafael, *Contracting Colonialism*, p. 113.

10. *Idem.*

myths, chronicles, and anecdotes related to fixed personalities, the animists had no literature and had no "memories" or "remembrances" linked to the *nonos*. Furthermore, as Rafael remarks, "Once one has eluded danger or obtained what one wants, one forgets about the *nono* until the next time they must be appeased: when one falls ill or must cross a river or a field or in any other way confronts a situation unknown or uncertain."[11]

Animism had little impact on the public life of the Filipinos. Political and public life was dominated by those who were educated in Church-backed schools or later in public schools during the American regime; here influences of animism were nil. Those who dominated the public life were also those who were influenced by Church-related organizations,[12] which had nothing to do with animism. Those leaders might still hold on to some animistic practices in their private homes and estates, but when they were in their public function, they had a different framework altogether. François Houtart, a Belgian sociologist, noted this, too, about animism: that it is a religion not having an "autonomy" or "control of the social mechanism (natural societies)."[13] Houtart claimed, moreover, that the praxis of animism "centered on the manipulation of the environment" in order to be responsive to "the immediate social and psychological needs of human groups,"[14] with no references to any divine-human relationship or to a long-term responsibility in history. This privatized religiosity, that is, one with little impact on the public life has influenced, too, present-day Catholics, whose Catholicism is more of a family religion.[15] Animism might be a thing of the past for

11. *Idem.*

12. See Raul Pertierra, "Forms of Rationality, Rationalization, and Social Transformation in a Northern Philippine Community," in Bruce Matthews and Judith Nagata, eds., Southeast Asian Studies (Singapore: Institute of Southeast Asian Studies, 1986) pp. 118-139.

13. François Houtart, "Religion and Development," *Religion and Development in Asia: A Sociological Approach with Christian Reflection* (Baguio Feres Seminar, 1976) pp. 2-89.

14. *Ibid.,* p. 30.

15. Niels Mulder. "Everyday Life in the Philippines: Religion is a Symbolic Expression of Family Relationships." *Appreciating Lowland Christian Filipino Culture.* Unpublished Book (1990), pp. 26-38.

today's Filipinos, but its incapacity for collective responsibility and action vis-à-vis public challenges remains.

Unique Lordship of Christ in the Context of Animism

There can be more than one perspective for viewing the uniqueness of the lordship of Christ but it seems that there is one which, according to Paul Knitter, rises from the monolithic and "perfect" culture of the classicists.[16] Here everybody sees truth as "one, certain, unchanging, normative."[17] The corollary is that if Jesus is the truth, this truth overwhelms all other truth-claims, cosmic and religious. This classicist culture, according to Knitter, dovetails with the Jewish eschatological-apocalyptic mentality" which when translated into the monotheistic experience of God in Jesus cannot but see this Son of God as "final and unsurpassable."[18]

Worth mentioning here is the effect of monotheism on the truth-claims related to belief. The first Christians were Jews who never left their monotheistic God in Judaism. This "one Father in heaven" was always in their consciousness. In this unique theism, could they, just as their Jewish ancestors did, set themselves apart and unique in a world of polytheism and syncretism? The lure of other religions was always there, especially when short-term alliances were needed and magical ways for instant results more promising. Given the "minority status" of Christians, the only way they could forestall loss of identity or absorption into a syncretistic world was to declare the exclusivistic uniqueness of Jesus' Lordship.

What are the implications of that traditional view and what is its impact on the religious life of the Filipinos? I would like to use as a given what Casalis[19] calls "theo-ideology," that is, "a theology of domination, produced by religious power of struc-

16. Paul F. Knitter, *No Other name? A Critical Survey of Christian Attitudes Towards the World Religions* (Maryknoll, NY: Orbis, 1985) p. 183.

17. *Idem.*

18. *Idem.*

19. George Casalis. *Correct Ideas Don't Fall From the Skies. Elements for an Inductive Theology* (Maryknoll NY: Orbis, 1984) p. 16.

tures in the service of the dominant classes of developed societies."[20] Here is the issue of uniqueness and consequently lordship
connected. Again, according to Casalis, making reference to Jean
Marie Aubert, power took over theology and "the process of
osmosis operated between ideology of the established order and
theology."[21] An example given by Aubert is that the title, "Son
of God, Savior," applied to Christ, was previously bestowed on
the emperor; which resulted in "Christ being the emperor."[22]
With that conceptualization of Christ came behavioral patterns of
missionary countries towards colonies. Accepting the unique
lordship of Christ could have meant accepting the powers and
structures brought about by Spain's cross-and-sword, religious-
military complex. The inseparability and the mutual dependency
of church and state in the Spanish regime bore this out; the
religious fiesta was also a municipal fiesta. The civil government
respected, as they still do today, the most important events of
Christ's life, like Holy Thursday, Good Friday and the Lord's
Nativity. The implication is that if the state respects the church's
affairs, the latter is expected to respect those of the former or, at
least, not to interfere with them.

The colonizers brought the devotion of the Santo Nino to the
Filipinos and with it a certain world-view and a certain religiosity
which we associate with a monotheistic, personalistic and historical religion. The Spanish *Santo Nino* fit in within the animistic
world of the *nonos* (tutelary or ancestral spirits) represented
through objects. The image of the *Santo Nino*, left to the Filipinos for thirty years before the return of the Spaniards, found a
home in these islands. The more systematic imposition of Spanish
institutions, including religion, must have caused disruption in
the systemic world of the animists. There were many repercus-
sions but our focus of attention in the discussion will only be on
the uniqueness and lordship of Christ. The animists had no
problem with the *Santo Nino* as another *nono* and uniqueness of
lordship could not have been brought up since *nonos* do not even
have personalities. They were beings one could relate to only in a
specific moment as when one is in a difficult or awkward situa-

20. *Idem.*
21. *Idem.*, p. 36.
22. *Idem.*

tion.[23] The problem arose when the official church introduced the *Santo Nino* in the context of "salvation history," or of the theology of the mission current in the sixteenth and seventeenth centuries. Furthermore, presenting Christ in the context of uniqueness, lordship, and insurpassability only confounded the problem. Eventually, the Christian perspective prevailed, but some animistic elements stayed.

The Santo Nino was presented only after categorizing the *nonos* as *genios*, *lares*, and *penates*, thus making the native beliefs pagan,[24] with all the negative connotations of the term "paganism." These "pagan" beings against which Christianity struggled could not just be identified with the natives' *nonos*. The natives gave the term *nono* to the spirits who "could appear anywhere at anytime." "They had no specific names and their genealogies were indeterminate." *Nono* was thus one way of designating what eluded naming. It was a means of identifying the source of events and occurrences that seemed to defy explanation.[25] The point of the ruling class that introduced the Santo Nino was, however, that all those spirits, mistaken as *genios*, *lares*, and *penates* should now be replaced by this new God in the form of a Child. To persist in believing them was to reject the Santo Nino, which in turn, would undermine the rulers' authority. As we know from history, the natives to whom the Spaniards presented the Holy Child accepted the cult, but with some sort of a vengeance; their acceptance was with a subtle resistance.

The Inculturation of the *Santo Nino* Cult

The natives' resistance found strength in the cult of the Santo Nino; after all, it merely confirmed them in their non-historical and non-development stance towards the world. In the *Santo Nino* was safety. It was a reinforcement of the animistic world of non-responsibility; it was a justification for passivity and a fatalistic attitude. This is a speculation corroborated by a spirituality in the spirit world in which one does not have a systematic way of

23. Rafael, *Contracting Colonaialism*, p. 115.
24. *Idem.*
25. *Idem.*

dealing with reality or an interconnecting network of beliefs. One responds to a situation or a moment where one ancestral or tutelary spirit is concerned. In other words, you only react to surroundings rather than control or systematically subdue them for one's gain.[26]

Introducing in Christ to the islands from the framework of a dominant ideology must have hit the native believers, already Christianized. As Hosillo said, the natives adopted the foreign ideology but changed or altered it in order to be original. The alteration can be seen from two phenomena related to the *Santo Nino*, the cult side by side with *Senor Nazareno* and the child in gala attire. Each phenomenon indicates a devotion that is simultaneously an inculturated acceptance of Christ.

The inseparability of the *Santo Nino* form the *Nazareno* and the *Santo Entierro* (the Holy Burial) tells us of the emphasis on sufferings and hardships. These images are in a way affirmations and acceptance of almost a futile condition in life, tinged with a fatalistic view of a world which could not be changed. We can look at the *Santo Nino* as a hermeneutics of their life, without yet falling into Marx's interpretation of religion as "opium of the people." Here, to borrow a phrase made famous by Tracy's book, operates "the analogical imagination."[27] Among the inarticulate, their incapacity to verbalize or conceptualize their experiences within accepted systems makes them resort to analogous images. Self-identification later gave rise to practices of flagellation and even actual crucifixion with nails and wounds but without the killing. This obsession with suffering must have been the motive for the many *Santo Ninos* that lean against the Cross; hence, the *Nino* of the Cross.

Another phenomenon related to the *Santo Nino* is the fiesta, which is more than just a seasonal celebration. It is also a structure and a behavioral ideology. First, let us give a description of the *Santo Nino* in the context of a fiesta. The Cebuanos' *Sinulog* and the Ilonggos' *Dinagyang* are some of the versions of honoring the *Santo Nino* of the Fiesta. The main feature of the festive celebration is the waving by a dancer, usually a female, of

26. *Idem.*
27. David Tracy, *The Analogical Imagination. Christian Theology and the Culture of Pluralism* (New York: Crossroad, 1981.)

a handy statue of the *Santo Nino* as she snakes her way in a
procession with two steps forward and one step backward. One is
reminded of a comic spectacle in the bible, when David was
dancing before the ark. Amidst the seriousness of religion and the
mortified life of its personnel, and amidst the severities of its
morality, here is a comical if not absurd act of dancing with
Christ.

What do the *Nino* of the Cross and the *Nino* of the Fiesta tell
us about the mode of inculturating Christ's uniqueness and
lordship? The *Nino* of the Cross is lord but we see what kind of
Lord he is, a fragile child leaning against a cross: two fitting
symbols of powerlessness. The seriousness of the Cross is tempered by the pleasant innocence of the child; this is a case of
coincidentia oppositorum, the jolting irony that makes the domi-
nator think hard of his domination. The *Nino* of the Fiesta, in the
frenzy and ecstasy of his celebrators is an indictment of the
calculated and well-drawn plans of the dominators. The non-
utilitarian dimension of the celebration offsets the rhythm of the
elite and the rulers. The *Nino* becomes a buffoon in the hands of
the dancer who is often painted and lavishly ornate.

The lordship of Christ is demythologized and even belittled in
the *Nino* of the Cross and the *Nino* of the Fiesta for in the former
he is identified with powerlessness and, in the latter, with buffoon-
ery. Both characteristics are not flattering for those who are
serious with lordship seen as unsurpassably unique. With such a
lord, who cares to be the subject, if such lordship is used to justify
the domination of its believers by its theology-backed rulers?

In the devotion to the Holy Child, there is a new twist to the
unique lordship, which was previously used as an ideology of
domination. In the Child of the Cross of the popular imagination,
that model of lordship which is one of domination is rendered
powerless and the seriousness for power is neutralized by the
playfulness of the Child of the Fiesta.[28] Doctrinally, however,
there is no denial of the uniqueness of Christ, except that it is one

28. See also Basilio Balajadia, "Mass Mediums: An Initial Study of Spirit
Possessions Based on Five Cases in Metro Manila." Unpublished Work (1990).
Here the *Santo Nino* was reported to have used women as mediums, prompting
feminist movement within the Church to say that the phenomenon was an act of
protest against a male-dominated clergy.

that is derived from what one theologian calls "an anthropology of love": for the divine love to be personalized it has to be unique.[29] The uniqueness of the Lord Jesus is a "break" from the sacralities of the cosmos,[30] where impersonal deities are believed to abound. This uniqueness of the Lord is inevitably derived from the mystery of the Incarnation. There is no other way to assume the human nature except through personalization from which uniqueness is inseparable.

The popular imagination's capacity to elicit sympathy for the vulnerable *Santo Nino*, is reinforced by inclusive participation, which is a corollary of "divine personalization." According to Thompson, in Jesus Christ's self — "a radically — sharing self," "Christology and ecclesiology intersect;" to be Christ is to be in solidarity with the people.[31] The *Santo Nino* cult based on this anthropology of love marks a radical break from the *nono*-inspired devotion to the Child. The adoration and reverence shown to the *Nino* overcomes the impersonal "use" of the *Nino*, as if this were just another tutelary spirit, which is only invoked when needed and deemed useful. Pertinent here is Walter Kasper's statement, "The personalization of God means that God is not an object to be judged by utility for us, but rather a sovereign subject."[32]

With the subsequent personalization of a *nono* in the *Santo Nino*, the function of memory comes to the fore, and with memory gratitude. The calling to mind of the suffering of the Nino of the Cross gives depth to the fiesta for true gratitude comes from a memory of a Savior who suffered and died for the people. This obviously destroys any pretensions for power and the change to dominate, for the christological basis of the exclusive uniqueness of lordship flies in the face of the popular imagination's all-embracing child, not to mention the inclusiveness of the anthropology of love.

In the development of the *Santo Nino* devotion, we have seen how the Filipinos used their creative imagination to neutralize any justification or rationalization for the dominant class theo-

29. Thompson, "Jesus," p. 105.
30. *Ibid.*, p. 106.
31. *Idem.*
32. Quoted by Thompson, "Jesus," p. 108.

ideology, but whether they really have gone beyond the fatalistic attitude is another question. The *Santo Nino* cult has also brought with itself the inherent weakness identified with some negative characteristics of a child: self-centeredness, no sense of responsibility, and absence of self-identity. Filipino christologists have practically turned into the conventional belief that our country's failure to develop and to be liberated from unjust structures, in spite of our Christian heritage, can be partly attributed to the people's "obsession" with the *Santo Nino* and the Crucified Christ, two images of inactivity and passivity.[33]

With regard to the rhetorical question: "With a Child who needs the Lord?," two qualifications can be made. The first is, if by "Lord" we mean we have a model of power that sees society divided into the elite and the disenfranchised, then, we do not really need such Lord. If, however, the bad side of childhood comes out through the negative characteristics, then we have to insist on a lordship that liberates. In any case, the *Santo Nino* in both the poplular imagination's sense of the Cross and the Fiesta and the incarnational theology's invocation of inclusive love, is liberating. This bears out the ever ancient and ever new christological title: "Lord and Savior Jesus Christ."

The novel way in which the Filipinos appropriated the devotion to the Santo Nino did not make a radical break from the "Christ" introduced by the colonizers. They merely re-rooted the devotion to the Christ of the gospels, who showed us a life through the narrow way and brought joy to the poor and the alienated. If, somehow, this was obscured by the dominant class who had their own agenda, other than those in the gospels, still a kernel of truth was not lost. It provided the seed of "protest" that would eventually take "vengeance" when manipulated. If the *Santo Nino* devotion were merely reduced to rational theology, then, the crafty wisdom of the world can easily use it to rationalize its oppressive designs; but, if the poor and the illiterate merely dance their faith in Christ, they do not have to justify it anymore, for faith is its own justification.

33. See, for examples, Douglas J. Elwood & Patricia Magdamo, *Christ in Philippine Cotnext* (Quezon City: New Day Publishers, 1971), pp. 8-13. Leonardo N. Mercado. *Christ in the Philippines* (Divine Word University Publication. Tacloban City, 1982), pp. 55-56. Chapter IX "The Re-Appropriation in the Filipino Context," pp. 299-343. Jose M. de Mesa and Lode L. Wostyn, *Doing Christology. The Re-Appropriation of A Tradition* (Quezon City: Claretian, 1989.)

TOWARDS A TRINITARIAN THEOLOGY
OF RELIGIONS

Gavin D'Costa

Introduction

In the modern world Christians cannot ignore the existence of other religions. Global communications, extensive travel, migration, colonialism, and international trade are all factors that have brought the religions closer to each other in both destructive and creative ways. The religiously plural world in which Christians live consists of ancient traditions, sometimes older than Christianity, with many millions of followers. These include Judaism, Islam, Hinduism and Buddhism. There are also numerically smaller groups with varying degrees of antiquity such as Jainism, Sikhism, Confucianism and African religions. Also, never far from western media attention, there are the new religious movements with complex relations to the more established traditions such as the Unification Church, the International Society for Krishna Consciousness, Rastafarianism, and New Age Movements. Religious plurality raises many practical and theological questions for Christians: should Buddhist meditation groups be allowed the use of Church halls; how should religious education be taught; what kind of social and political co-operation or opposition is appropriate with people of other faiths; and how should Christians react to forms of what they percieve to be injustice within certain faiths? There are also fundamental theological issues at stake. If salvation is possible outside Christ/Christianity, is the uniqueness of Christ and the universal mission of the Church called into question? Or if salvation is not possible outside Christ/Christianity, is it credible that a loving God would consign the majority of humankind to perdition, often through no fault of their own? Can Christians learn from other faiths? Can they be enriched rather than diluted or polluted from this encounter?

There have been many different Christian responses to the world religions in the modern age. Equally, there are many different motives behind these attitudes involving theological, political, social and economic factors. For Christians living in the twentieth century there is also the recent history of colonialism and imperialism in which many parts of the non-Christian world have been subjugated by white Christian powers. Furthermore, the Christian west lives with the scars of two world wars and the destruction of nearly a third of Jewry. This chequered history has caused a crisis in confidence both within Christianity and also in its relation with the world faiths.

No set of categories is adequate to analyse and deal with the complexity of the topic, but it may be helpful to label three types of theological responses to other religions for heuristic purposes. There are of course considerable differences between theologians belonging to the same 'camps' and some overlap between different approaches. I shall call these three approaches: *pluralism* (that all religions are equal and valid paths to the one divine reality and Christ is one revelation among many equally important revelations); *exclusivism* (only those who hear the Gospel proclaimed and explicitly confess Christ are saved); and *inclusivism* (that Christ is the normative revelation of God, although salvation is possible through religions other than Christianity). Various presuppositions undergird each approach, often revolving around Christology and the doctrine of God. It might also be said that the three approaches are derived from the emphasis given to either one or both of two crucial theological axioms: firstly that salvation is given by God in Christ, thereby emphasising the *particularity* of Christian revelation - and secondly, the axiom that God loves and desires the salvation of all men and women, thereby emphasising the *universality* of grace. Those who emphasise the former move towards exclusivism, and those who emphasise the latter tend towards pluralism. I shall argue that a fully Trinitarian theology can hold together both the particular and universal in a manner appropriate for a fruitful Christian theology of religions.

Exclusivism and Pluralism

The early work of Karl Barth can be used to examine some of

the theological issues raised by exclusivism, although strictly speaking, Barth considered in totality is not an exclusivist. Nevertheless, he is important in influencing some rigorous exclusivist theologians. I use Barth only to illustrate some general points. Barth's theology was propounded in the light of two basic theological convictions. The first, common to a number of Christian denominations (although stressed to different degrees) concerns the fallen state of men and women. Because human beings live in a sinful state, all religion, including the Christian religion in certain circumstances, is *idolatrous*. All human formulations concerning God are precisely that - *human formulations*, falling short of the real God and threby inevitably idolizing a false human-made God. Such was the import of Barth's classic essay, "The Revelation of God as the Abolition of Religion."[1] You will notice that the title also reflects Barth's second premise concerning the revelation of God. For Barth, one premise rests upon the other. The other being that God uniquely discloses himself in Christ. Consequently, all "religion" and all human culture is judged in the light of Christ. By the standard of Christ, human history is judged as idolatrous. Barth's theology is profoundly *Christocentric*.

The attitude to the world religions that can be generated from this Christomonism is exemplified in the following story. D.T. Niles, the Indian Christian theologian, recalls a meeting with Barth in 1935. Barth asserted that "other religions are just unbelief." Niles replied, asking "How many Hindus, Dr. Barth have you met?" Barth's unhesitating reply was "Not one." To this, Niles pressed the issue a little further: "How then do you know that Hinduism is unbelief?" Barth's answer, which took Niles by surprise, was quite simply "A Priori"![2] Barth was simply expressing the logical implications of his exclusivist Christocentric theology.

I have taken Barth as a representative figure and do not want to discuss *his* views in any detail as I only wish to highlight some of the theological issues at stake. Some of Barth's followers have

1. K. Barth, *Church Dogmatics*, Vol. 1/2 (Edinburgh: T. & T. Clark, 1970) section 17.

2. D. Niles, "Karl Barth - A Personal Memory," *The South East Journal of Theology*, Vol. 2 (1969) 8-12.

developed his suggestions in various ways which remain exclusivist in as much as for those who do not encounter Christ, there
is no salvation. Hence, the proclamation of the Congress on
World Mission: "In the years since the war, more than one
billion souls have passed into eternity and more than half of these
went to the torment of hell fire without even hearing of Jesus
Christ, who He was, or why He died on the cross of Calvary."[3]

This type of exclusivism faces a number of theological objec-
tions which have caused me to reject it while also acknowledging
much that is of value in it. First, while valuing its Christocentric
emphasis I would criticise its *use* of this Christocentric emphasis.
As a Christian I believe that God has unreservedly disclosed
himself in Christ. *But* the God disclosed in Christ is a God of
universal love, mercy and judgement. Central to the Christian
tradition's emphasis on Christ, has always been an emphasis on
God's loving nature and desire to save all men and women. A
God of infinite love, mercy and justice, could surely not condemn
the majority of humankind to perdition, most of whom have
never even heard the Gospel, let alone rejected it. Such a God
could only be deemed an unjust tyrant. I think that the simple
historical fact that most of humankind have never encountered
the Gospel, coupled with the theological doctrine of a God of
universal love, begins to undermine a rigorous exclusivist position.

Another objection to such a view lies in the notion of *grace*
often implicit within such exclusivist positions. While wishing to
retain the conviction that God discloses himself unreservedly in
Christ, it is theologically and historically untenable to maintain
that saving grace is limited to only those who submit to Christ. In
traditional Christian theology, Judaism, up to the time of Christ,
was certainly accorded revelatory status. That is, it was believed
that God both revealed himself and acted salvifically within
Judaism. This is why the Hebrew Bible is part of Christian
scripture. In fact, Marcion (second century) was deemed heretical
for just such an exclusion of the "Old Testament." If my point is
accepted, in principle it may also be true that God has acted

3. See ed. J. Percy, *Facing the Unfinished Task* (Michigan: W. Eerdman, 1961)
9; and also the Frankfurt Declaration (1970), the Lausanne Statement (1975).

salvifically in various ways and in different degrees throughout human history. And given the doctrine of a God who desires the salvation of all men and women, such a possibility is not altogether unlikely.

Besides the history of Israel testifying to salvific grace outside the particular event of the historical Jesus, there are also a number of passages within the New Testament that highlight the importance of *loving action*. If for instance, a person's courageous self-sacrificing love is due to certain demands within their religion, can these acts of response to grace be divorced from the mediators of such grace? Or, can the humanist's self-sacrificial love for another, so powerfully portrayed in Camus' *The Plague*, have nothing to do with Jesus' implied teaching that "as you did it to one of the least of my brethren, you did it to me." (Matthew 25:40)? I do not want to conflate religious truth with loving acts, but I would question whether the two can be completely separated. Accordingly, a person's way of life, and not simply their assent to a set of beliefs (concerning Christ), is of great importance.[4]

My basic objection to exclusivism is its emphasis on the particularity of Christ at the cost of the universality of God's grace. In contrast, pluralism tends to reverse this emphasis. In the symphony of Christian history pluralism has been a very minor melody, whereas exclusivism has often been the dominant key. The pluralist position is nicely exemplified in a poem by John Saxe entitled, *The Blind Men and the Elephant*. The poem highlights the conviction that the different religions are equal paths to the one divine reality and exclusivist claims can only lead to gross distortion:

It was six men of Hindostan,
To learning much inclined,
Who went to see the Elephant,
(Though all of them were blind):
That each by observation
Might satisfy his mind.

4. I have paid attention to this problem in more detail in *Theology and Religious Pluralism* (Oxford: Basil Blackwell, 1986); see also J. Kellenbreger, *God-Relationships With and Without God* (London: Macmillan, 1989); Y. Congar, *The Wide World My Parish* (London: Darton Longman & Todd, 1961) ch. 10.

The first approached the Elephant,
And happening to fall
Against his broad and sturdy side,
At once began to brawl:
"Bless me, it seems the Elephant,
Is very like a wall."

The second, feeling of his tusk,
Cried, "Ho! what have we here
So very round and smooth and sharp?
This wonder of an Elephant
Is very like a spear."

The Third approached the animal,
And happening to take
The squirming trunk within his hands,
Then boldly up and spake:
"I see," quoth he, "the Elephant
Is very like a snake."

...

And so these men of Hindostan
Disputed loud and long,
Each in his opinion
Exceeding stiff and strong,
Though each was partly in the right
And all were in the wrong.

When religions claim exclusive rights to the truth, pluralists claim that they are like the blind men. John Hick is a leading proponent of pluralism. If Barth was *Christocentric*, Hick is avowedly *theocentric*. He asks: "Can we ... accept the conclusion that the God of love who seeks to save all mankind has nevertheless ordained that men must be saved in such a way that only a small minority can in fact receive this salvation?"[5] Hick's answer is "no"! He also argues the case that Christians should view Christ as just one revelation amongst other and equal revelations; one myth, in a world of many religious myths. He suggests: "May it not be that the different concepts of God, as Jahweh, Allah, Krishna, Param Atma, Holy Trinity, and so on... are all images of the divine, each expressing some aspect or range

5. J. Hick, *God and the Universe of Faiths*, London: Fount, 1977) 122.

of aspects and yet none by itself fully and exhaustively corresponding to the infinite nature of ultimate reality?".[6] In his more
recent work, Hick has had to move away from his theocentric
basis to accommodate non-theistic religions, but as I am simply
using Hick to highlight some general issues, I will not pursue this
development here.[7]

As with the position of exclusivism, there are a number of
points that lead me to fundamentally disagree with this pluralist
stance while valuing some of its concerns. What I value is its
openness to the universality of God's grace and love; that God is
salvifically present in other religions and non-religions. What I
object to is its attempt to establish this universality by bypassing
the particularity of Christ. That is, the attempt to speak of God,
while being a Christian, without reference to Christ as the basis
and norm for the revelation of who God is. Pluralism attempts to
reach the universal without the particular.

If we return to the elephant and blind-men parable my point
can be illustrated more clearly. Saxe's poem omits reference to
the prince who conducts the experiment, and if it was not for his
particular vantage point from which he is able to say that "each
was partly in the right," how can we know that the "elephant"
was not in fact a "wall" rather than a "spear" or "snake"? Or
how could we know that the blind men were in fact touching the
same object? If we are to say that God is possibly present in the
religions, how are we to identify, recognise and justify this claim?
Why, for instance, should Nazism be denied the self-claimed
status (supported by many of the German churches at the time)
as being part of God's unfolding revelation? If we do not have
some criteria by which to identify and recognise the action of
God, the valuable openness of the pluralist position collapses into
a self-destructive and theologically uncritical stance.

If exclusivism tends towards restricting God to Christ, Hick's
pluralism moves in the opposite direction. He denies any normativity to the revelation of God in Christ in his attempt to break
away from the exclusivist coupling of God and Christ. In follow-

6. Hick, *ibid.*, p. 140.
7. See my "Taking Other Religions Seriously: Some Ironies in the Current
Debate on a Christian Theology of Religions," *The Thomist*, Vol. 54, No 3 (1990)
519-529.

ing this strategy, pluralists tend either to utilise an abstract and non-revelatory notion of God, or to operate with hidden assumptions that really run counter to their pluralist position. For example, Hick is increasingly unable to account for his doctrine of God as any attempt to give normative weighting to any particular tradition is unacceptable on his own criteria. Ironically, in trying to take the diversity of religions seriously this form of pluralism ends up by taking none of the religions seriously. All normative claims generated from the particularites of history are deemed mythological, analagous to Hick's interpretation of the incarnation, and thereby provisional and not ontologically binding. This runs counter to the self-understanding of most religious believers including Christians.

This relates to another major problem. Most religious and non-religious believers hold the conviction that what they are talking about is *true*; that their language actually relates to reality, the state of things as they are. The difficulty with pluralism is that it too easily bypasses the very genuine problem of conflicting truth claims. None of the examples I give are necessarily intractable, but they *do* pose genuine problems that must be faced fairly and squarely - and also peacefully and charitably. These examples are random: did Jesus die on the cross as Christians claim or is the Qur'an correct in saying that he did not die on the cross? For Christians this issue is paramount. Or, is the theistic God of Semitic religions only a provisional and inadequate representation of the divine which is, as Radhakrishnan claims, ultimately non-dual and identical to the soul: ie. Atman is Brahman.[8] Examples can be multiplied.[9] Does pluralism arrive at its solution far too quickly and far too easily? I think that it does.

It will be clear by now that I have only one option left and I wish to devote the rest of this paper to outlining a Trinitarian form of inclusivism which does justice to both the irreducible particularity of Christ and the gratuitousness and universality of God's grace.[10]

8. See S. Radhakrishnan, *A Hindu View of Life* (London: Unwin, 1980) ch. 2, and pp. 23f.

9. See W. Christian, *Opposition of Religious Doctrines* (London: Macmillan, 1972.)

10. The Trinitarian aspect of the debate has been somewhat neglected, with

Trinitarian inclusivism

Broadly speaking I believe that the Trinitarian doctrine of God facilitates an authentically Christian response to the world religions because it takes the *particularities* of history entirely seriously as well as the *universality* of God's action. This is so because the doctrine seeks to affirm that God has disclosed himself unreservedly and irreversibly in the contingencies and particularity of the person Jesus. But within Trinitarian thinking, we are also able to affirm, in the action of the third person, that God is constantly revealing himself through history by means of the Holy Spirit. The Spirit in this activity serves to deepen and universalise our understanding of God in Christ, a process that is incomplete until the parousia. The Father, therefore, is never fully known "face to face" until the eschaton. Yet, the Father is known through Christ and the Spirit, and it is only on the basis of this particularity that we are able to affirm the universal agency of God's redeeming activity, for the God who redeems is always and everywhere the triune God revealed in Christ. Such a Trinitarian orientation thereby facilitates an openness to the world religions, for the activity of the Spirit cannot be confined to Christianity. This frees us from the *a priori* tendencies of both exclusivism and pluralism: the *a priori's* of denial and affirmation, respectively. Furthermore, Christians are called to really listen and learn from (as well as to share with) the religions of the world and in this process be open to the judgment of God upon the Christian community.

In this short space I can only indicate possible avenues for further exploration within this Trinitarian orientation. I would like to do so by proposing two theses for consideration.

Thesis one: A Trinitarian Christocentricism guards against exclusivism and pluralism by dialectically relating the universal to the particular

The Trinity safeguards against an exclusivist particularism and

important exceptions such as R. Panikkar, *The Trinity and the Religious Experience of Man: Icon-Person-Mystery* (London: Darton, Longman & Todd, 1973.)

a pluralist theocentricism, such as I have already outlined, for it stipulates against an *exclusive* identification of God and Jesus as well as a *non-normative* identification of God and Jesus. George Lindbeck, following Bernard Lonergan, correctly points out that Athanasius's understanding of consubstantiality instantiates the rule "that whatever is said of the Father is said of the Son, except that the Son is not the Father."[11] The unity and distinction between the persons of the Trinity allows one to combat both the extremes of exclusivism and pluralism. Against exclusivists, it must be stressed that the "Son is not the Father." Hence although we come to know God through Jesus, we cannot turn Jesus into an idol and claim that the Father is exclusively known through him. It is through the Spirit *and* the Son that God is disclosed. Hence, any attempt to limit or monopolize God in terms solely of Jesus turns into a binatarianism or unitarianism which fails to account for the fullness of the Trinitarian self-disclosure of God in history.

Against pluralism, it must also be stressed that "whatever is said of the Father is said of the Son." We cannot, as Christians, speak of the Father without the story of Jesus. The Father cannot be conjured up through speculation, abstractions or from non-particularities, but is revealed in the contingencies of history. It is central to the Christian tradition that God's nature is disclosed irreversibly and eschatologically in the story of the Son, understood and interpreted through the illumination of the Spirit within the community of the Church. It is through constantly attending to the particularities of Jesus' story that we come to know who God is - which is the reason why the liturgy is at the heart of the Christian community. We cannot divorce our understanding of God from the story of Jesus and rend assunder the universal and particular.[12] But, as I have indicated, the story of Jesus is incomplete until the end of history and through the Spirit, is constantly unfolded. I will return to this point shortly.

A third point also follows from the above which is not in itself

11. G. Lindbeck, *The Nature of Doctrine: Religion and Theology in a Post-liberal Age* (London: SPCK, 1984.)

12. I fear that Pannikar's work is tending in this direction, especially in "The Jordan, the Tiber, and the Ganges," in eds. J. Hick & P. Knitter, *The Myth of Christian Uniqueness* (New York: Orbis, 1987) 89-116.

Christological and Trinitarian, but is a result of such reflections. [13] If Christians are sensitive to the particularity and universality of their own tradition, they will be prompted to take seriously both the particularity and universality of the traditions they encounter - whenever these categories are appropriate. Pluralism tends to diminish the force of the universal claims generated by the particularities of the various traditions as we have seen above. Hence, particularities are evaporated to make way for the all controlling universal *idea* of "God" to which all particularities are conformed. On the other hand, exclusivism in some of its forms does not take seriously the universal claims made by other religions, but dismisses them a priori. One must resist imposing any overarching interpretative scheme upon the world religions which surpresses or distorts the intractible and particular claims they make and the universal binding force they imply. Each tradition must be encountered within its own particular uniqueness and only from this starting point is a viable theology of religions possible.

I would like to conclude this first thesis with some comments on the use of the world "uniqueness" in the debate on the religions. It may be more appropriate to argue that Jesus Christ is the *normative*, rather than on the one hand the exclusive or unique revelation of God, or, on the other hand, simply one among many equal revelations. By normative, one affirms more precisely the important connotations of exclusive and unique. Normative implies that nothing which is of God can contradict what we know of him through Christ. An analogy may help. We are not simply discussing the question of the best image of God, as if we were choosing from different photographs the best likeness of a friend. Rather, to continue the analogy, Jesus is the friend that we know and in this respect all other images are judged by this one. This is certainly one measure by which the Spirit may be discerned - in its conformity to Jesus Christ. But as I shall point out shortly, Jesus is not a static norm.

Furthermore, normative is better than unique for after all, every particular thing, event or person is unique. So while every

13. I am indebted to C. Schwobel for this point: C. Schwobel, "Particularity, Universality, and the Religions," in ed. G. D'Costa, *Christian Uniqueness Reconsidered* (New York: Orbis, 1990) 30-48.

person is unique, it cannot be said of every person that they are normative for the meaning of history. However, there is one sense of the term unique which should not be obscured and that is the beliefe that in Christ, God has uttered himself unreservedly; has given of his very self. This after all is central to maintaining the identity of the immanent and economic Trinity. It is to say that in this one particular time in history God has spoken irreversibly and with a finality that is the basis of all Christian hope. Hence by virtue of being normative, it is being said of Jesus that here is the decisive self-utterance of God - and in this respect the important sense of uniqueness is retained in the clearer term: normative.

One final point about the term normativity. When we speak of Jesus as normative it includes the understanding that it is through Christ that salvation has entered the world in a way in which it has until then, always been ambigious and unclear. It is this revelation that brings salvation into the world by the irreversible self-utterance of the Father, so that all salvation is salvation from the God that we know as Triune, and whom we come to know in Christ.

The Trinitarian Christology I have been advocating is rooted in the particularity of Christ, but without being exclusive or on the other hand, relativizing. But, the particular is related to the universal and it is to God's universal agency and to pneumatology that I now turn.

Thesis two: The Holy Spirit allows the particularity of Christ to be related to the universal activity of God in human history

The doctrine of the Holy Spirit allows us to theologically relate the particularity of Christ to the entire history of humankind. One may note the biblical testimony to the creative, prophetic and saving action of the Word and Spirit from the time of creation. The fact that this testimony is primarily related to the Jewish-Christian tradition should not blind us to the possible reality of God's creative, prophetic and saving activity elsewhere, as I have argued earlier. There are no good theological reasons to suggest that God's activity has stopped, but rather, given the universal salvific will of God revealed in Christ, we can have every expectation that God's activity in history is ongoing and certainly not limited to Christianity. The logical point I am making is this: All history, both past, present and to come is potentially a particularity by which God's self-revelation is mediated. Chronologically and geographically there can be no preset limitations to this: "The Spirit blows where it will." Ecclesiologically this is affirmed in the condemnation of the Jansenist teaching that "outside the church no grace is granted."[14] In our present discussion, this clearly indicates that the history of the religions must be taken seriously as possibly testifying to the power and promptings of the Spirit. Clearly, there can be no *a priori* judgment on this question, but rather an attentive, careful and critical discernment of the tradition we may encounter.

One can develop this pneumatological insight in a Christological and ecclesiological direction by means of a brief meditation on John 16:12-15. In John's Farewell Discourses, Jesus speaks of the Holy Spirit's relation to himself and the Father. "I have yet many things to say to you but you cannot bear them now. When the Spirit of truth comes, he will guide you into all truth; for he will not speak on his own authority, for whatever he hears he will speak, and he will declare to you the things that are to come. He will glorify me, for he will take what is mine and declare it to you. All that the Father has is mine; therefore I said that he will take what is mine and declare it to you." John was not of course addressing the question with which we are dealing but I believe that the hermeneutical spiral present in this passage is pertinent for our purposes.

The full richness and depths of God are yet to be discovered even though in Christianity it is claimed that God has revealed himself definitively in Christ. "I have yet many things to say to you" is indicative of this recognition, which also poses this question: How is this deepening process of disclosure to take place? The answer given here is through the work of the Spirit, who will "guide" and "declare." What is interesting in this passage is the ongoing hermeneutical spiral underpinning John's Trinitarian theology. The process of guidance and declaration, or

14. See Denzinger, 1379. Before Clement's condemnation see Pius V (1025), and Innocent XI (1295); and my examination of this in "Extra ecclesiam nulla salus - revisited," in ed. I. Hamnett, *Religious Pluralism and Unbelief* (London: Routledge, 1990.)

what we might call the continuing disclosure of the fullness of revelation, is authorised and measured insomuch as it is in conformity to Christ. Hence Jesus says of the Spirit: "He will glorify me, for he will take what is mine and declare it to you." This conformity to Christ is itself only authorized because of his relationship to the Father ("All that the Father has is mine"). The riches of the mystery of God are disclosed by the Spirit and are measured and discerned by their conformity to and in their illumination of Christ. Insomuch as these riches are disclosed, Christ, the universal Logos is more fully translated and universalized, while not diminishing his particularity. In this sense Jesus is the normative criteria for God, while not foreclosing the ongoing self-disclosure of God in history through his Spirit.

The most important Christological feature of this hermeneutical spiral is the way in which Christ is both the norm for the understanding of God and yet not a static norm, but one that is being constantly transformed and enriched through the guiding/declaring/judging function of the Spirit. This can be seen in the history of Christology, whereby Christians in different periods have sought to express the reality of the incarnation in very different ways and often discerning very different implications. Of course, not all such expressions can be considered as promptings of the Holy Spirit. This view of the open centrality of Christ is why in Roman Catholic theology it is maintained that revelation was "closed" with the death of the last apostle, *not* in the sense that God speaks no more, but that Christ's revelation is definitive.[15]

The ecclesiological implication of this Johannine passage is germane. The dialectical relation between Son and Spirit in disclosing God must necessarily remain unresolved until the eschaton. This means that the Church should always be open to the Spirit of God within the world religions in anticipation of understanding Christ more deeply, and thereby the mystery of God. If we have good reasons to believe that the Spirit and Word are present and active in the lives lived within the religions of the

---

15. See K. Rahner, "The Development of Dogma," *Theological Investigations*, Vol. 1 (London: Darton, Longman & Todd, 1961) 37-77; E. Schillebeeckx, *Revelation and Theology*, Vol. 1 London: Sheed & Ward, 1967) 66ff.

world (in ways which cannot be a priori specified), then it is intrinsic to the vocation of the Church to be attentive to the world religions. Otherwise, it wilfully closes itself to the Spirit of truth, which it requires to remain faithful to the truth and thereby be guided more deeply into it. The doctrine of the Spirit thereby provides the opening in which the testimonies of peoples from other religions, in their own words and lives, can unmask the false ideologies and distorted practices within Christian communities. This relates well to the teaching that the Church stands under the constant judgment of the Holy Spirit and Christ if it is to be maintained in truth. At the same time, it allows Christians to be aware of God's self-disclosure within the world's religions, and through this process of learning, enrich its own self-understanding. Without listening to this testimony, Christians cease to be faithful to their own calling as Christians, in possibly being inattentive to God.

Conclusion

In this essay I have not tried to examine the interface of the particular encounters that Christians do have with the religions of the world. I have also not illustrated the theological points with examples from the history of encounter. I have been solely concerned with certain theological issues that face Christians when they reflect on the problems and promise of the meeting with the world religions. I have been particularly concerned to show how a Trinitarian Christology and Pneumatology is open to the world religions in refusing to make either *a priori* positive affirmation or critical judgments, but rather suggests the orientation and rules by which such important tasks may be undertaken within the specific contexts of dialogue. It does not try and fit the other religions, unhistorically, into an all-encompassing schematization in terms of characterizing them as "partial anticipations," "equal paths to God," "sinful human-made systems," and so on. It is also open in that it fully acknowledges and looks forward to hearing the voice of God, through the Spirit, in the testimonies of peoples from other religions. Such testimonies can and do open the eyes of Christians to the many and diverse ways in which God acts in history. Such testimony may also be the vehicles of judgment upon Christian theology and practice — and in both ways Christians must be attentive to other religions in order to be faithful to their own. Christian life and thought will be transformed in the meeting of religions, a process which is already clear in the history of Christianity. Inasmuch as such testimonies may reveal a self-deceiving or enslaving way of life counter to the Good News, Christians may have to question and confront the world religions. Hence, in a religiously plural world there are a variety of specific, though related, inter-religious and intra-religious tasks. If I have been able to clarify some of the issues and tasks before Christianity in a religiously plural world, my aim will have been achieved.

IN THE NAME OF JESUS CHRIST:
CHRISTOLOGY AND THE INTERRELIGIOUS DIALOGUE

Wiel Logister

Between 1950 and 1980 a major thrust in theology was a new interest in and a sensitivity toward the humanity of Jesus Christ. The background included the experience that the evidence on which the Renaissance and the Enlightenment understood human beings and the Mystery of God (the asymptotic ground of human existence and life) had fallen into smithereens. Man had become, once more, a question for himself because of his alienation from the industrial and capitalist culture, and by the alarming view of the cultural pressures which often accompanied Christian missions and evangelism.

These questions were exacerbated by the World Wars and the local conflicts which did lay bare the more brutal side of the human race, and by the protests of many people who thought their concerns, their sorrows, or their sexual orientations were not taken seriously. At the same time, this critique of religion made clear that often communication with the Mystery of God is corrupted by secret feelings, desires, and projections. In this situation it was no longer possible to continue along the traditional paths. Already in 1896, Troeltsch said "Everything staggers!" Naked and displaced, Christianity was thrown back on its most profound root, the desire for the experience of him who is the cornerstone of Christian belief and inspiration, Jesus of Nazareth. Dislocated in our sense of God and of man, we once more look to Jesus to discover the realities behind the basic words, to what they evoke, rather than the 'clear and distinct ideas' which can be juggled or argued with mathematical precision.

Since 1980, theology has turned more and more to the encounter of all the religions of the world, confronting the notion that a number of different ideas and attitudes about the world, man, and God intersect in them. In a very new way theology is looking at this common gathering of different cultures and religions. A lot of people experience this sort of re-union as an enrichment, while others think it indigestible and an unendurable complexity, needing 'sorting out'. Many fear that this confrontation will result in a new intolerant fundamentalism that will menace the future of all humankind.

Heinz Robert Schlette asks that all religous groupings, especially those who claim a universal relevance for themselves, start to look at their ability to communicate with others in a humble manner, in a self-critical approach, and certainly without an imperial and violent attitude. If we really want to grow into a commonality of all men, the religious communities do have to reflect seriously on their own motives and discuss openly and freely their universalist claims. [1]

Paul Knitter suggests that truth is present in different ways in different religions. "Because God cannot be reduced to a Oneness that removes all unremovable differences, so too for the world of religions each form of Oneness that denies the differences between the different traditions is forbidden". [2] He therefore rejects all forms of all-inclusive thinking, and with William Thompson speaks of a "complementary uniqueness". [3] What does this mean practically for the Christian experience of Jesus Christ?

John Hick and others seek a basis for interreligious dialogue and reflection on religious pluralism, and on exclusivism or inclusivism, either from the idea of Justin the Martyr that the Logos sows his seed on all people and cultures, or in the insight that the Holy Spirit also sows indiscriminately. For centuries, theology has discussed such a universal revelation, the beneficent and salvific presence of God among all peoples and cultures. This theme has been much developed by Reformed theologians such as Abraham Kuyper and Harrie Kuitert, [4] and also has been discussed by Rahner and Schillebeeckx in presenting their views on the interrelations between creation, anthropology and sacred his-

1. H.R. SCHLETTE, "Zum Universalitätsanspräch von Religionen," *Orientierung* 54 (1990) 99-102.

2. P. KNITTER, "Grundfragen zu einer Theologie der Religionen," *Evangelische Kommentare*, 23 (1990) 607.

3. *Ibid.* 609.

4. See H. BERKHOF, "Neocalvinistische theologie van Kuyper tot Kuitert," in K.U. GÄBLER, et al. *Geloof dat te denken geeft* (Baarn, 1989) 30-48.

tory.[5] No doubt this approach reinforces the respect for other religions, but do we really gain anything here? Can we speak still about the world as a creation of God in such a general sense?

The Chinese theologian, Zhang Shi Chong, cautions against such an abstract consideration of universal revelation. He says, "Universal revelation is exactly the particular culture, the specific culture, the multiplicity of particular cultures".[6] So the 'particular culture' is precisely the universal revelation. The presence of God as Creator is always concrete, expressed in the forms of a definite time and a definite culture.

This leads to the real question: how does one tradition of God's presence match up with other traditions of God's presence? Is each tradition entirely distinct? Does each one claim exclusivity? Or does the new sense of complementarity indicate that each tradition ought to be at the same time so rich and yet so humble that, out of its own experience with, and trepidation before, God, it can unite with other cultures and can acknowledge God's presence in them?

For Christianity, universality has to do with Jesus Christ. Christian belief is centered on Jesus. He is the Way on which the Christian wishes to proceed, convinced that such a life brings peace and justice and does not oppress, or deny the good and truth, of other people. In this fashion we learned between 1950 and 1980, we do not have to cease concentrating on Jesus. But now, in conformity with the Second Vatican Council, we are encouraged to join this "step to a more credible authenticity" with a step toward a greater universality.[7] Will this be possible "in Jesus' name" or is this way closed to believing Christians?

Theologians who try to develop their thought in this direction are often under the suspicion of ignoring the divine nature of Christ, and rather of falling into a subordinationist Christology. Does not this approach have the consequence that the 'Jesus-event' no longer qualitatively differs from the experience of the

5. See K. RAHNER, *Grundkurs des Glauben. Einführrung in den Begriff des Christentums* (Freiburg, 1976) 147ff; E. SCHILLEBEECKX, *Wereld en Kerk. Theologische Peilingen, III* (Bilthoven, 1966) 142ff.

6. See L.A. VAN PEURSEN, "Evangelie en cultuur," *Evangelisch Commentaar*, 14 (1990) No. 12, 8.

7. L. HONNEFELDER, "Ein Gespräch," *Herder Korrespondenz* 45 (1990) 25.

divine on which all other religions rest? And did not the attempts
to rethink the mystery of Christ along these lines lead to a serious
crisis at the level of mission and evangelism? Do not these
attempts lead to a rejection of the teachings of the Church? Do
not they reduce the particularity of Jesus to something which can
be encountered in all religions? Or, in the terms of Pohier: "As
soon as the contingency is acknowledged, it seems that what is
necessary loses its necessity". [8]

Especially in regions where Christians are a minority, theologians no longer wish to shape their thought on the old models,
and so they seek to courageously break new paths. "As people
contemplate Christianity as one religion among others, they are
required to cease thinking of God as they have in the past, fixed
in an exclusive, intolerant tradition which subjugates other traditions to itself. Rather, He becomes a mystery, an eschatological
problem for the meeting of cultures in their insurmountable
differences". [9] This leads to another perspective: "The Church is
not Catholic because it brings the truth to all people in all times,
but also because it needs the collaboration of all civilizations, the
contributions of all men to illuminate its dominion, as it carries
out the task with which it is entrusted, the building of God's
eternal city". [10] It also calls to mind the practice among the
Christians in Antioch in the fourth century of attending the
Jewish as well as the Christian liturgy, [11] as well as the plea of
Aloysius Pieris and others for a *communio in sacris*. [12] Would this
be possible? Often it has been denied in the name of Jesus
himself. But recently Jacques Pohier did formulate the following
disturbing thesis: "To take on in our speaking and thinking the
contingency, the finite nature and the plurality of Jesus Christ. .

8. J. POHIER, "Het absolute van God en de contingentie van het christendom", *Informele Priestergroep Gent*, 18 (1991) 10.

9. A. NGINDU MUSHETE, "Het begrip waarheid in de Afrikaanse theologie",
Concilium (1987/4) 50.

10. *Ibid.*, 53.

11. See G. STEMBERGER, *Juden und Christen im Heiligen Land. Palästina
unter Konstantin und Theodosius* (Münich, 1987) 71.

12. A. PIERIS, *Liebe und Weisheit. Begegnung von Christentum und Bud-
dhismus* (Mainz 1989) 175-177.

.has as a necessary condition, that we really could live in Jesus Christ and that Jesus Christ could live in us".[13]

So, to find a new Christian attitude toward people of other religions we have to look at the concrete way Jesus did live his human existence in the face of God, and at the way Jesus himself did shape human life because of his relation to God.[14] The belief in the humanity of Jesus implies that his human history is determinative for Christian ideas on God and man. Belief in the human nature of Christ does not only say that he had a human soul and a human body, but also and especially that as the Son of Man and the New Adam he did reveal how humanity has to see itself and God. Christians want to learn from the specific, particular and contingent story of Jesus how to express the mystery of God and the mystery of man. He thus is the norm or criterion for the spirituality with which we have to encounter people of other cultures and beliefs. But, even as the norm, Jesus does not lose his contingency. The amazing point is that Jesus' way of living his contingency reopens the possibility of living with God and with other peoples without premature absolutisms.

What we must do with this exciting datum requires much, maybe too much from us. That is why we tend to deify Jesus at the cost of his contingency — in spite of the warnings of the Gospel of Mark. Pohier repeats these warnings against our feeling "that there cannot be any absoluteness, any presence of the absolute or any contact with the absolute in the contingent, the finite and the plural".[15] Is not this open to the trap of monophysitism and a theology of Incarnation that forgets to take its starting point in the concreteness of the humanity of Jesus?

---

13. POHIER, *Het absolute van God en de contingentie van het christendom*, p. 19.

14. SCHUBERT M. OGDEN, ["Gibt es nur eine wahre Religion oder mehrere?," *Zeitschrift für Theologie und Kirche*, 99 (1991) 81-100], rightly asks: what is the argument for pluralism? His own thesis is that we cannot exclude the possibility of more true religions because of our belief in the love of God, but that only an extensive inquiry can show, if and how this possibility actuality is realized, I agree with this point of view. But I want to add that the Christians therefore first have to look to Jesus himself and to consider again their own belief in him.

15. POHIER, *Het absolute van God en de contingentie van het christendom*, p. 23.

It is not easy to begin with the existential individualness of Jesus Christ as sketched in the different writings of the New Testament.[16] It is not at all simple to bring to light the person and life of Jesus which ties together a whole series of interactive and fine-spun relations. When in him the mystery of God and man becomes visible "without mix and without division," then it is not permissible to mix one through the other, nor to lay down one cleanly separate from the other. The way in which things come together in the person and history of Jesus, or in which they flow from him, requires considerable caution on our part. How quickly we can be 'beside the mark' on this point has been proven by Albert Schweitzer in his *Geschichte der Leben-Jesu-Forschung*. But the problem is not hopeless. Understanding the fact that we cannot understand Jesus without the Writings he did read (Tanach) and without the community in which he did live (Judaism of the Second Temple Period) can certainly help us. In addition, we do not have to read the Old Testament only in the schema of 'promise-fulfillment', but also as the first basic Testament. Lastly, the New Testament itself, because of its own plurality, warns us against any one-sided views.

The challange to account once again for the structure and nature of the belief in Jesus Christ cannot mean simply to cut away some difficult points or simply to reduce the Good News to what is also found in other religious traditions. In serious theology the question is: do we understand the Gospel of Jesus Christ in the right way? In what sense will a serious interrogation of his Good News create links and/or oppositions to the convictions of other religions? Christians confess that the eschatological truth of God is manifest in Jesus. For that reason Jesus is named the Christ and the Son of God. The question now arises how can we render this confession in a Christological theory or model. For this we can distinguish two major possibilities.

---

16. This idea is taken from S.M. OGDEN, *The point of Christology* (London, 1982) 39-40. The point here is not a Christology from below in search of the historical Jesus behind the New Testament, but rather the way Jesus is painted in the New Testament, and not only in the Gospels, but also in the other writings. Within the scope of this essay, we can only take a very small sampling of these sketches.

The Classic Christological Model

The classic expression of this view is succinctly summarized by Jean Mouroux: "Because this man is the Eternal Word, he becomes at once and down into his temporal existence 'He in which God lets dwell all completeness' (Col 1,19), the Fulness of the Universe and of Time itself. He becomes the one in whom everything is born, exists and comes to completeness; the one who is the princple, the center, the end of cosmic time in its totality. He is the Eternal, personally engaged in the becoming. In his own humanity he founds, opens and marks time. This *Epha-pax* of the Christ makes him the *absolute hapax*. *Once* sent and appeared, *once* born, died and resuscitated; *once* penetrated in the heavens at the right hand of God to advocate our cause; *once* the Savior of the World, the Head of the Church, Alpha and Omega". [17] Therefore Christ is "predestined to be *the Chief of all men*, following the totality of the time of the world". [18] There is no single aspect of human life which is not taken up in Christ, touched and healed. "The Christ *attracts the whole man to himself* because he has completely passed though him: though the whole corporeal in his efforts, his works, his tears, and his death; through the whole psychical in the joy, the fear, the disgust and the terrible agony of death, and through the whole spiritual in his contemplation, his freedom, his true, crucified and blessed love". [19]

Yet when Mouroux speaks about the humanity of Christ, the point of departure and the perspective is not the man Jesus as a historical and contingent being in the midst of Israel. For Mouroux Jesus is the Christ. This does not so much refer to the biblical Messiah, rather the structual framework is provided by an abstract doctrine of the Incarnation together with an equally abstract doctrine of the Trinity. In Jesus here, the eternal Son of the Father is made manifest, he as a man lives through all human sentiments and feelings, drawing upon the power of his divinity, and consequently purifies, elevates and orients them in the man-

17. J. MOROUX, *Le mystäre du temps. Approche théologique* (Paris, 1962) 91-92.
18. *Ibid.*, 95. Cfr. Eph 1,10.
19. *Ibid.*, 149. Cfr. Joh 12,32.

ner in which God experiences his own being. All the mediation of
the Old Testament is forgotten, so that Jesus, compared with
Israel, is directly and immediately unique as God's partner and
relevator. Hence the ontology of Mouroux runs outside the idiom
of Israel.[20]

After Chalcedon (451), this Christological vision associated
with Cyril of Alexandria in a certain sense gained exclusive rights
in theological discourse, and more or less closed the matter at the
second council of Constantinople (553). Chalcedon, commenting
on the two-fold confessional formula affirming Jesus as "God of
God" and "man for us men" only said that it meant "one and
the same." Already before that time, and certainly after 451, this
unity was interpreted as a compound in which the *hypostasis* (or
concrete nature) of the Eternal Son of God bore the weight. That
poses all sorts of questions about the truth of Jesus' human
nature, exacerbated by issues involving his knowledge and his
will. Grillmeier recently has comprehensively described this history. One of his conclusions reads that "on the whole Byzantine
Christology did not succeed in developing a convincing evalua-
tion of the human knowledge and will of Christ, and also of his
freedom".[21] He continues, "Basically until now we do not have a
generally accepted and uncontradicted theory of the knowledge of
Jesus".

Must we not expand upon this conclusion? In general, the
Cyrillic model has difficulty giving a clear place to the concrete
humanity of Jesus. Here we do not question the meanings and
intentions of this thought model, but rather its possibility of
doing complete justice to all the elements of the Gospel. Its result
is an exclusive declaration of the *ephapax* of Jesus. He is the
absolute unique and exhaustive Incarnation of God. He is ontologically and radically above and opposed to all others. At the
same time pronouncements about God and his nature arise from
an almost unquestioned theological standpoint. Not in Chalce-

---

20. See F.-W. MARQUARDT, *Das christliche Bekenntnis zu Jesus, dem Juden*
(Münich 1990) 299.

21. A. GRILLMEIER, *Jesus Christus im Glauben der Kirche*, II/2 (Freiburg,
1989) 533.

don, but here, it might be said, was Christianity hellenized. More and more in this history we see a Christology wherein the concreteness of the humanity of Jesus and his sustained zeal to honor the God of Israel fully and radically became overshadowed by speculative ideas that were foreign to his own faith. In consequence, the *ephapax* of Jesus was interpreted ontologically in such a way that his being came to stand radically above, and even, opposed to all others.

A New Model

In recent decades there have been many attempts to develop a Christological model which will do more justice to Jesus' struggle to bring his concrete experience of God into the human quest for God's truth and for the truth of the human person and of the human community. The very fact that Jesus is the Son of God within time demands our attention in a very precise manner. Typically, Jesus has become a fascinating intersection for a number of aspects of life, both from the side of God, and also from the side of mankind. In this 'Christology from below,' the concern is not a denial of the divine nature of Jesus, but a conviction that the very concreteness of Jesus is a 'given' which must not be forgotten or transgressed. This Christology is primarily intrigued by the concrete way in which Jesus manifests himself as a religious man, a Jewish 'zaddik' with the inclinations of a wisdom teacher and a prophet. If he did award himself a central place in the mystery of God's gracious care for his people, and if he, after Easter, was called the Son of God by his disciples, all this must be understood on the basis of concepts and sentiments which were present in Israel. They should not arise directly from the thought patterns of other nations.

The concreteness of Jesus is connected with his conviction that God's nearness to mankind (first to Israel and then to 'the nations') is not a future affair, but is happening here and now. Thus he believed it was possible to live in the 'here and now' as new persons, converted, permeated with the Spirit, able to maintain the Torah. This would not happen automatically, but by the presence of God and God's Spirit it would be possible for people dependant on God to turn to a life of peace and righteousness, and away from violence toward others. This violence would especially be a pressure to uniformity and toward domination of others, giving monopoly to one set of convictions and subjecting others to them.

That the struggle against this violence lay at the very center of Jesus' soul, and that he was willing to lay down his life for it, became steadily clearer in the course of Jesus' ministry. It is not entirely clear to what extent Jesus himself interpreted the fusion of his most intimate being with God's nearness to men through such metaphors as "the Messiah," "the Son of Man," or "the Son of God." He apparently lived in such a way that one or the other of these titles could have been given to him. But Jesus' style of life was so impressive that, after he had given his life as a last, comprehensive witness to his faith in God's forgiving and nurturing love for mankind, his disciples used such metaphors (titles) to express the meaning of his person and the nature of his being. By doing this they reinterpreted the metaphors and gave them a new concrete reference. This belief in Jesus as a messenger and prophet of God was not only based on his own claims; the Easter experience told them that this was also true in the eyes of God.

When Jesus received the title "God of God," it involved the One, the God of Israel, as interpreted and experienced through Jesus. The idea of oneness does not argue against multiplicity as such, but against a multiplicity, as well as a uniformity, which does not do justice to the way in which God revealed himself to Israel. Jesus allowed this God to be in him in such a way that God's love for mankind expressly came to light in and through him, "full of grace and truth" [John 1,14]. This cannot be understood on the basis of abstract concepts about God, on 'oneness' or 'revelation' for example, but must clearly be based on the concrete events in Jesus' life-story. This concreteness must not lose its form or become lost in thought models which originate in the belief that Jesus is "God of God."

All of the above implies that the confession of Jesus' universality cannot be maintained as a 'supra-historical' or 'contextless' fact. Although a claim to truth implies universal validity, and although we believe that in Jesus truth had been manifest in the name of God, it is still valid that the universal meaning of Jesus must again and again be discovered and unfolded in his concrete reality. If we say that 'God received a definitive form in Jesus,' that is a statement about a Jesus who in his concrete way makes men free to live selflessly *coram Deo*. With the multiple theological and Christological varients of the New Testament which do not contradict one another but cohere in the concrete questions and situations confronted by the sacred writers, it becomes clear that this can only be considered concretely.

Moreover, this new model of Christology is connected with the 'great shift' in metaphysics. The Christologies of Karl Rahner, Edward Schillebeeckx, and Hans Urs von Balthasar no longer build on a foundation of an onto-theology in a mere theoretical sense, but they take the theoretical and practical reflection on mankind together. With their approach it is impossible to lay down first the metaphysical or ontological divinity of Jesus, and only then secondarily to speak of his human nature. In the context of a transendental anthropology, in the light of Old Testament religious thinking, and from an implicit Christian belief, the new Christologies seek to detect the divinity of Jesus by looking at him as he exists concretely, as an historical human being, a man with a special behaviour and a special fate.[22]

A Break with Tradition?

These Christological shifts necessarily bring with them fundamental theological questions, which will not be about only marginal aspects of the whole body of doctrine. Christology is correctly by most theologians — though often from quite diverse starting points — regarded as an *articulus stantis et cadentis ecclesiae*. Faith is fundamentally at issue. In the eyes of many, such a new approach to Jesus is a betrayal of the New Testament, of tradition, and of the authority of doctrine. It is a radical 'earth movement' by comparison to classical Christology. Can one change such a paradigm of faith, especially in view of the

22. See P. HÄNERMANN, "ber den Verständnisrahmen der Christologie," in L. HAGEMANN and E. PULSFORT, "Ihr alle aber seid Bräder." *Festchrift für A.Th. Khoury zum 60. Geburtstag* (Wärzburg-Altenberge 1990) 405-419.

immense tradition behind the 'classic Christology' as we have seen it expressed by J. Mouroux?

This new view of Christology implies a critical reconsideration of the history of dogma, and it brings up questions about the way Scripture is to be read as the primary source of faith. It raises further questions about the evidence by which Christianity has imagined itself to possess the truth. Here I do not proceed from the supposition that the history of faith is a radical *Abfallsgeschichte*, but it would be foolish not to take into account the fact that belief can become caught up in models which, in the long term, work to entangle it. It is not an easy matter to acknowledge this. The problems of classic Christology come together in such a way that obedient to the concreteness of the Scriptures we must patiently re-examine them, on the one side encouraged by the liberating power of God's presence, and on the other, taking into account the possibility that sometimes we can lose our way (Ps. 139,24).

At its deepest level, this re-orientation can not be made independent of fundamental alterations in theology. Two theological currents are steadily coming clearer. Beside the first, or traditional, model of the "'glaubenswisenschaftlichen' reconstruction of the *scientia Dei* for the use of the doctrinal representation of the system of revelation," the second model, the "glaubenswissenschaftlichen Hermeneutik," exists.[23] While these two models are not in all respects totally opposite to each other, they do breath out of a very different atmosphere.

This second model is not enthused about the idea "that the Word of God is a static doctrine or that theological theory continues to explain and understand ever more fully his content".[24] This is not to say that the second model seeks an a-dogmatic Christianity, a faith in which everything is relative, or a theology empty of truth. People in this model are guided explicity through a Scripture-based understanding of life that depends upon the whole cluster of revelation-experiences surrounding the First and Last manifestation of Jesus, the *Alpha* and the *Omega*. The radiance of the Divine does not really lead once

23. M. SECKLER, "Theologie als Glaubenswissenschaft," *Handbuch der Fundamentaltheologie IV* (Freiburg, 1988) 203.

24. *Loc. cit.*

and for all to clear and detailed insight into the nature of God or the structure of the world, but rather it is a challange to obedience in all possible circumstances — the breaking in of the Mystery's love of humanity so that we will not become crazed with 'fear and trembling'. In all the traditions given in Scripture it is said repeatedly that a life *corum Deo* is beneficient, giving people the possibility of encircling their lives with solicitude and creating wholeness. äIn the course of time it came into concrete existence as a broad tradition with rules for life, devotion, and symbols. It existed not so much as a system of doctrine, but as a wisdom distinguishing between journeying in God's space, and the space of the Evil One. Scripture and tradition do not lead to a detailed and unalterable truth. They contain, rather, memorable distillations that awaken the creative sense, but which cannot be taken over indiscriminately in an ever changing culture and/or in new circumstances. People attempt to learn in the sense that they avoid old mistakes, biases, and excesses, but they do not cherish the illusion that they will slowly but surely succeed in letting the music of the spheres be heard once for all. In distinction to scholastic theology, therefore, stands a rabbinic and mystagogic wisdom-theology in which all sorts of reflections and concrete observations are loosely connected with one another, and with only here and there an anathema!

According to this new Christology, the essence and value of the early Christian councils, for instance, lies in their protest against aberrations (*anathema sit*) and reminding the Church of its hermeneutical point of departure, rather than the unchangeable content of its pronouncements. The conciliar confessions are to be understood here as norms or boundaries for the reading of Scripture, not as verities whose contents are in themselves valid as premises for speculation, and capable of leading to clearer understanding.

In the light of these norms, it is the present task of theologians to initiate a dialogue between the present situation with all its possibilities and difficulties, and the way in which mankind directed by Scripture has responded to life. Scripture, exactly in and through its historicity, opens horizons to readers of all times, and has the power to challenge lives in other times and to bring them to fullness. This fact does not say that we possess the answers to all questions. Confrontation with Scripture often has something alienating and challenging about it, and most properly works in the dialectic between creativity and fantasy. Thus we sometimes face questions and challenges on which the Scripture does not speak. This should not surprise us, because Scripture itself is a historical tradition in which we find a blending of various horizons, and repeatedly the new and the surprising comes into play in Scripture under new circumstances. Only constant re-reading and having an eye for the historical context of the various parts of the text may challenge one to risk one's own interpretation.

In this way, by confronting present-day questions with the light of Scriptural tradition, the theologian takes part in applying faith to contemporary circumstances. This presupposes acquaintance with the contemporary situation and schooling in the world of the Bible. Starting with these points of focus, the course of investigation and judgement seeks to clarify each of these questions as they intersect with each other, and explicitly mediate between them, a process in which familiarity with the history of tradition and the experience of the Church plays no small part. Here it is particularly important to establish the centrality of the theological dimension, and not lose oneself in historical, psychological, or sociological minutiae. This is indeed difficult because the theological dimension cannot be extracted from such details, but is interwoven with them. The *viva vox Evangelii* or the breath of the Holy Spirit rips itself free from the lines of the stories, devotions, and wisdom meditations from which the particularities of history, mentality, and society cannot be eliminated. So the theological dimension is present in the traditions of the one great Tradition.

This blending of points-of-view is not without dangers. All sorts of 'hidden agendas' and sentiments can come into play. Therefore, from the very beginning of the investigation one must state with great clarity what questions are being asked of Scripture. Justice must be done to the historical characteristics of the text, and the leitmotif which runs through the Scripture binding together its varied books into an intangible unity must be sought out carefully. This will not lead to a fixed and frozen systematic theology. We must repeatedly take up the Scripture with its different books and genres, to look again how the leitmotif is perceptible variously in the texts.

Because that leitmotif of Scripture is not fully objectifiable, and because every explanation is influenced by its contemporary context, its questions and its options, not all the themes of faith come to light in the same manner in different ages. However the reality of the Scriptures does determine our approach to the present-day context, leading our imagination to a specific understanding of our own time. In the interplay of all these contexts and horizons we come to a concrete description of faith's meaning for our own time and situation. In doing so, no timeless dogmatics comes into existence, but space is created in our own time for belief (without making everything possible or legitimate), and room for the realization of our human and Christian destiny.

After this interlude on fundamental theology, we can return to the question: what is the stance toward other religions created by belief in Jesus? Can we uphold the reality of God in Jesus, or confess that he is the image and human face of the liberating God, without unavoidably discriminating against other religions, or seeing them as somehow 'variations on a theme.'

The Absolute in the Relative

Christians are convinced that it is possible "to admit to a 'not-itself-absolute absoluteness'".[25] "God's definitive, irretractable form or redemptive revelation"[26]can be "reflected in the historically relative," but retains "a nevertheless absolute meaning".[27] This possibility of the 'Eternal-within-time' underpins all of Christology. But which shape does this possibility take in Jesus Christ? How is he God's Son within time? Often we are very

25. *Ibid.*, 17.
26. E. SCHILLEBEECKX, "Identiteit, eigenheid en universaliteit van Gods heil in Jezus," *Tijdschrift voor Theologie* 30 (1990) 267.
27. *Ibid.*, 268.

impressed with the idea that the contingent being cannot support a real presence of the Absolute and that we cannot contact the Absolute in the contingent finite being, or in the plurality. From this presumption we cannot really believe that the Word can be made flesh. But the puzzling point of the Bible is that the divine can appear in a concrete human life, in the ethical/spiritual experience and behaviour of a concrete person or a concrete society.

If we call Jesus *vere Deus*, it is not merely sujective rhetoric. There is a place for "a translation of God's being in and through the contingent, historical, genuine humanity of Jesus," yet there remains "a tension between Jesus' identification with God and Jesus' own identity".[28] The Christian Gospel identifies Jesus as one absolute, unforgettable characteristic of the specificity of God. What does this mean precisely and concretely? And which possibilities does the concrete truth of Christian belief offer for an authentic, open, critical, and self-critical dialogue with people from other religions?

Our perception of the Absolute in Jesus is often translated into a position that says that 'the other' is always inferior compared to him. The missionary call is often understood in this sense. "The Christian claim for absoluteness determines the relation to the non-christian in such a way that the non-christian is devalued."[29] That danger certainly did not become less after the conversion of Constantine, but more often it took the shape of a "naive, unproblematic and therefore unreflected self-sufficiency".[30]

This was not a responsible stance in the past, and certainly is not in our time. Not only to do justice to other religions, but also to do justice to the Gospel, the absolute demands of our faith must be clearly distinguished from our inclination to prejudgements of superiority and exclusivity. Have we in the Christian faith not too easily accommodated ourselves to our desire for clarity and order?

---

28. *Ibid.*, 271.
29. R. BERNHARDT, *Der Absolutheitsanspruch des Christentum. Von der Aufklärung bis zur Pluralistischen Religionstheologie* (Gätersloh 1990) 18.
30. *Ibid.*, 29.

Have we not too conveniently used our formulas of faith, which
are really doxological and self-implicating rather than rational/
insightful principles with sharp contours? Is faith in Jesus Christ
shaped by these formulas not too simply conceived as the true
knowledge of all reality? Did not Christianity derive too 'hard and
fast' absolute and irrefutable claims from this approach?

'Monos' in a Biblical Sense

Because of Biblical monotheism, Christians cannot begin by
assuming the equality, or even the equal truth, of all religions.
The very fundamental experiences of the faith-history from
Moses to Jesus bear witness to the fact that not every religion is
legitimate. Moses not only attacked the Pharaoh, but also the
very foundations of Egyptian religion. Jesus was crucified in the
name of religious values, whether they be understood to be of
Roman or Jewish origin. But does that mean that we, today, have
a universal standpoint or a settled answer in all dialogues?
Because Christians here and now do not possess divine insight,
there remains room for a "breath of theological agnosticism",[31]
for *docta ignorantia* and eschatological reservations. Rather 'I
know not', than a knowledge that wraps itself all too quickly in
the robes of the Almighty! Therefore Christians should not go
forth to meet non-christians with too much of an air of infallibil-
ity.

In this connection it is reasonable to ask how we approach the
oneness of God, or understand Biblical monotheism. Is this
monos identical with "exclusivity"? In the first instance, Biblical
monotheism is a form of protest: the Mystery of God may not be
understood on the basis of the theology of Egypt or Canaan, and
the accompanying anthropological and social concepts. It is not
an abstract speculation on the category of "one" or "oneness,"
but a reordering in which neither the theoretical nor the practical
may be given up: the concept of God cannot tolerate a concept of

31. BERNHARDT, *Der Absolutheitsanspruch des Christentum*, 236.

integration or a social system in which the Pharaoh is the *only* son of god whom all other men must serve. Neither will it tolerate polytheism in which the struggle for life has the last word, nor a hierarchically structured caste system. The monotheism of Israel separates itself from such understandings of life, and stubbornly and unyieldingly maintains that the first theological principle is that God cares for the oppressed and the dispossessed. This one concept is the foundation on which Israel stands. Any social, philosophical, or theological system that denies or marginalizes this concept fundamentally and essentially threatens Israel's faith in God. [32]

This critical monotheism contains a warning against attempts to choose an abstract/general point of departure for dialogues between religions. From the outset, Scripture lays upon the table a question, a norm, a basic criterium. At least somewhere in the dialogue the question must be directly asked: What are the power relations? What is your point of departure? In the relations between religions, the issues cannot be dealt with as abstract and general questions, but must focus on specific, concrete realities. "A doctrine that wants to be universal but does not respect this 'Vorläufigkeit *sub specie aeternitatis*,' has to be cricized because of its very absolutism; the same must be said for a particularistic-Christian absoluteness, that forgets its Vorläufigkeit". [33] While "the understanding of revelation out of the Platonic-Neoplatonic concept of truth tends to an contemplative-theoretical narrowing," in Judaism and Christianity it involves an "operative-practical understanding of truth". [34]

By analogy, the same is true with regard to Jesus. His universal meaning is not abstract, but concrete. If Christians confess that God is made manifest in Jesus, they therefore must speak about very specific and concrete circumstances. On every occasion, such particularity must necessarily be addressed. When, for instance, theology speaks of Jesus' *anhypostasis* and his *enhypostasis*, these

32. See W. Logister, *Een mensenleven door God getekend. Inleiding in de christologie* (Averbode-Kampen, 1987) 57ff. Id., "Het unieke van Jezus - een systematische vingeroefening," *Tijdschrift voor Theologie*, 28 (1988) 247-271, particularly 255ff.

33. Bernhardt, *Der Absoluteitsanspruch des Christentum*, 237-238.

34. *Ibid.*, 61.

ontological terms must be understood in the light of the concrete ways in which Jesus acted and spoke in the name of God, the ways in which he maintained the distinctions between himself and God through his self-abnegation, and how he left others with no impression of pedantry or dogmatism. It is with these attitudes in mind that Christians should step toward others. We believe that these are Godly attitudes, and are therefore fundamental both to individual human conduct, and for the building up of human community. To someone like Jesus we can say "please, be more of yourself," without the exclusion of others. Jesus does not lead to "the system of the excluded third".[35]

However, it is certainly not true that Christians enter into dialogue with non-christians completely without presuppositions. They can never deny the concrete, absolute demands with which Jesus has confronted them. In certain situations, witness to this must be radical and without reservation, as in the case of the Barmen Declaration, or when in the name of Christ Christians in the first centuries refused to acknowledge the power of the Caesars and their gods. This unyielding witness is demanded in situations in which there is absolutely no freedom permitted for that style of life which Jesus, by his own life and death, brought forward in God's name as fundamental for his followers. That such a witness is required in circumstances which manifest the radical antithesis of Jesus, does not mean that in all other circumstances there is justification for taking up the same oppositional posture.

More than Moses

The Christian tradition discovered something in Jesus which previously was not present in Judaism in the same personal/concrete way. Jesus had a peculiar qualitative depth which could not be reduced into other qualities. It concerned both his proclamation and his style of life in which the closeness or presence of God's love for mankind stood central. This is reflected in his conviction that he was beginning a new connection with God.

35. POHIER, *Het absolute van God en de contingentie van het Christendom*, p. 20.

When we consider the meaning of this, we must not forget how Jesus characterised the similarities and differences between himself and David, Jonah, and Solomon, among others. In comparison to them, Jesus is greater. What that 'greater' is, can only be established in an experimental and concrete way; it cannot be determined *a priori*. On every occasion it must appear concretely, or it must be demonstrated. When Jesus characterised himself in comparison with certain figures in his own Jewish tradition, he did not consider them as figures of less value. Nor was he saying that he substitutes for them once and for all. This when properly observed makes it difficult to point out precisely what is the specific character of Jesus. It is not a matter of absolute opposition nor of radical exclusivity.[36]

By doing so, Jesus undoubtedly revealed something of God's Mystery. Christian theocentrism is not so vague that it can mean everything. The God of Jesus cannot be harnessed to every wagon. Jesus spoke of God in a specific way, with human titles for God, with the concrete demands that God laid upon mankind. Notwithstanding, Jesus left the Mystery of God intact. "The Father is greater than I." The fact that God has drawn near to us in Jesus gives us no hold over God; rather, it is God's hand that helps us to be human, no more and no less than to be human *coram Deo*. In this sense the descent of the Word in Jesus strengthens the possibility of experiencing and thinking about God, without making us the master of the Mystery.

Schillebeeckx shows this dilemma, when he speaks both of "*an* eschatological - that is, definitive - revelation of God within our history, which can never be withdrawn" as well as "*the* decisive and definitive, in particular eschatological, 'revelation of God'".[37] On this basis Knitter says, "Schillebeeckx obviously understands 'definite and decisive' in a way that likewise definite and decisive revelations elsewhere are not excluded".[38]

---

36. Recently, in an exigesis of the Transfiguration (Mk 9,2-8), Hartmut Gese on the one hand did emphasize the new revelation of God in Jesus his Son, but on the other he acknowledged the identity between Jesus and the Torah and the Prophets. See H. GESE, "Gottes Bild und Gottes Wort," in E. LUBAHN & O. RODENBERG, *Von Gott erkannt. Gotteserkenntnis im hebräischen und griechischen Denken* (Stuttgart 1990) 56ff.

37. SCHILLEBEECKX, *Identiteit, 261 and 262 (italics added)*.

38. KNITTER, "Grundfragen zu einer Theologie der Religionen," p. 609.

This dilemma cannot be resolved through abstract or purely terminological descriptions of the meaning of revelation in Jesus or his universal significance. The meaning and significance of Jesus' person and his way of living must be described as concretely as possible; not by a historical-critical analysis that looks for a 'Jesus behind the Gospel,' but by reading the Gospel itself as accurately as possible. Only in doing so can we prevent the veiling of our own feelings of superiority under 'divine glamour,' and the supression of Jesus' personhood. When setting forth the meaning of Jesus, we cannot begin from a number of eternal verities, but must constantly give attention to the concrete ways in which he turned toward others, to bring them to truth in thought, in word and in deed. Belief in Jesus is not concerned with an abstract universality or commonality, but with the specific ways in which he conducted himself. His words and acts cannot be isolated from their context, any more than it can be done in a laboratory when molecules or atoms are studied. Words and actions always have a concrete relation to their environment. In order to discover their meaning for our own time we are directed to our own creative intelligence, which hopefully is so selfless or *anhypostatic* that the Spirit of God can enter.

Terms such as 'unique', 'absolute', 'universally valid', 'exclusive', and 'inclusive' are indications of a certain direction of thought rather than clear or self-evident concepts. When they are used in the language of faith, they do not point to eternal and unchanging verities that we can appropriate as our own, but are doxological confessions from which neither sober understanding nor human assertiveness can draw quick conclusions. Undoubtedly they give us something to think about, but because of the nature of the terms, this thought must be slow, careful and insightful.

Simeon called Jesus "a light that will bring revelation to the Gentiles, and glory to your people Israel" [Luke 2,32 RSV]. Does not that shine a 'light' on Jesus' universal meaning? That seems to be an unavoidable conclusion. But before we agree, we have to listen to the sound and color of Simeon's language. What thoughts and sentiments do they evoke in us? How are we to understand 'the nations' and 'Israel'? To what sort of posture does it lead? Does 'Gentiles' have the same meaning as 'heathen' had fifty years ago? Does Simeon intend the Israel-theology of the old Good Friday liturgy (prior to 1955), or is he an early forerunner of the Rheinische Synod of 1980?

The sense in which Jesus has a proper and typical universal meaning can only become clear in a reflection which from the very start pays attention to the concrete meaning and experience of 'the nations' and 'Israel.' This consideration does not begin with Jesus in opposition to other salvation and revelation traditions, but by extension of the way he himself related to Israel and to the Gentiles. This by no means excludes critical examination of 'Israel' and 'the nations.' The way in which salvation and revelation were manifested in Jesus raises the question of how we speak of salvation and revelation in relation to 'the nations' and 'Israel.' This requires specific investigation. How such investigation must proceed becomes clear in the New Testament in Jesus' conversation with the Syrophoenician woman, and in Paul's 'sermon' on the Areopagus where he is preaching the Jewish God in light of the Jesus-event.

One consequence of this is that the systematic theologian cannot speak on his own about the universality of Jesus in relation to Israel and other nations. He must work together with experts who have studied Israel and other religious traditions, or he must build his own expertise concerning them. This personal expertise is all the more necessary now that cultures are less shaped by the Christian Churches alone, and the fact that soon practically all communities will be multi-religious. When such a theologian speaks about 'the nations' he will be speaking about his friends and neighbors! And since we have become conscious of the *adversus Judaeos* tradition as the left hand of Christology, Judaism looks over its shoulder if we call Jesus the Messiah and the Son of God.

Teach All Nations

What meaning does all of this have for preaching the Gospel and missionary effort? Can or must the idea of mission not be replaced by the concept of an open *communicatio in sacris*, a mutual exchange of that which people consider the mystery of life

and, ultimately, salvation in the way of God? I will answer these
questions by a short examination of Matthew 28,18-20, a text
which has played a major role in Christian missions. "All authority in heaven and on earth has been given to me. Go
therefore and make disciples of all nations, baptizing them in the
name of the Father and of the Son and of the Holy Spirit,
teaching them to observe all that I have commanded you; and lo,
I am with you always, to the close of the age." [RSV]

What are the implications of these words? äWhich Christological profile comes to the fore here? What do they say about
other peoples and their cultures and religions? What does this
mean for mission and dialogue? Does this give any reason to
speak of singleness (unicity) and/or absoluteness? Of course, all
of the New Testament does not meet in these lines, nor is this the
last word regarding Jesus and the mission of the Church. But if
we wish to find a responsible approach to mission and dialogue,
then this is certainly an important text. On the basis of this text, I
wish to demonstrate how a critical examination of a Christian
truism offers greater possibilities for dialogue with other religions
than had previously been suspected.

The imperative *mathäteusate*, "make disciples," is the center of
Jesus' words. All of his other instructions are placed around this
imperative as participles. Karl Barth remarks on how striking this
term is: "Von *mathäteusein* ist in jenem Befehl auffallenderweise
die Rede - nicht, wie man erwarten sollte, von *kärussein* oder
euaggelizesthai".[39] Making disciples was the goal of Jesus' efforts
and actions. In the course of the gospel of Matthew, the circle of
this action becomes steadily wider: it broadens out from the Sea
of Galilee (4,18) to all Galilee (4,23), the land of the Gadarenes
(8,28), the region of Tyre and Sidon (15,21), Caesarea Philippi
(16,3), and via Jericho (20,29) to Jerusalem (21,1). When 28,19
speaks of *panta ta ethnä*, it appears that Israel and Judaism is not
excluded. Now the disciples are given a task in this steadily
widening movement. They are addressed as 'wandering prophets'
and told: "Go, therefore" (*poreuthentes*).

This discipleship is not something completely new, but a radi-
calising of what Moses had taught: to do the will of God. "Das

39. K. BARTH, *Kirchliche Dogmatik IV/4* (Zärich, 1967) 105.

Lehren ist bei Mt ausgerichnet auf das, was zu tun ist, auf den Willen Gottes, so wie ihn der irdische Jesus verkändete, vor allem in der Bergpredigt, auf seine Weisung, seine Gebote... Im Gehorsam gegenäber dieser Weisung realisiert sich das Volk Gottes, wahres Israel".[40] In that sense the disciples must teach (*didaskontes*) others "to observe all that I have commanded you" (vs.28), that is to say, the Torah as Jesus taught it to them. This does not directly involve the person of Jesus *in abstracto*, but the commandments, which became the heart of his being. The commandments are also the criteria used in the Last Judgement (Matt. 25). The circle of disciples must be opened on all sides to win people to the observance of the will of God. There is no prohibition on witness among Jews. This was not excluded by Jesus himself nor by Paul. But that witness does not have to take the form of an exclusive *Christus solus*, in whom all the truth and all the spiritual experiences of humanity are included.

Next there is a reference to *baptizontes*. Baptism indicates the radical seriousness of renewal of life in which Jesus explained the Torah. And Baptism was the giving of grace and power to fulfill the commandments of the Torah. More than simple daily ablutions or baths, 'baptism' here refers to an eschatologial renewal in which the disciple no longer merely looks forward to the approach of God, but accepts it as a 'real presence' that grants him or her a new heart and a new spirit for the rest of their lives. Because the kerygma of and about Jesus is not just another addition to the works of the Tannach, but a very specific sharpening and fulfillment of the Torah, "die Konfrontation met dem Wort des Evangeliums allein"[41] is not sufficient. Here to be serious they have to lose themselves before the God of Jesus and his Holy Spirit.

Baptism takes place *eis to onoma tou patros kai tou huiou kai tou hagiou pneumatos* (vs.19). Through baptism a person receives a place in the sphere of God-Abba, accepts the appeal of Jesus, and receives the power of the Spirit. Based on Jesus' preaching and example, this flows out from Jesus' own baptism in the name of the Father and the Spirit. The person being baptized is taken

---

40. Joachim Gnilka, *Das Matthäusevangelium*, 2 (Freiburg, 1988) 590-510.
41. *Loc. cit.*

into the ambit that is evoked by the words "Father, Son, and Spirit". Being baptized "in the name of..." "is a way saying that the person belongs to the one whose name is mentioned".[42] What 'belonging the Father and Spirit' means in concrete terms is to be seen in the action and authoritative teaching of Jesus. This is not a point of speculative trinitarian theology, but the concrete sense in which the authority of Jesus must be understood.

This is the background of the words, that "all authority in heaven and on earth has been given to" Jesus (vs. 18). What do these words mean? "The statement of fullness of authority is expressed here mainly because of the command that follows. . .to underline the origin of the obligation of the command that follows".[43] These words form "a fitting conclusion to the presentation of Jesus throughout the Gospel as the one possessing authority. At the same time this assertion causes the reader to reflect backwards in the Gospel for evidences that the assertion is plausible. This is the function of the Matthaen redaction".[44] Previously the redactor has regularly pointed out the authority of Jesus: at the baptism ("This is my beloved Son, with whom I am well pleased" 3,17) and again at the transfiguration ("This is my beloved Son,. . .listen to him" 17,5). That he once again brings the authority of Jesus to the fore at this point, the heightened climax to the Gospel, underscores the demand to maintain his teachings. The authority of Jesus has a relationship to his teachings (see, for example, Matthew 7,29). His death has not altered this; quite to the contrary. Jesus still has authority, and still approaches mankind in the name of God.

The Christian witness undoubtedly involves a specific experience of God which would be impossible to conceive without the name of Jesus. That becomes clear in the closing words: "And lo, I am with you always, to the close of the age" (vs. 20b). These words form an inclusion with Matthew 1,23 "Immanuel, God with us." That "God with us" is given a face and power in the Risen One who is the same as the man Jesus who did live on earth.

42. O.S. BROOKS, "Matthew xxviii 16-20 and the design of the first gospel," *JSMT* 10 (1981) 4.

43. B.J. MALINA, "The literary structure and form of Matt. XXVIII. 16-20," *New Testament Studies* 17 (1970-71) 89.

44. BROOKS, *Ibid.*, 3.

What then are the implications of these closing words of the Gospel of Matthew? Do they imply an absolute opposition between Jesus and other religions? One can only with great caution speak of the way in which the will of God is known in Judaism and elsewhere, and even more, about the spiritual power that is present in them to do this Will. Notwithstanding all his personhood and newness, according to Matthew Jesus does stand in the same line with Abraham and David (1,17). The light he manifests is not out of line with the wisdom of 'the nations' who are represented by the Magi (2,1ff). A faith may come forward among 'the nations' which Jesus never found in Israel (8,1-12). When we are in touch with Jews and others, the greatest caution is commended to us by Jesus himself.

This is not to deny the individuality and authority of Jesus, but rather the caution proceeds from his hope to make Christians and others better believers — that is, people who live according to God's will. The caution, preventing us from filling in the discipleship of Jesus with glib claims of 'greatness,' belongs to the norms which Jesus laid down for his disciples. It is one of those criteria with which Christians consider the nature and purpose of salvation in other religions.[45] Therefore we must say that Christian orthodoxy "only implies that certain doctrines are true about God, and so that their contradictories are false, without entailing the blasphemous conclusion that they exhaust the whole truth about God".[46]

This short attempt to re-read the New Testament has to be followed up with more probing. The Christology of the Fourth Gospel particularly seems to be an unsurmountable difficulty for

45. See W. LOGISTER, "Ann de overkant van exclusiviteit en inclusiviteit," *Tijdschrift voor Theologie*, 29 (1989) 379-387. Recently Pannenberg has connected this open stance with the fact that we do not yet live in the fullness of the eschaton [W. Pannenberg, "Die Religionen als Thema der Theologie," *Theologisches Quartalschrift*, 169 (1989) 99-110]. I consider that standpoint dangerous, because in this manner the claim that the fullness of salvation in all possible situations is to be found in Jesus is implicitly maintained. I have argued elsewhere that this claim does not necessarily have to be read into the "Cosmic Christology" of Ephesians and Colossians [W. LOGISTER, *Reïncarnatie. De vele gestalten van een oud en nieuw geloof* (Tielt, 1990) 99-114].

46. H.A. MEYNELL, "The Conditions of Christian Uniqueness," *Journal of Ecumenical Studies* 26 (1989) 70.

this approach. In this Fourth Gospel the mystery of Jesus has been pinpointed to emphasize 'the given' that the Word of God has been found in a contingent human being. This underlines one side of Jesus: that in his person and life God really did become flesh. From this point of view, our reading of the synoptic Gospels is in the correct direction; but also, in these Gospels, the contingency of Jesus has not been suppressed. The Jesus of the New Testament reveals God and the destiny of humanity in a very specific and concrete way. We discover this not by refusing to look at other prophets and saints, but by concentrating our attention looking for the breakthrough of God in the histories and narratives of ordinary men and women. We must look at the old and the young, mostly at the poor, but also at the comfortable. We must look at all those who live without blowing up their own significance. And we must not deny that in simple contingency the Mystery of Divine Grace can reveal itself.

THE ELEVEN THESES OF FRANK DE GRAEVE:
A CRITICAL APPRAISAL

Catherine Cornille

The thesis-form has become an apt way to express one's views on the theology of religions. [1] As pointed out by Jan Van Bragt "it is good scholastic practice, and, while laying the writer wide open to critique, it is conducive to further discussion." [2] In the course of developing and teaching courses in the theology of religions at the universities of Notre Dame and Leuven, Frank De Graeve also came to express his views on the topic in the form of theses. They were published under the playful and imaginative title "From O.T.S.O.G. to T.A.S.C.A.S., Eleven Theses toward a Christian Theology of Interreligious Encounter." [3] With the first acronym of the title, which stands for "On The Shoulders Of Giants," De Graeve pays tribute to some of his teachers and main sources of inspiration: Louis Monden, Mircea Eliade, Joseph Goetz, Paul Tillich, Wilhelm Dilthey, Hans-Georg Gadamer, Schubert Ogden, David Tracy, a.o. "Standing on their shoulders," he writes, "I was no longer dwarfed by their height, but able to look a little beyond their own horizons to the new one that would be mine." [4] The acronym T.A.S.C.A.S. then refers to the attempt to develop his own conclusions, and to rethink and rephrase venerable but dusty pronouncements of the Church and tradition as "Tossing Around Some Curves and Spitballs."

The eleven theses took definite form during the Second Vatican Council. They bear its open attitude toward other religions while

1. There are the five (in this volume two) theses of Gavin D'Costa in G. D'Costa (ed.), *Christian Uniqueness Reconsidered. The Myth of A Pluralistic Theology of Religions* (New York: Orbis, 1990.) and the ten theses of Jan Van Bragt, *Toward a Theology of Religions* (Tokyo: Oriens Institute for Religious Research, 1984.)

2. J. Van Bragt, *Toward a Theology of Religions*, p. 5.

3. In *Louvain Studies* 7 (1979) 314-325.

4. *Ibid.*, p. 316.

carrying this a little further. Their pioneering and still timely nature can be appreciated when compared with the main paradigms of the early sixties and with those developed nowadays. Prior to, and to a large extent also during and after the Second Vatican Council, the attitude toward non-Christian religions was dominated by exclusivistic and fulfilment theories. Other religions were viewed at best as a "praeparatio evangelica," awaiting fulfilment in Christianity. De Graeve, however, saw the openness toward other religions introduced in the Vatican documents *Lumen Gentium* and *Nostra Aetate* as an invitation to develop ideas which had obviously been lurking for some time, but which only now could come into the open.

For three decades, they have shaped the thoughts of many a student, and have proven a fertile ground for further reflection. De Graeve's many foreign students have carried his thought from India to Australia, from the United States to the Filipines and to Africa, where they often surface in their own teaching and writing. These eleven theses have thus in their own way contributed to the contemporary theology of religions, and to the ongoing debate.

In this essay, I have taken the liberty of rearranging the theses on the basis of four major topics around which they seem to evolve: religious pluralism, the uniqueness of Christianity, the convergence of religions, and the role of Christianity in that convergence.[5]

Religious Pluralism

The Second Vatican Council was a landmark or watershed in the attitude of the Catholic Church toward non-Christian religions. The first thesis of De Graeve reflects this radical opening toward other religions in stating that *All authentic religions are valid, lawful, legitimate as social, institutional communities of men who, within their own existential situation, respond in their own way to God's salvific revelation as manifested to them.* This thesis

5. In changing the sequence of the theses, their meaning may be somewhat modified. But throughout the years, De Graeve himself often presented them in differing order.

bears the direct influence of Karl Rahner, who has been called the "chief engineer" of Vatican II. The "validity, lawfulness, and legitimacy" of other religions is based on the belief that they contain not merely elements of natural knowledge of God (as had hitherto been the extent of Christian openness toward other religions) but also supernatural elements. The other religions are regarded as different responses from within their particular contexts to God's salvific revelation. Here, one can discern the influence of Mircea Eliade, who emphasized the need to understand religions from within "the situations and positions that have induced or made possible their appearance or their triumph at a particular historical moment."[6] But this thesis goes beyond a historical or phenomenological understanding of other religions to an explicitly theological acknowledgement of them.

Christian missionaries have always encountered authentically holy people in religions which were regarded as pagan. This constituted an enigma. How could evil or erroneous religions give birth to saints? The problem was resolved by speaking of "pagan saints," saved in spite of their religion. With his first thesis, De Graeve directly reacts against this approach. The so-called "pagan saints" are according to him not the exception which prove the rule, but the very evidence of the validity of these religions as "social and institutional communities of men (and women)." This belief in the soteriological power of the institutional and ritual dimensions of other religions may be seen as a Catholic embracing of the temporal reality. It must be said, however, that very few have been able or willing to go that far.

This acknowledgement of the soteriological potential of other religions, however, does not imply a naive and uncritical acceptance of any and all non-Christian religions. The thesis applies to all "authentic" religions. With Paul Tillich, De Graeve distinguishes an authentic religion from a quasi-religion, which looks like a religion but is not, and from a pseudo-religion, which claims to be a religion but is not. The latter distinction has often been applied to the difference between the established and the new religions, sometimes appearing as veiled economic enterprises or harmful

6. M. Eliade, "History of Religions and a New Humanism" *History of Religions* 1 (1961) 3.

therapeutical groups. While some so-called new religions may indeed be deceptive, there does not seem to be any ground for excluding a priori all the new religions from the openness manifested toward other non-Christian religions. This is an area into which the theology of religions has yet to venture.

Granted that every religion, especially when seen in its social and institutional dimensions, is an amalgamy of authentic and inauthentic forces, elements of magic and superstition and truly spiritual characteristics, De Graeve emphasizes in his second thesis that *In "sizing up" or evaluating "other" religions theologically, we have to discover their authenticity, their specificity, their integrity, particularly in their Founders, prophets, saints, and mystics.* In former, and sometimes even in contemporary apologetic discourse, the opposite has often been the case. A caricature of the non-Christian religion is compared to an idealized view of Christianity. Beliefs and practices strange or superstitious to Christian eyes are taken out of context and exposed or ridiculed. Painfully aware of the damage which this has caused to the understanding of, and the dialogue between religions, De Graeve has been untiring in insisting on the need to comprehend the other religion through its most eminent representatives, its most elevated practices and beliefs, and its most sophisticated philosophical systems. This requires the capacity for analogical imagination and cross-cultural symbolic thinking of which his teaching and writing is eminent evidence. The golden rule of reciprocity, to treat other religions as you would have them treat yours, has always been his adage.

While this attempt to understand a religion in its ideal form was a necessary correction to the previous approach, it may also distort one's view of that religion as a lived reality. Hinduism cannot be understood only through the reading of the Upanishads or the Bhagavad Gita, or Buddhism grasped through the Dhammapada or a figure such as Nagarjuna. Religions being a composite of abstract philosophical and folk traditions, superstition and spirituality, morality and corruption, dialogue may also be undertaken in the spirit of mutual suspicion, criticism and correction.[7]

7. J. Milbank, "The End of Dialogue" *Christian Uniqueness Reconsidered* (G. D'Costa, ed., Maryknoll, N.Y.: Orbis books, 1990) 190.

The Uniqueness of Christianity

The unique soteriological function which Christianity attributes to the figure of Jesus Christ has been the main stumbling-block in the dialogue with other religions. It has thus been the focus of apologetical discourse and critical self-reflection in the Christian theology of religions. New Christologies have been developed from the encounter with different religions and cultures, the category of uniqueness reconsidered, and the original Christological formulas reinterpreted. Some have been prepared to abandon altogether the Christian faith in the uniqueness of Christ while others have held fast to the established conceptions. In spite of his respect and reverence for the best in the non-Christian religions, De Graeve has always held fast to the uniqueness of Christianity which for him is the uniqueness of Christ: *In Christ, the "eschatos Adam" and "Son of God," not just a revelation of God, but God revealed, the response of man has been definitively identified with the Word of God himself, realizing the divine plan of salvation in the human dimension of time.* The traditional conception of the uniqueness of Christ is here viewed from the particular perspective of religious pluralism. The expression "not just a revelation of God, but God revealed" is meant to emphasize the difference or discontinuity between the figure of Jesus Christ and God's revelation in other religions. Jesus Christ is, according to De Graeve, "not just one more in the series of messengers of God to man (Heb 1:1) known in the History of Religions, nor in that of god's mystical avatars and hierophanies, nor in that of mythical or historico-mythical culture heroes. He is the God he reveals."[8]

While the uniqueness of Christ has come to be interpreted in functional and hermeneutical terms in the contemporary theology of religions, De Graeve in this thesis retains the traditional ontological understanding of Christ's uniqueness. This is established through explicit comparison with the saviour figures of other traditions. Every saviour, however, is conceived within a particular hermeneutical framework from which it cannot be isolated for comparison.

8. *Louvain Studies* 16 (1979) 321.

At the same time, De Graeve emphasizes that this does not imply that the Church is the sole path to salvation: *The claim of the Church to be a "home" to the religions is not a claim for her specificity, but a claim for the uniqueness of Jesus as the Christ.* Here the expression "extra Ecclesiam nulla salus" is put on trial.[9] De Graeve argues that in its original use, this thesis was meant for heretics and schismatics. As such, it was an appeal to fidelity for those who were members of the Church, rather than a denunciation of all those who were not. The biblical passage upon which it is based (1 Peter 3:20) compares the necessity of baptism for salvation to the ark of Noah, rather than to the bark of Peter, De Graeve points out. The negative meaning of the axiom was, however, later developed through Augustine's conception of the "massa damnata" and officially pronounced in that sense at the Council of Florence in the fifteenth century. This eventually called for the idea of "baptism by desire" to allow for exceptions, and carries all the way to Karl Rahner's notion of the "anonymous Christians."[10] In this thesis, De Graeve argues that the exclusive claims of the Church are not grounded in its own temporal nature, but in the uniqueness of Jesus as the Christ. A severing of the monolithic identification of the Christ and the Church is one of the direct consequences of the recognition of the salvific potential of non-Christian religions. While some then come to completely ignore the role of the Church, De Graeve emphasizes that the Church preserves a vital and indispensible function in proclaiming the Christ: *The message of the Church for the "Gentes" is: that the salvation of all mankind is "now" (eschatological "nun," "nunc") being offered as a living communion with the incarnated Son of God.* In the midst of what has been referred to as the "anti-missionary syndrome of the Western Church,"[11] De Graeve has held firmly to its missionary function.

9. For a discussion of the axiom, see G. D'Costa, "Extra Ecclesiam Nulla Salus Revisited" *Religious Pluralism and Unbelief* (Hamnett, Ian, ed.) (London: Routledge, 1990) 130-148.

10. While De Graeve fully sympathizes with Rahner's intent, he points out that the notion is a "non sequitur because it implies that the non-Christian does not know what he is but we do. If he were an anonymous Christian, he would know, but we wouldn't."

11. V. Neckebrouck, *De Stomme Duivelen. Het anti-missionair syndroom in de Westerse Kerk* (Brugge: Tabor, 1990.)

While he rejects the old attitude toward mission as the Church's propagation of itself, he emphasizes that the Church continues to have an indispensible role in proclaiming the Christ. Rather than making it obsolete, respect for other religions and a true interreligious dialogue presuppose the desire to share one's own faith with others. This is part of the natural dynamics of faith. Nor is anything less expected by the partners in dialogue.

The missionary responsibility also challenges the Church to live up to her own ideals, to give witness to the experience of living communion with Christ. In the following thesis, De Graeve argues that only then is conversion to Christianity justified: *The "Church" becomes a demand for them, if and when she actually and convincingly appears as the offer of salvation, which could not be rejected in religious integrity*. This is a reaction against missionary methods and many of the conversions which took place during the Conquista in South America. Christianity as represented by the conquistadores was a brutal, arrogant, and inhumane religion. The conversion to such a religion could thus not be regarded as an act of religious integrity. With Francisco de Vittorio, De Graeve regards these conversions as nothing but "levity of heart," and the rejection of such a religion as an act of religious integrity.

De Graeve contrasts this with the missionary ideal as realized by a figure as Roberto De Nobili, s.j., one of the first Catholic missionaries to India.[12] In spite of much opposition from within the Church, he abandoned the Western form of Christianity and became a *brahmacharin*, a student or disciple within the Hindu tradition. He dressed and lived like a Brahmin and studied Tamil, Sanskrit, the Veda, and Hindu philosophy. Presenting himself as a Brahmin from Italy, he entered into discussions with Pandits. Many (according to some accounts more than eight hundred Indians) became his disciples and viewed him as a guru with his own particular teaching.

Though this attempt to live among the people, study their tradition and present Christianity in familiar categories may be seen as pioneering, De Nobili's approach was not unambiguous

12. F. De Graeve, "Roberto De Nobili: A Bold Attempt at Inculturation," *Religion in the Pacific Era* (eds. F. Flinn and T. Hendrickx; New York: Paragon House, 1985) 31-42.

and has not been free from critique. He adopted the Brahmin way of life and Hindu categories, less out of respect for the Hindu tradition itself than as a means to gain converts. Most of his disciples were ignorant of the fact that they had converted to a different religion, and spontaneously returned to their former Hindu tradition after De Nobili died. The ambiguity of De Nobili's approach surfaces nowadays in the fact that, when seen in line with the efforts of Roberto De Nobili, contemporary attempts at inculturation through Catholic ashrams[13] are mistrusted by some Hindus as no more than a ruse, a last desperate attempt of Christianity to convert the unweary masses.[14]

The Convergence of Religions

Here I have isolated two theses of De Graeve which express his views on the future of religious pluralism. While the awareness of religious pluralism has often led to a focus on the common origin or essence of religions, De Graeve's vision is directed less to the past or the present, than to the future unity of religions. He expresses this in terms of Teilhard de Chardin's notion of convergence: *The "conversion" to which all religions, including Christianity, are constantly called, is not so much a "turning away from" as a "turning to": conversion is convergence.* Conversion is here understood in the context of the process of self-purification and growth within every particular religion. Based on Teilhard's principle that "everything that rises must converge," De Graeve sees this process of inner conversion as one of convergence of all religions. The image is that of one pyramid of which the various religions, themselves represented as pyramids, form the basis. The basis may be endlessly enlarge to reveal common elements and mutual influences. As the religions rise, their peaks approach one another and may be subsumed in a higher reality until all religions finally meet in the eschatological unity of religions.

13. On the attempts at inculturation through Catholic ashrams see C. Cornille, Catherine, *The Guru in Indian Catholicism. Ambiguity or Opportunity of Inculturation?* (Leuven: Peeters Press, 1991.)
14. This stance is most forcefully expressed in: S.R. Goel, *Catholic Ashrams. Adopting and Adapting Hindu Dharma* (New Delhi: Voice of India, 1988.)

As is generally the case with images, that of the pyramid representing the unity of religions is revealing but also problematic. It allows for every religious tradition to preserve its own specificity and uniqueness, even within the higher unity. This is expressed in the thesis: *The variety of religions, as the variety of existential situations themselves, is a sign of the creative abundance that is supposed to enhance unity, and not necessarily a sign of particularism that precludes it.* De Graeve insists on the preservation of the diversity of cultural and religious identity in his vision of the eschatological convergence of religions. This is based on the belief that "history is not the only cause of plurality and that therefore plurality cannot completely disappear in fulfilment."

Since the ultimate unity of religions is conceived of as an eschatological reality, no single religion can claim absolute truth and hegemony over the other religions. Rather than turning away from one's own tradition, and against the supermarket mentality of running from one religion to the next, De Graeve here pleads for a deeper grounding in, and a higher realization of one's own particular tradition. In doing so, he believes, one naturally approaches the other religious traditions.

This utopian view of a future unity of religions has not found many adherents among the contemporary theologians of religions. It is a modification or an extension of the belief that all religions meet or merge in the religious experiences of their respective mystics and saints, eloquently and enthusiastically advanced by authors such as Aldous Huxley, William James and Frithjof Schuon, and severely criticized by Steven Katz. Since this is a problem which by its very nature cannot be resolved, it has lost many advocates. Current emphasis is more on the necessary particularity of divine revelation and religious experience, and on differences between the goals of the various religions.[15] From this perspective, religions are characterized by their incompatible or conflicting truth claims. Moreover, the notion of a "higher" truth is contrary to the self-understanding of most religious traditions. The belief that religions are progressively moving toward a higher unity may be seen as tempered by the growth of religious fundamentalism over the past few decades.

15. G. See D'Costa (ed.), *Christian Uniqueness Reconsidered* (Maryknoll: Orbis, 1990.)

The Uniqueness of Christianity and the Convergence of Religions

While the conception of the convergence of religions transcends every particular religious tradition, Christianity included, the notion of eschatological fulfilment is necessarily expressed in categories and symbols belonging to a particular religion. From within the Christian tradition, De Graeve states that: *The fulfilment and consummation of all religions is what could be called "Christ-ianity," the integration of the religious intentionality of man in the growth of the once-for-all redeemed mankind toward the "full adulthood" of Christ, the "pleroma of God."* This thesis may appear to rejoin the traditional fulfilment theories of the relationship of Christianity to other religious traditions. But while such theories considered Christianity in its historical and institutional form to be the fulfilment of other religions, De Graeve refers to the aforementioned eschatological reality as "Christianity". This term, borrowed from Col. 2:8-3:11 and Eph. 1:9-23, is used as "a theological stenogram for Christ's anonymous presence in all religions, really the 'Christ-ness' of religion."[16] The term "consummation" refers to a bringing to perfection of what is already present within a religious tradition in terms of a higher synthesis, rather than absorption in any other particular religion. This is what is understood by the Christ-ness of religion.

This rendering of belief in the universal salvific will of God and of faith in the uniqueness of Christ recalls Raimundo Panikkar's emphasis upon the Cosmic Christ.[17] While Panikkar points to the need to sever the Cosmic Christ from the historical Jesus in order to recognize grace and salvation in other religions, De Graeve develops a more dialectical relationship between incarnation and transcendence: *The relation of "Christ-ianity" to the religions (and Christianity), one of fulfilment to previous phases of growth, is characterized by a dialectic of incarnation (i.e. really "present" in the "human sphere") and transcendence (i.e. never exhaustively present in the human sphere, never utterly reducible to it.)* In this thesis, the Christian dialectical tension between the already and the not-yet is applied to other religions. De Graeve

16. *Louvain Studies* 16 (1979) 321.
17. Cfr. R. Panikkar, *The Unknown Christ of Hinduism* (First published: London: Darton, Longman & Todd, 1964.)

emphasizes that "the Christian theology of non-Christian religions will always be an Incarnation Theology." His understanding of the activity of God's grace in other religions is based on a dynamic view of the incarnation which is both a once-and-for-all event and a continuous process. In this view, the Pleroma of God will not be fulfilled until Christ has become realized in all cultures. Rather than identifying the incarnation of Christ with a particular tradition, De Graeve here emphasizes the element of transcendence as expressed in the traditional Christian notion of "eschatological proviso." This precludes the possibility of manipulation and abuse inherent in religions where the transcendence of the divine is less emphasized.

The dialectic of incarnation and transcendence may thus be seen as constituting the essence of the mission of the Church. The historical manifestation of the Christ in the figure of Jesus of Nazareth allows for a positive proclamation and a normative perspective, while the element of transcendence permits both openness and a critical (and self-critical) attitude toward other religions. This is expressed in the final thesis which argues that *In accepting and fulfilling her mission, the Church realizes her own conversion to Christ-ianity: she ensures her salvation by sharing it with others, she as well as the others become more what they are by growing closer together*. Here, De Graeve's conception of mission comes into full perspective. The proclamation of Christ to the nations is vital, not only for the "peoples" but for the Church herself. It is through the process of inculturation -through the knowledge of Christ which is realized in different traditions-that the inculturation unfolds. The mission of the Church is thus as much a matter of listening as of speaking. In becoming incarnated in a particular culture and tradition, a new understanding of the Christ may emerge to enrich traditional Christology. In discovering Christ in other religions, Christianity itself comes to a fuller understanding of Christ thus growing closer to "Christianity". De Graeve emphasizes that the same principle may apply to other religions. Just as Christians come to a fuller understanding of the Christ through inculturation and dialogue with other religions, so Buddhists, for example, may develop a deeper comprehension of the "Buddha-nature" through contact with Christianity. Religious pluralism challenges every particular religion to live up to its own ideals, and to discover and realize its fullest potential.

General Conclusion

I have elaborated Frank De Graeve's theology of religions through a rearrangement, clarification and reflection upon his eleven theses. In doing so, I hope not to have wronged or diminished them.

Since Vatican II, a wide variety of theories (become paradigms) have been developed to couch the Christian attitude toward non-Christian religions.[18] If placed within the more or less helpful distinction between the exclusivistic, the pluralistic, and the inclusivistic attitude toward religious pluralism, De Graeve's theses clearly fit within the latter. They are profoundly inspired by Rahner while adding their own flavour to the paradigm. The inclusivism advanced by De Graeve is one in which all religions, Christianity included, are moving toward a transcendent, eschatological unity which, from the Christian perspective, is understood as Christ-ianity. This process of growth is brought about by sharing with other religions and by reaching a fuller understanding of the reality of Christ through inculturation and inter-religious dialogue. De Graeve thus believes that bringing the Christian message in a pluralistic world involves a dialogical theology for which he prescribes the basic attitude: "One enters into a dialogical theology without expansionistic or annexationistic motivations, lethal for true communication, trusting that one's own faith can be brilliantly reflected through the prism of other traditions, and in the gettin' up morning, through that of their sum total."

That most of De Graeve's reflections on the theology of religions have since been incorporated into the general discourse illustrates their pioneering nature. They touch upon issues which are now at the core of the theological debate: the emphasis on the particularity of religious traditions, the need to preserve the belief in the uniqueness of Christ and Christianity without identifying

18. G. D'Costa, *Theology and Religious Pluralism* (Oxford: Blackwell, 1986.)

the historical with the eschatological Church, and the under-standing of interreligious dialogue as a goal in itself and an essential part of the mission of the Church. His vision of the eschatological convergence of religions -though itself too utopian and evolutionistic for current thought- is based on some of the same fundamental hermeneutical and theological principles as the latest inclusivistic approaches to the theology of religions: the need for a particular approach to the divine, the necessary normativity of Christ, the possibility of finding Christ in other religions and growing through interreligious dialogue. [19]

Of late, the question of the particular uniqueness and normati-vity of Christ has come increasingly to the fore. It is at the core of discussions between soteriocentric and Christocentric approaches to religious pluralism. While the former emphasize the potential for liberation of a religion as the only legitimate normative principle in a religiously plural world, the latter argue that this very orientation is and can only be based on a Christocentric approach.

Even though some of De Graeve's theses have not found continuity in the current debate, and do not explicitly deal with certain issues which have since become crucial, the majority of the theses still constitutes the essence of Christian theological reflection on religious pluralism. Frank De Graeve may thus without reservation be counted among the pioneers and founding fathers of the contemporary theology of religions.

---

19. Compare with the latest collection of essays on the topic in G. D'Costa (ed.), *Christian Uniqueness Reconsidered* (Maryknoll: Orbis Books, 1990.)

Aylward Shorter is currently president of the Missionary Institute in London. For many years he taught pastoral anthropology in various institutions in West Africa. He has published numerous works on African theology and this book *Toward a Theology of Inculturation* (London: Chapman, 1988) has become one of the most famous fundamental works on the topic.

Jacques Dupuis is professor of dogmatic theology at the Gregorian University in Rome. He lived for more than two decades in India where he taught at the *Vidyajyoti* Jesuit institute in New Delhi. He is the author of several works relating to Indian Christianity and the theology of religions. His most recent publication is *Jesus Christ at the Encounter of World Religions* (Maryknoll: Orbis, 1992).

Jan Van Bragt is a member (former director) of the Nanzan Instituut for Religion and Culture in Japan. He has been in Japan for over thirty years, and has become one of the main translators of the Kyoto School of philosophy to the West: cfr. his translation of Nishitani Keiji's *Religion and Nothingness* (Berkeley: University of California Press, 1982).

Arnulf Camps is professor emeritus of missiology and comparative religion of the University of Nijmegen. He studied and worked for several years in Pakistan where he became involved with the dialogue with Islam. His main work in the area of the theology of religions is *Partners in Dialogue: Christianity and the Other World Religions* (Maryknoll: Orbis, 1983).

Lambert Bartels has been working as a missionary in Ethiopia for many years. As an anthropologist, he lived and worked among the Oromo people, about whom he published the book *Oromo Religion: mythes qnd rites of the Western Oromo of Ethiopia — an attempt to understand* (Berlin: Reimer, 1983).

Jose de Mesa is professor at de la Salle University in the Philippines. He has published widely on the topic of the inculturation of Christianity in the Philippines. His books include *In Solidarity with the Culture: studies in theological re-rooting* (Quezon City: Maryhill School of Theology, 1987).

Jimmy Belita is professor at de la Salle University in the Philippines. His research has focussed on issues relating to the inculturation of Christianity in the Philippines, such as the possibility of "a Filipino Eucharist."

Gavin D'Costa is professor of theology and religious studies at the University of Bristol. He has become widely known as one of the most eloquent and ingenious spokesmen for an inclusivist approach of the theology of religions. His publications include *Theology and Religious Pluralism* (Oxford: Basil Blackwell, 1986) and more recently (ed.) *Christian Uniqueness Reconsidered* (Maryknoll: Orbis, 1990)

Wiel Logister is professor of special dogmatics at the University of Tilburg. He has published many articles in the area of the theology of religions focussing mainly on the Christological questions. His publications also include the book *Reincarnatie: de vele gestalten van een oud en nieuw geloof.*

Catherine Cornille is professor of comparative religion at the University of Leuven. Her focus is mainly on the question of inculturation and the emergence of new religions and new religious phenomena from the meeting of religions and cultures. Her publications include *The Guru in Indian Catholicism: Ambiguity or Opportunity of Inculturation* (Leuven: Peeters Press, 1991).

ORIENTALISTE, P.B. 41, B-3000 Leuven